ISLAND VISIONS

Throughout this book, we seek to acknowledge the traditional custodians of this place and all land upon which we stand. We understand the importance of recognizing this area's rich history and culture, both past and present. We pay respects to the Chumash Elders past, present, and future for they hold the memories, the traditions, and the culture of this area, which has become a place called home for people from all over the world.

ISLAND VISIONS

Copyright © 2020 by Pedal Born Pictures LLC

The information in this book was correct at the time of publication. The Author does not assume any liability for loss or damage caused by errors or omissions.

Sample scenarios in this book are fictitious. Any similarity to actual persons, living or dead, is coincidental.

ISBN 978-1-930194-05-2

This project was a joint publication of:

Pedal Born Pictures
www.PedalBornPictures.com

Santa Barbara Middle School
www.SBMS.org

Maps.com
120 Cremona Dr. Suite 260. Santa Barbara, CA 93117
www.Maps.com

Printed in Canada. First Printing, 2020

ENVIRONMENTAL BENEFITS STATEMENT

Island Visions saved the following resources by printing the pages of this book on chlorine free paper made with 100% post-consumer waste.

TREES	WATER	ENERGY	SOLID WASTE	GREENHOUSE GASES
161 FULLY GROWN	13,000 GALLONS	68 MILLION BTUs	550 POUNDS	69,700 POUNDS

Environmental impact estimates were made using the Environmental Paper Network Paper Calculator 4.0. For more information visit www.papercalculator.org.

FSC
www.fsc.org
MIX
Paper from responsible sources
FSC® C016245

WHO WROTE THIS

214 Plankton
5 Students
10 Scientists
3 Dolphins
2 Sailors
1 Otter

6 Activists
145 Fish
5 Fishermen
2 Foxes
∞ Ancestors
9 Harbor Seals

5 Artists
4 Trees
10 Teachers
7 Historians
4 Boats
345 Tacos

6 Business Owners
30 Elders
3 Surfers
4 Jellyfish
2 Rangers
18 Rocks

As brothers, we grew up exploring the beaches, trails, and peaks of a place that many now call Santa Barbara. Gazing out to sea we saw the Channel Islands—purple and blue smudges of mystery just out of reach. On a ninth grade outdoor expedition with Santa Barbara Middle School we had the privilege to experience the wonders of these islands. It was also at SBMS that we met ocean filmmaker Mike deGruy. Mike taught us that every place, every creature, has a story.

A lot has happened since our first trip to the islands. Inspired by filmmakers like Mike, we started Pedal Born Pictures. We have traveled the world seeking out stories of wonder, but have never forgotten the Channel Islands or Mike's reminders about the stories in our own backyards. *Island Visions* is our effort to help share these tales. It is a collaboration between Pedal Born Pictures and SBMS, fueled by Mike's passion from above, and guided by a group of elders who live and breathe this incredible place.

-Jacob and Isaac

EDITED & WRITTEN BY
Jacob Seigel Brielle

DESIGNED & ILLUSTRATED BY
Isaac Seigel-Boettner

DEVELOPMENT DIRECTOR
Brian McWilliams

ADVISORY BOARD
Mimi deGruy
Laura Francis
Peter Schuyler
Scott E. Simon

DEVELOPMENT MANAGER
Phoebe Hitchman

WITH SUPPORT FROM
Nancy & Henry Armstrong
Laura Francis
Sally Kurnick
Peter Schuyler
Christie & John Glanville
Blake & Emily Jones
Chris & Wendy Blau

CULTURAL CONSULTANT
Mia Lopez

COPY EDITOR
Laurie Deans

PROOFREADER
Nicole Wald

FACT CHECKERS
Kyle Byrd-Fisher
Michele Johnson

DON'T LOOK AT THE BIG, OVERWHELMING ISSUES OF THE WORLD.
LOOK IN YOUR OWN BACKYARD. LOOK IN YOUR HEART.
WHAT DO YOU CARE ABOUT THAT ISN'T RIGHT WHERE YOU LIVE?
FIX IT.

-Mike deGruy
Filmmaker and Ocean Storyteller
1951-2012

CONTENTS

ISLANDS

OCEAN

FIRST PEOPLE

NEW CLAIMS

OFF THE COAST,

hiding in the fog, lies a small chain of rugged islands. They are home to families of tiny foxes battling extinction, enormous blue whales with hearts the size of small cars, and towering undersea forests of kelp. The Chumash people inhabited these islands for more than 13,000 years. They crossed the channel in masterfully-built redwood plank canoes, only to be "discovered" by Spanish explorers, then replaced by Mexican and American ranchers. Every island resident, be they flippered, pawed, finned, or footed, has a story to tell. Forget dragons. Here there be wonder. Welcome to the Channel Islands.

While they appear distant from the mainland, these islands are closely connected to California and our planet as a whole. We are bound to them by the air we breathe and the currents that carry water from our shores to theirs. How we live on the mainland impacts the climate, landscapes, and seascapes of this magical place. The Channel Islands teach us that there really is no such thing as an island. Our entire planet is connected. The connections between the islands themselves—and the islands and the mainland—have helped create the wonderfully complex stories that you are about to read.

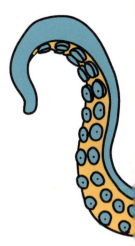

A note on places and names: there are eight Channel Islands—four northern (San Miguel, Santa Rosa, Santa Cruz, and Anacapa) and four southern (Santa Barbara, San Nicolas, San Clemente, and Santa Catalina). All eight could fill their own volumes of stories. In order to remain a manageable size, this book focuses on the northern four. Unless otherwise specified, the label "Channel Islands" in the following pages refers to just these islands. Over the centuries these islands have had different names. Today we often use names given to them by Spanish explorers. For thousands of years they were known by Chumash names. In the following pages we will often include these Chumash names along with their Spanish counterparts. The Chumash have several different languages. In this book, we will be using words from the Shmuwich language spelled phonetically and italicized for these island names, as well as key cultural and religious concepts.

When you gather a group of people in a room, you notice differences. Some people may speak different languages or have different beliefs. Arguments may break out. If they listen, everyone will gain a better understanding of their neighbors' views. This is the power of diversity. Keep it in mind as you hear from the storytellers in the following pages. All have unique perspectives that come from years of experiencing the islands in their own ways. You may notice authors disagreeing with each other. Take note. Only by paying attention to all these voices can we begin to understand the islands. Only by building this understanding can we begin to conserve them.

ISLANDS

TUQAN
"SAN MIGUEL ISLAND"
Area : 3,790 hectares / 14.6 square miles

Tallest Peak : 253 meters / 831 feet

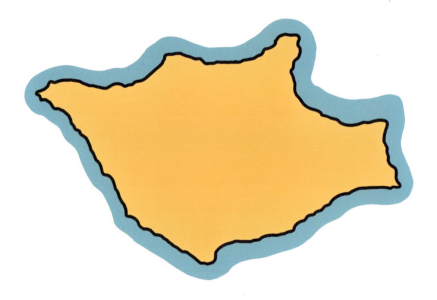

WIMA
"SANTA ROSA ISLAND"
Area : 21,596 hectares / 83.4 square miles

Tallest Peak : 484 meters / 1,589 feet

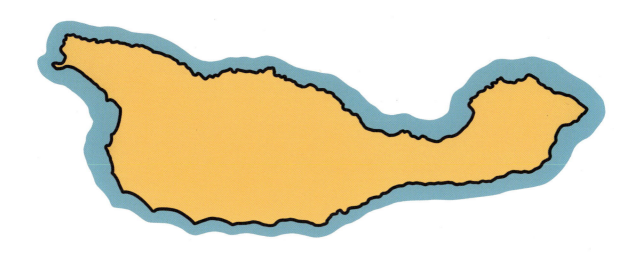

LIMUW
"SANTA CRUZ ISLAND"
Area : 24,864 hectares / 96 square miles
Tallest Peak : 747 meters / 2,450 feet

'ANYAPAX
"ANACAPA ISLAND"
Area : 295 hectares / 1.1 square miles
Tallest Peak : 283 meters / 930 feet

Photo by Pedal Born Pictures

WHAT IS IT THAT DRAWS US TO ISLANDS?

These small smudges of land float on the horizon, seemingly remote and mysterious. Up close, they become more knowable. Unlike with a continent, we can often sail, swim, paddle, or hike around an island in a day. We may struggle to grasp the size of North America, but tiny Anacapa is much more imaginable.

The Channel Islands' mysteries have inspired generations of storytellers, sailors, and scientists. Their small size and isolation make them the perfect places for new species and cultures to evolve. But this all comes at a cost. These tiny spots of wonder are vulnerable. Though we may not realize it, our every action on the mainland can impact these not-so-far-off isles.

LAND HO!

by Liz Clark – *Sailor*

AGE 2

Started sailing with her family to Catalina and the other Channel Islands.

AGE 9

Took epic family sailing trip: 5,000 miles, San Diego to Mexico.

AGE 21

Won national college surf championship. Given sailboat by mentor.

AGE 25

Set sail on her childhood dream: a round-the-world surfing adventure.

At the hint of dawn, Venus shines above the dark silhouette of the mountains as Katie and I motor past the rows of boats in the harbor. As we enter open water, the beam of my headlamp helps me raise and set the mainsail. I push out the boom to catch the light offshore breeze. Katie rolls out the headsail. Sitting at the tiller, we point the bow offshore and watch the coastal features of downtown Santa Barbara—the pier, harbor, buildings, streetlights, and car headlights—shrink into the distance behind us. We have four days to leave it all in our wake!

The darkness slowly breaks into shadowy grays, lightening in shades across the sky and blanketing the sea in silver. A fog bank squats resolutely offshore. It's been only an hour, but the serenity of sea already feels soothing. As day breaks, the wind shifts to the west and I pull my beanie low over my ears to block the cold, damp breeze. Katie appears with two cups of hot tea.

By mid-morning our little sloop approaches the unrelenting fog, and soon we're swallowed into soggy whiteness. Thankfully we meet no towering steel beasts while crossing the shipping lane, and instead enjoy the company of a pod of common dolphins. They don't seem to mind the fog, frolicking and leaping from the sea all around us.

Near midday, the fog begins to break up and patches of sunlight leap on the deep sea blues. We're chatting and snacking on sunflower seeds when, all at once, we sail into clear skies and behold our island destination boldly bathing in sunshine dead ahead!

As we near her windswept shores, the sailboat accelerates with each strengthening gust and we watch the island grow into detail. A rocky crag tumbles seaward, backed by steep, flat cliffs covered in dry grasses. The meadow atop the cliff rolls west into the slope of a mountainous backdrop. There's not a single building or boat or another human in sight. Our welcome party is a flock of pelicans flying in formation above.

As we approach the southern side of Santa Cruz Island, I'm awed by the complex geography—striated sedimentary cliffs, inviting nooks, sandy shorelines, dramatic rock formations, and sea caves awash in the churning seas. Seeing the unaltered island wilderness sprawling for as far as the eye can see quenches an inner thirst I can't explain. I pull in a deep breath; it smells of summer adventures—salt, seaweed, guano, tar, and parched earth. I exhale all my land-bound worries.

We trim the sails as we round the south end of the island. My fingers tingle with excitement when we see what we were hoping for—a south swell! We can't contain our smiles, as large lumps of water rise and fall beneath the hull. We drop the anchor in a horseshoe-shaped bay that will be home for tonight. We square away the decks and peel off our layers and boots to slip into 4mm wetsuits. The sea welcomes us in its chilly embrace as we plunge in with our boards and start the paddle towards the break. The kelp waves as we pass, and a sea lion breaks the surface to check out the newcomers. Katie catches the first wave but we both squeal with delight as she glides down the face, awash in gratitude, wonder, and freedom! Our island adventure has just begun!

Photos courtesy of Liz Clark Collection

Isle Wisdoms

Throughout history, islands have played a central role in religious texts, campfire stories, and spiritual beliefs across the globe. These mysterious places have helped us answer the big questions: Where did we come from? Where do we go when we die? Where does the sun go at night? Islands float just out of reach—the perfect home for the magical and unknown.

Home

The Chumash tell of how human life began on the Channel Islands. *Hutash*, the Earth Mother, grew the first people from seeds on *Limuw*, which some now call Santa Cruz Island. Hutash's husband *Alchupo'osh*, the Sky Snake (a.k.a. the Milky Way), wanted to make the people happy, so he gave them fire with a bolt of lighting from his forked tongue. The Chumash prospered, and the islands became one of the most densely-populated regions along the west coast of North America.

Gods

Ancient Chinese emperors sent expeditions in search of the legendary island of Penglai. Home to gods and goddesses, its pure white mountains were dotted with beautiful palaces made of gold and silver. Jewels and gems grew on the trees. Somewhere on Penglai was a potion of immortality. Unfortunately, the island didn't want to be found. Whenever an intrepid explorer got too close a vicious wind would blow them off course, leaving Penglai untouched by human hands.

ANSWERS

In the Slavic mythology of Eastern Europe, the mysterious island of Buyan is the source of those natural forces that we struggle to explain. It is the home of the North, East, and West winds , and the place where the sun sleeps at night. At dawn the Morning Star opens the palace gates on Buyan to let the sun journey across the sky. Each night when the Sun returns, the Evening Star closes the gates behind him. Hidden from mortals, Buyan will disappear if you sail too close.

ORIGINS

The Samoan people live on a chain of islands in the South Pacific Ocean. They describe the creation of these islands as the work of the god Tagaloa. In the beginning, the world was covered in water. Even mighty gods need a place to rest their feet, so Tagaloa created the first island. With his feet finally planted, Tagaloa set his sights on the horizon. He broke up the island, creating god-size stepping stones that allowed him to cross the ocean. This is how the islands of the South Pacific were formed.

AFTERLIFE

Greek philosophers spoke of the Isles of the Blessed, where the greatest of heroes go after their deaths. Located far out in the Atlantic ocean at the world's edge, this idyllic island had fields that produced fruit without needing to be farmed. The worst weather that the Isles' heroic residents could expect was a pleasant blanket of morning fog. There was no wind. Winter never came here. What better place for your soul after a long life of vanquishing monsters?

MAGIC

The island of Avalon was the mysterious setting of several key moments in the legend of King Arthur. Said to be full of magic, it was here that Arthur's legendary sword Excalibur—the sword in the stone—was forged. After being mortally wounded in battle, Arthur was taken to this same island to be healed. As the story goes, the Avalon's powerful magic keeps him alive to this day. On this island's shores, he stands ready to return and save England in her darkest hour.

PARADISE

Saint Brendan the Navigator was a curious Irish monk born in 484 CE. On one of his voyages across the Atlantic, he got lost in a fog bank. When the mists parted, he found himself on the shores of an island full of lush green forests. Saint Brendan's Isle found its way onto the maps of many European explorers in the centuries that followed. Did this wayward saint actually stumble upon North America? Or is his island just another story of our constant search for untouched paradise?

ANCESTORS

According to the Chumash, the population of the Channel Islands eventually grew beyond what the land could support. *Kakunupmawa*, the Mystery Behind the Sun, saw this and told the Chumash that some would have to leave. He built a giant rainbow connecting the islands to the mainland. This allowed the Chumash to spread across what some now call California, where many live to this day. [To read the full story of the rainbow bridge, as told by Chumash elder Georgiana Valoyce Sanchez, go to page 108.]

Imagination will often

carry us to worlds

that never were.

But without it

we go nowhere.

- Carl Sagan

Anacapa, Santa Cruz, Santa Rosa, and San
Miguel Islands (bottom to top) from the air.
Photo by Wayne Hsieh

IF ISLANDS COULD TALK

by Ian Williams – *San Miguel Island Ranger*

AGE 1	AGE 16	AGE 22	AGE 31
Parents took him to nature to meet the trees before meeting family.	Met ranger in Kings Canyon, knew that was what he wanted to be.	First job with Park Service playing a cavalry trooper from the 1870s.	Hired as ranger of San Miguel Island. Spent next 26 years working there.

"Tell me a story," the camper asked as we hiked up Nidever Canyon on the north side of San Miguel Island.

I pointed to the dry waterfall that stretched up the steep west wall of the canyon. I told her how I had watched an island fox spring back and forth like a mountain goat from the cattails on the canyon floor all the way up the wall. The fox had bounded straight up the hillside canyon in a fraction of the time it had taken us to hike up the trail.

Nidever Canyon is full of stories. It is named after George Nidever, who was a story in and of himself. He was a mountain man who turned to the sea. Nidever hunted otters, harvested gull eggs, and in 1850 started sheep ranching on San Miguel, something that would change the island's landscape forever. Nidever even found the lone woman of San Nicolas Island (inspiration for *Island of the Blue Dolphins*) and brought her to Santa Barbara.

Hiking up the Nidever Canyon trail is a walk through history. For more than a century it has been the only path leading up from the beach. When you hike it, you follow in the footsteps of every boater, camper, researcher, ranger, and rancher who has gone before you. What is now a trail was built as a road by William Waters, back in 1888. He used it to haul wool down to the beach to be loaded onto boats to the mainland during the years that the island was a sheep ranch. That was the business of San Miguel for 100 years.

His wife, Minnie Waters, told the story of the building of that road in her diary. In the spring of 1888 she wrote about the days spent blasting rocks to carve out the trail. In places, you can still mentally excavate the dirt that has slumped down and picture the path being the width of a wagon.

Even the story of San Miguel's geology is told in the canyon. Magnetic readings from a core drilled in volcanic rocks told geologists that the island had rotated 90 degrees since those rocks cooled 17 million years ago. This would mean that San Miguel started out underwater, near present-day San Diego. [See the illustration on the following page for an explanation of how this happened.]

The steepness of the trail gives you a lot of excuses to stop and enjoy the view as you catch your breath. That's a good thing to do because the canyon is one of the most natural places on the island. The slopes are covered with native and endemic (found nowhere else on Earth) plants. They tell the story of how they survived in places that were too steep for the sheep to eat them.

The canyon is one of the few places where you find surface water on San Miguel. Ravens bathe in the pools and do aerobatics over the canyon. The songs of sparrows, wrens, and warblers echo off the canyon walls as they tell their own stories.

When you hike the trail up Nidever Canyon, you'll surely come away with a few stories of your own.

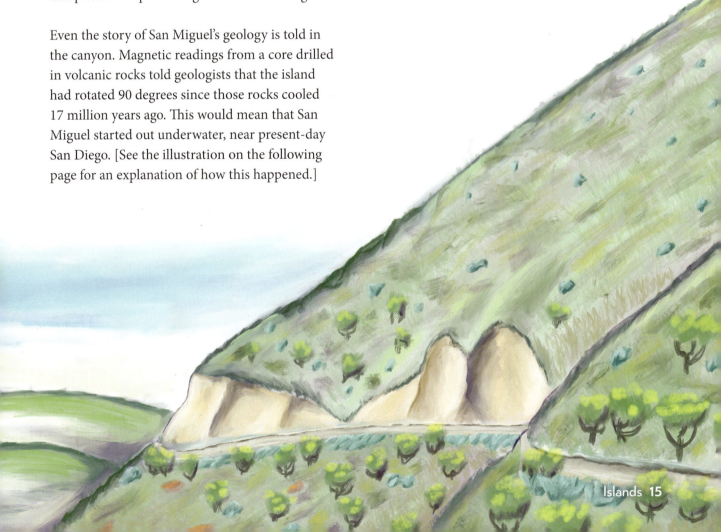

How They Formed

18,000,000 Years ago

The Pacific Plate pushed northwestward past the North American Plate. A piece of the Earth's crust that would become the Channel Islands broke off along this border and began to **rotate**.

5,000,000 Years ago

By this time, the piece had rotated by about 90 degrees. The Pacific and North American plates began to squeeze this piece, **pushing up** the islands and coastal mountains.

20,000 Years Ago

By the height of the last ice age, this squeezing had caused the south edge of this piece of crust to **pop up**, creating the single island of Santarosae.

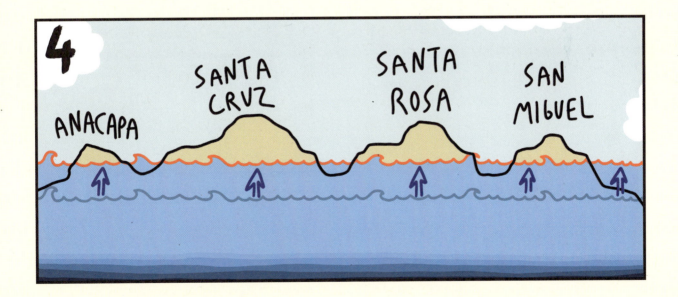

5,000 Years Ago

At the end of the last ice age, sea levels had **risen**, separating Santarosae into a series of smaller land masses that became the modern Channel Islands.

SANTAROSAE

SANTA ROSA ISLAND

CURRENT COASTLINE

ISLAND

SANTA CRUZ ISLAND

10,000 - 15,000 YEARS AGO

MMM ROCKS

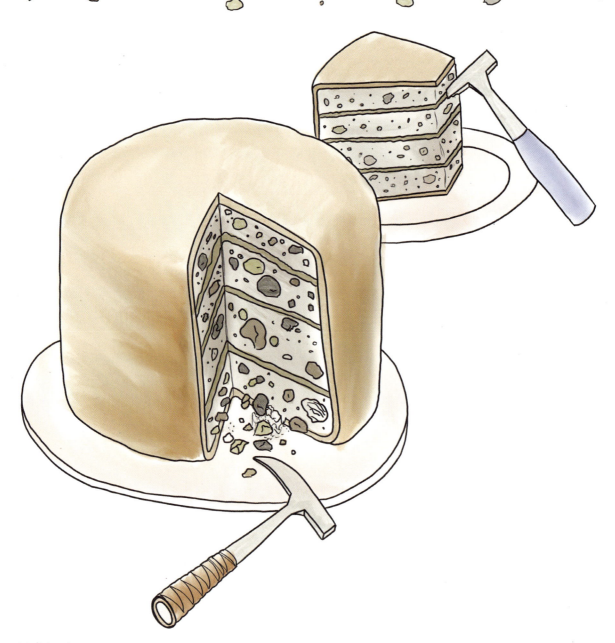

with Tanya Atwater – Geology Professor, UCSB

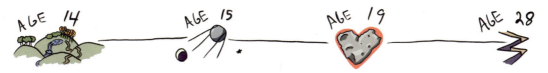

AGE 14 — Grew up exploring the hills above Santa Barbara with her sisters.

AGE 15 — Saw Sputnik launch. Knew she wanted to become a scientist.

AGE 19 — Attended a geology camp in Montana, fell in love with shapes of the landscape.

AGE 28 — Published a paper on the history of the San Andreas Fault system.

What first drew you to the Channel Islands?

I grew up in Los Angeles, but moved to Santa Barbara when I was 14. After so much time in \the big city, I loved the smallness of Santa Barbara and the wildness that was all around. My sisters and I spent lots of time hiking on the mountain trails and swimming in the creeks and ocean.

After I went away to college and learned about geology, and then came home again, I was amazed at how much more I could see in my favorite mountains. It felt like I had been blind before! Suddenly I could see what the mountains were made of and why they had the shapes they had; why the trails up them were so steep and stony in some places and so smooth in other parts.

And I loved the views, with the islands out there seeming to float in the mist. They seemed so near, yet so far and mysterious. When I first went out to the islands, I was happy to see that they were very wild too. I have since learned about their geology and found that they are a lot like our mountains, just partly hidden under the sea water.

If the rocks on those mountains—and islands—could talk, what would they say?

They would tell us lots of things about the time long ago when they were formed. They could tell us what was going on then, such as volcanic eruptions, earthquakes, floods and big fires, so we might know what we should be ready for. They might tell us what kinds of creatures were alive, what they were doing, and what the climate was like. They could tell us what kind of soil they form, so we would know what kind of crops would be the best to plant there. They could tell us where to look for resources that we need, like oil, metals, even gold!

In a way, they do talk about a lot of these things, if we can just decipher their languages. That's what geologists are trying to do. One big problem is that most of the rocks that form don't last. They get eroded away, leaving us with rocks from a few periods of time. We can travel around and find some more rocks from a few other ages, but our story is always very patchy. To fill in the missing parts, we have to assume that Earth's processes in the past weren't too different from those active today. And we have to guess a lot.

Is there a particularly memorable field discovery on the islands that sticks with you?

In my particular field of study—geophysics—a really important discovery was that of the unusual magnetic directions that are frozen into our local rocks. We might expect them to point north, the way a compass needle does. But when scientists measured the magnetic directions, many of them pointed east, not north. We theorize that this shows that the islands, together with our coastlines and mountains, were originally lined up north-south, and since then they have been rotated around to their present east-west orientations.

This rotation idea fits very well with our understanding of the San Andreas Fault. The San Andreas Fault is caused by the Pacific Plate going past North America toward Alaska and dragging the edge of the continent along with it. We imagine that our particular piece of land had one end stuck in the continent, so the Pacific Plate just snagged the other end and dragged it around. This is sort of like a log floating down a river but with one end dragging along the shore.

Can you describe some of the unique geological features that one might encounter hiking on or paddling around the islands?

The profiles of the islands show us an interesting story. Many of the high parts of the islands have flat tops. Sometimes you can see two or three flat benches at different heights, sort of like a staircase. The island rocks weren't formed that way; something eroded them into their odd shapes. We think that each of the flat sections was ground down by ocean waves along a coastline when they were at sea level. There is

a big, slow geological collision happening that is pushing crust under the islands and lifting the rocks up to their present heights. In fact, that's why the islands stick up out of the water.

Another thing to look for is rock layers of the Monterey Formation. These rocks are white or very light-colored, with very thin beds that can be deformed into wild folds. They are made of microscopic sea creature skeletons that collected on the ocean floor under a shallow sea. You can find them here and there on the islands and the mainland, including on very high places. This also supports the idea of a big uplift of the land.

You often use animations to show why our planet looks the way it does today—especially when it comes to the formation of the Channel Islands. What attracted you to this medium?

Growing up, I wanted to be an artist. When I thought about anything or I read a book, I would see pictures in my head. I loved maps. I always had them open during family trips, to keep track of where we were going. It was like being a bird high in the sky, watching our car go along the roads.

Later, after I became a scientist and was trying to explain something to someone, I always drew pictures and diagrams. I also used words, of course, but they were mostly to point out and explain things that were in my pictures.

When I started to study continental drift and to teach about it, I was always trying to show how pieces of the earth were moving around past other pieces. That was not easy to do using still pictures; I always wanted parts of the pictures to move. Then a friend showed me how to use one of the first computer animation programs. I immediately put some of my drawings in there and made them move. It was wonderful to see!

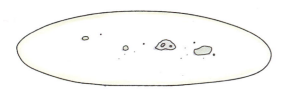

When I started making animations, I was surprised at how much people liked them and understood them. It makes me think that we humans are born with a special ability to understand moving things—especially if the moving things have big teeth! I have especially enjoyed figuring out how to make animations that teach the viewer a particular story that I want to tell. There can be a lot going on in an animation, but our eyes are especially drawn to bright colors and to any object that is moving faster than the rest.

What advice would you give to a student who is just beginning to learn about our planet and the forces that created the Channel Islands?

I hope you have a good world map to study and enjoy or, even better, a globe. If you don't have a globe, see if your parents will get you one. I recommend that you get a "physical" globe—one that concentrates on Earth's features: mountains, rivers and river flood plains, ocean floor, etc.—instead of, or in addition to, a "political" globe—one that shows countries.

Our Earth is very beautiful and a little more fragile than we used to think. It will be you and your friends' job to help humanity learn to live in balance with Earth's life-giving systems. I am sure that you will do it. We humans are really good at figuring out what to do, once we realize that there is a problem to solve. So don't worry too much, but do learn all you can about Earth and its atmosphere, weather, and waters. Then, when the time is right, you'll know what to do.

ISLAND FEATURES

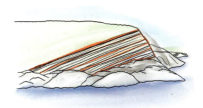

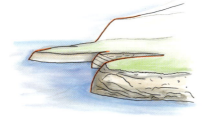

Many cliffs and hills of the islands have thin white stripes. This **Monterey Formation** is made of the skeletons of tiny, long-dead sea creatures, evidence that the islands used to be underwater.

If you look out at the islands you may notice that parts look like giant stairs. The flat **marine terraces** may have once been at sea level but were pushed up as plates beneath Earth's surface collided.

Santa Cruz Island's **Painted Cave** is one of the largest sea caves in the world. Longer than four football fields, it gets its name from the brightly-colored lichen and algae that cover its walls.

ISLAND EVOLUTION

Being a new bird on this island is tough. The best food here is a rock-hard local nut. One of your friends has a particularly sharp beak and can crack twice as many nuts in a day as you can. They eat like royalty, while you and your dull beak go hungry. Guess who everyone in the flock wants to have babies with?

Fast-forward a few dozen generations. Many of the birds on the island are descendents of your friend and sport that same sharp beak. A visiting scientist classifies these descendents as their own species. We call this process **evolution**, and it often happens rapidly on islands.

Evolution is defined as the changing of an organism's genes from generation to generation. **Genes** are the materials within an organism's cells that shape its physical characteristics. Individuals with characteristics—like your friend's beak—that help them live better, are more likely to survive, reproduce, and thus pass on these characteristics—and genes—to their offspring.

SPECIATION

Evolution often occurs when a small group of organisms gets separated from the rest of their species. This small group frequently evolves into a new species, as happened with the birds on the previous page. This is called **speciation**. Organisms can get separated and evolve into new species in a variety of different ways:

VICARIANCE

Vicariance occurs when the territory where a species lives gets split into pieces.

Plate tectonics separate land

Glaciers split populations

Mountain ranges rise

DISPERSAL

Dispersal occurs when a portion of a species moves to a new territory, such as an island.

Lack of food forces migration

A group rafts across water to new land

Animals transport seeds in poop

Dwarfism

Many new species have evolved on the Channel Islands. In some cases, these species have become smaller than their mainland counterparts. We call this type of evolution **dwarfism**.

About 40,000 years ago, Columbian mammoths—roughly 4.3 meters (14 feet) tall—swam out to Santarosae. Eventually the mammoth's height decreased to 2 meters (6.6 feet). Scientists think these smaller **pygmy mammoths** were better adapted to the limited amount of food on the island.

The **island fox** evolved to be 30 percent smaller than its mainland grey fox cousin. This also may have been because of the limited food on the islands. [Check out page 188 to learn more about how these cute and crucial creatures nearly became extinct.]

Gigantism

Not every species on the Channel Islands has evolved to be smaller. Some organisms have become significantly larger through a form of evolution known as **gigantism**.

The **giant coreopsis** is a huge daisy-like flower straight out of a Dr. Seuss book. It can grow up to 1.8 meters (6 feet) tall. This coreopsis may have evolved to be so big because of the lack of large plant-eating predators, such as deer, on the islands.

The **island scrub-jay** is another island giant, growing larger than its mainland cousin. It lives only on Santa Cruz Island. Interestingly, scientists have found diverse jays living right next to each other, each with their own unique beak adapted to specific types of nuts.

Island Rules

In 1964 scientist J. Bristol Foster hypothesized that when a large animal arrives on an island it will evolve to become smaller, and that when a small animal arrives on an island it will evolve to become larger. This became known as the **island rule** and appeared to be a good explanation of why island dwarfism and gigantism occur.

However, over the last several decades other scientists, including Ted Case, have found countless exceptions to the rule. Some now hypothesize that when an animal arrives on an island, it will evolve in whichever size direction allows it to occupy a position on the food chain that is currently unoccupied.

Confused? Then you are paying attention. Scientists constantly struggle to better explain the world without oversimplifying it. A model or rule might sound great and stand for decades, only to be blown apart by a shocking discovery. Only by continuously testing a hypothesis—and then retesting conclusions—can we get closer to understanding. This is the beauty of science.

Paleontologists carefully unearth a pygmy
mammoth on Santa Rosa Island in 1994.
Photo by Bill Faulkner / National Park Service

Unearthing Mammoths

with Don Morris – Archaeologist

Read *Digging in the Southwest*. Decided to become an archaeologist.

Started backpacking and mountaineering during first year at U of Arizona.

First permanent job for National Park Service at Wupatki Nat'l Monument.

Became official archaeologist at Channel Islands National Park.

How did you first hear about the pygmy mammoth skeleton on Santa Rosa?

In the late 1980s, new dating techniques made me curious about retesting the famous Arlington Springs Man skeleton to secure a more accurate age. [Read more about this theory-changing set of bones on page 98.] This meant heading back to the original dig site in Arlington Canyon on Santa Rosa Island.

While exploring a sea terrace on the dig, a friend approached and said "Tom [Rockwell, the expedition geologist] thinks he has found a complete mammoth. You haven't found many of those, have you?"

"Many? We haven't found any!" I replied. Nearly all of the mammoth material collected prior to then was single bones.

When did you realize that this mammoth was different?

We realized we had something different immediately. We didn't know precisely what it was, but it was clear that digging would be a major project, if done correctly. Our summer plans would have to change! We needed expert identification—and that meant calling in Dr. Larry Agenbroad.

Can you walk us through what a day on the 1994 dig was like, from sunrise to sunset?

The dig team was based in trailers at the National Park Service facility at Bechers Bay on Santa Rosa Island. We rose around six every morning and ate, then traveled 8 kilometers (5 miles) by vehicle and on foot to the site. Then we started digging.

This project was exceptional because the skeleton was covered in dune sand that was very easy to remove—about the easiest digging I have ever experienced. Around 10 a.m. visitors would arrive. We were able to arrange for them to come and stand on the edge of the dig and observe and ask questions. Larry was quite good at handling this, and it did not usually interfere with our work.

We had a small tent nearby for shade during lunch and water breaks. Around 5 or 6 p.m. we packed up, returned to camp, showered, and ate dinner. Repeated as necessary. After about two weeks of work, we were finished.

Given the island location of the dig, were there any unique challenges that you faced?

The dig site was fairly accessible, but it was about 9 meters (30 feet) above a sheer, 15-meter (50-foot) cliff that plunged directly to the sea. The slope was about 45 degrees, so we installed a retaining fence that would hopefully catch any tools, specimens, or paleontologists that would roll down.

In doing any work in a National Park, you must consider the impact. We had to descend a steep slope, traversing a field of endangered plants. The park botanist worked with us to lay out a trail, marking some specific plants that we had to step over and avoid on each trip. There was also concern about disturbing nesting seabirds with the helicopter operations. There is a danger of catastrophic erosion when digging in sand dune material, and we had to install shielding as our excavation deepened.

We were fortunate in being able to accomplish the excavation so soon following discovery. We also made the discovery at almost the perfect time. Rain during the following winter would have undoubtedly degraded the material.

It was a very constructive and worthwhile project. My wife was working alongside me, and the crew and all associated worked together very well. This was the beginning for me of a 20-year

Pygmy mammoth dig site on Santa Rosa Island. Work had to be done slowly, so as not to damage the fossil.
Photo by National Park Service

collaboration with Larry Agenbroad—a real high point in my career.

What was the significance of that 1994 discovery?

This was the first reasonably complete pygmy mammoth skeleton ever recovered, and it gave us a more complete picture of the entire animal. Later study showed that, as the pygmy evolved on the islands, the ratio of the length of the upper and lower leg bones—relative to its ancestor—had changed. This meant that the pygmy was able to climb steeper slopes than a normal mammoth: up to 35 degrees instead of just 25 degrees. This gave the pygmy access to more of the island and its food resources. And its smaller size meant it needed less food. Larger size was not necessary since there were no predators on the island.

When we dated the remains, we found that the pygmy mammoths were around at the same time as the Arlington Springs Man, 13,000 years ago. People and pygmies were on the island together. How did they interact? Could human activity have caused the extinction of the pygmy mammoth?

What advice would you give to an aspiring archaeologist?

Archaeology touches on many different disciplines, so brush up on your geology and biology. Anyone doing fieldwork should be comfortable in outdoor situations, and be adaptable and versatile. You will be dealing with many different physical situations and collaborating with fellow investigators. Do it right, and you will have both a rewarding career and lifelong friends in the field.

Remains of a pygmy mammoth tusk on Santa Rosa Island, in marine deposits dated to roughly 80,000 years ago. *Photo by Daniel R. Muhs / U.S. Geological Survey*

COME HERE

While the mammoths are long gone, the Channel Islands today are home to dozens of species found nowhere else on this planet. To experience the wonder of this not-so-remote place, grab your flippers or hiking boots. The "Galapagos of North America" are just a short boat ride away.

CROSS

It takes about one hour to get from Ventura Harbor to Santa Cruz Island by boat. Keep an eye out for pods of dolphins and migrating whales.

LEARN

Before you go, check out the Channel Islands National Park Visitor Center in Ventura Harbor.

LOS ANGELES

VENTURA

OXNARD

SANTA BARBARA

POINT CONCEPTION

ANACAPA

SANTA CRUZ

SANTA ROSA

SAN MIGUEL

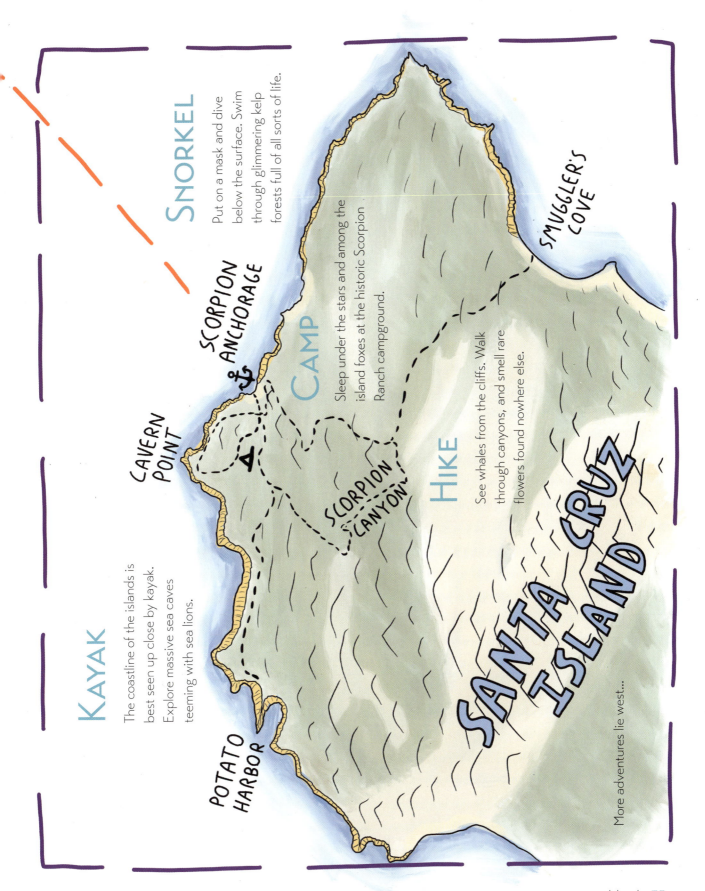

KAYAK

The coastline of the islands is best seen up close by kayak. Explore massive sea caves teeming with sea lions.

POTATO HARBOR

CAVERN POINT

SCORPION ANCHORAGE

SNORKEL

Put on a mask and dive below the surface. Swim through glimmering kelp forests full of all sorts of life.

SMUGGLER'S COVE

CAMP

Sleep under the stars and among the island foxes at the historic Scorpion Ranch campground.

HIKE

See whales from the cliffs. Walk through canyons, and smell rare flowers found nowhere else.

SCORPION CANYON

SANTA CRUZ ISLAND

More adventures lie west...

PLANT VOICES

by Peter Schuyler – *Botanist*

AGE 9
Begging his dad paid off! First trip to Santa Cruz and San Miguel Islands.

AGE 17
Sailed to the islands— explored, hiked, dived— and repeated again.

AGE 20
Journeyed into botany and plants using Islands as a natural laboratory.

AGE 26
Got paid to live and work on Santa Cruz for The Nature Conservancy.

The four northern Channel Islands are a botanical wonderland. Giant yellow coreopsis straight out of a Dr. Suess book dot the hills. Stealthy succulents hide beneath the soil, popping up only in the winter when there is water. Rugged pine trees grow into incredible shapes, sculpted by the powerful winds that blow across the islands.

Many of these species are endemic, meaning that they are found nowhere else in the world. Some were once widespread, but are now just memories of a climate long-gone; we call these relicts. Other more common varieties have evolved into new forms, some growing larger, others becoming dwarfs, still others losing chemical defenses or thorns due to the lack of predators such as deer.

The islands are unfortunately also now home to non-native plant species from around the world. Some cause no problems while others are highly invasive and have altered the fragile plant communities that call these places home. The worst threaten the very existence of the islands' endemic species.

Each plant has its own story. Some shout it loudly from the ridgetops. Others whisper quietly from beneath the soil. By listening to all of these plant voices, we can better understand the wonder of the island ecosystems. It is only through this understanding that we can preserve them for future generations.

up to 15.2 meters / 50 feet

up to 20 centimeters / 8 inches

Santa Cruz Island Ironwood

Lyonothmnus floribundus subsp. *asplenifolius*

White flowers, red bark
Memories of long ago
Clinging to a cliff

A member of the rose family, this tree can reach up to 15.2 meters (50 feet) tall. It has peeling reddish bark, white flowers, and shiny dark green leaves. Finding an ironwood grove on steep rocky slopes means you are exploring the islands' hidden landscapes. Ironwoods rarely reproduce by seed; all trees in a grove are clones of each other. Fossils from the mainland indicate that ironwood trees were once widespread in the western United States. The Santa Cruz Island ironwood is the official Santa Barbara County tree and can be seen planted by the freeway!

Santa Cruz Island Live Forever

Dudleya nesiotica

Low coastal land spit
One of a kind succulent
Live forever, alone

This tiny succulent plant, only a few centimeters in height, is found only on a small windswept portion of Santa Cruz Island. Nowhere else on the island...or in the world! Subject to salt spray and threats from invasive plant species, the live forever survives in a harsh environment. Rounded reddish leaves emerge in the winter months, with small star and v-shaped white flowers following in late spring. By the end of summer, little trace of the plant can be found as it goes dormant. Think of this like a deep sleep.

up to 2.4 meters / 8 feet

Giant Coreopsis

Leptosyne gigantea

Beauty and the beast
Blaze of yellow–green come March
Summer stark desert

Giant coreopsis undergo radical seasonal change. With thick succulent stems and delicate green leaves in winter, it becomes a mass of bright yellow flowers which can be seen from the mainland (!) in early spring. By late summer it enters a Dr. Suess-like dormant phase with only bare stems and dried leaves and flowers hanging on, helping it survive the long dry summer. The giant coreopsis used to exist only on remote cliff faces, beyond the reach of ranch animals. With the removal of these creatures, it has spread to open fields.

up to 15 meters / 49.2 feet

Santa Rosa Island Torrey Pine

Pinus torreyana subsp. *insularis*

Long blue gray needles
Windswept bonsai monument
Rarest of the rare

This extremely rare tree has two subspecies, one found only on the Del Mar coast near San Diego, and the other found only on Santa Rosa Island. The Torrey Pine was down to about 100 reproductive wild individuals in the early 20th century. Conservation efforts have increased the population to more than 3,500 trees. Often twisted into beautiful contorted shapes by the high winds found on Santa Rosa, the Torrey Pine grove epitomizes the wild, unique landscapes found on the islands.

up to 70 centimeters / 2.3 feet

HOFFMAN'S
ROCKCRESS

Boechera hoffmannii

Thought lost for all time
Your purple flowers returning
Slowly now faster

This federally-endangered mustard family species for many years was thought to be extinct. Rediscovered in the 1980s in two small populations on Santa Cruz Island, its recovery was slow for decades. In the spring of 2019, after a long rainy season, a dramatic boom occurred. Numbers greatly increased, and new populations popped up in unexpected sites. Land managers had to rethink what conditions the plants needed to thrive. It goes to show that continual exploration, an open mind, and a good dose of optimism can pay off.

up to 2.5 meters / 8.2 feet

SWEET
FENNEL

Foeniculum vulgare

Carpets of yellow,
Creeping across the landscape
Natural trouble

Originally from Europe and used as a spice and condiment, fennel has been present on the islands since the 1800s. Kept somewhat in check by cattle and sheep, the removal of these grazers presented a conservation puzzle for island managers. Take away one invasive, and another may thrive. The explosive growth of fennel on Santa Cruz Island following the removal of animals in the 1980s highlighted the need for future restoration programs to expect unexpected consequences from conservation actions.

ISLAND HOMES

The Channel Islands and their surrounding waters are home to a vibrant ecosystem like no other on this planet. If you were to cram all of this life onto a single isle, it might look a bit like this:

MIGRATION

Many animals come through the islands and the surrounding waters on their way up or down the Californian coast. Some stop for food and shelter; others are looking for a safe place to give birth to their young.

Brown pelicans roam California, but nest mainly on these islands.

Island scrub-jays have different beaks depending on what they eat.

Grey whales swim through on their way from Alaska to Baja California and back.

ROOKERIES

Unlike those on the mainland, the islands' shores are largely undeveloped. Seals and sea lions come here to raise their young in giant colonies called rookeries. Point Bennett on San Miguel is one of the largest in the world, with more than 30,000 residents!

Male elephant seals fight to be the boss of the beach and impress females.

Sharks love rookeries too! It's where their food grows.

I seal you.

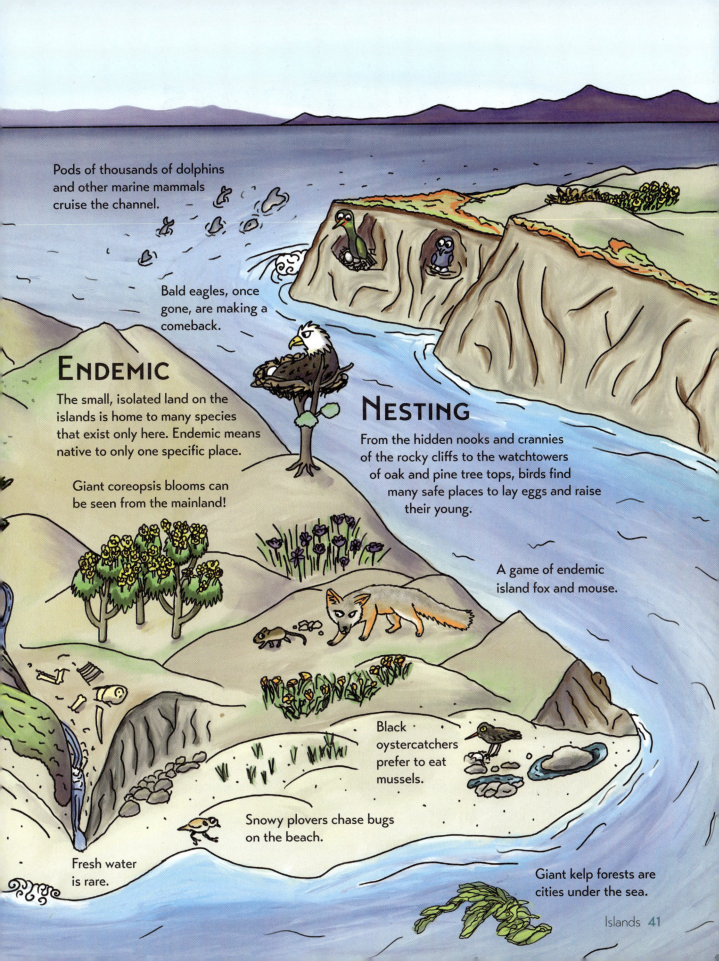

Pods of thousands of dolphins and other marine mammals cruise the channel.

Bald eagles, once gone, are making a comeback.

ENDEMIC

The small, isolated land on the islands is home to many species that exist only here. Endemic means native to only one specific place.

Giant coreopsis blooms can be seen from the mainland!

NESTING

From the hidden nooks and crannies of the rocky cliffs to the watchtowers of oak and pine tree tops, birds find many safe places to lay eggs and raise their young.

A game of endemic island fox and mouse.

Black oystercatchers prefer to eat mussels.

Snowy plovers chase bugs on the beach.

Fresh water is rare.

Giant kelp forests are cities under the sea.

A Pelican Island

by Amelia Jade DuVall – *Ecologist*

AGE 18 — Fell in love with the Pacific. Moved from Florida to California.

AGE 19 — Volunteered at a marine mammal rehabilitation center.

AGE 20 — Visited Channel Islands National Park. Vowed to see all the islands.

AGE 26 — Got job monitoring breeding seabirds on the Channel Islands.

The first time I tried to count California brown pelicans it was so hard that I went home and cried.

Earlier that day I was sitting on the bow of a National Park Service boat, binoculars pressed to my face, looking south towards West Anacapa Island. We were stopped about 150 meters (492 feet) offshore, in front of a massive bowl cut into the face of the island, appropriately dubbed the "Amphitheater." It was the middle of the breeding season, and hundreds of pelicans were nestled among the canyons and rocky cliffs, many of them hunkered down on large nests with their chicks.

Anacapa is historically the largest and most consistent breeding colony in the United States for the California brown pelican. In some years pelicans have built more than 5,000 nests and raised more than 3,000 chicks on West Anacapa alone. The only other major breeding location in the United States is found on Santa Barbara Island. While many visitors flock to the islands for

A flock of brown pelicans flies over Arch Rock on Anacapa Island.
Photo by Robert Schwemmer

a glimpse of the charismatic island fox, seabirds nest in larger numbers on Anacapa and Santa Barbara precisely because they are the only Channel Islands without foxes. Foxes are known predators of eggs, and pelican nests are especially vulnerable because they are often out in the open and on the ground. These small islands provide pelicans a safe refuge, away from mammalian predators as well as human development and disturbance, which can cause them to abandon their nests.

That day on the Park Service boat, we were counting adult pelicans, nests, and chicks to document how their breeding population was doing. At a distance, the adults in their bright breeding plumage, red pouches, and white heads looked like small Q-tips. I would tell myself to focus on the Q-tips, and start all the way at the top: "1, 2, 3…" and inevitably, somewhere around 47, or 86, or 292, I would lose my place and have to start over. I was completely overwhelmed. The sun in my face and the rocking boat only added to my frustration.

But, the truth is, it was exhilarating to see so many pelicans. In 1970 the California brown pelican was listed as federally endangered. That year only one chick on Anacapa Island survived. The nearby Montrose Chemical Corporation plant and other chemical production facilities had been discharging pesticides into the ocean for decades and contaminating the marine ecosystem. The main culprit at hand, the pesticide known as DDT, interferes with calcium deposition during shell formation, resulting in the production of thin-shelled eggs that are susceptible to water loss and being crushed during incubation. DDT was banned in the United States in 1972, and the Montrose plant was shut down. [Learn more about the Montrose disaster on page 188.] As a result, California's brown pelican population began to recover in the 1980s. The brown pelican was removed from the Endangered Species List in 2009.

Counting pelicans has become easier over time. But despite their incredible recovery, the California brown pelican still faces threats from oil spills, overfishing, human disturbance, invasive species, and climate change. Through continued research and conservation we can protect this magnificent species—and be lucky enough to have trouble counting all of them out on Anacapa.

Right on the horizon are these little spots of wonder,
little spots full of life found nowhere else on our planet.
Until you really see the Channel Islands,
from their peaks to the depths off their shores,
it is hard to believe that places like this really exist.
Once you understand how utterly magnificent they are,
that horizon will never quite look the same.

– Mike deGruy, Filmmaker and Ocean Storyteller

Photo by Robert Schwemmer

CHAPTER 2

OCEAN

PACIFIC

CHANNEL ISLANDS

OCEAN

Photo by NASA

ASTRONAUTS LOOKING DOWN FROM SPACE SEE MOSTLY BLUE.

From this universal perspective water makes every piece of land—from giant Africa to tiny Anacapa—an island. Yet that which separates also connects. No matter which island you are standing on, you are linked to the ocean in countless unimaginable ways.

The very water that makes our planet blue also keeps us and all the creatures on the Channel Islands breathing. Despite this, we know next to nothing about its depths. We often don't notice our impact on the ocean until it is too late. The solution: strap on a pair of flippers. Dive in. Discover blue that makes this marble our home.

How Much Ocean?

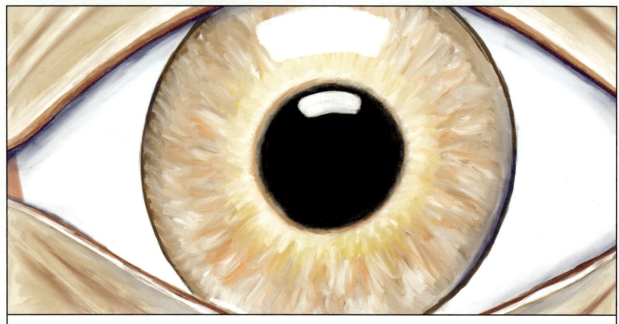

Human Eye = **2.4 centimeters** (0.94 inches) tall

Human Face = **24 centimeters** (9.4 inches) tall

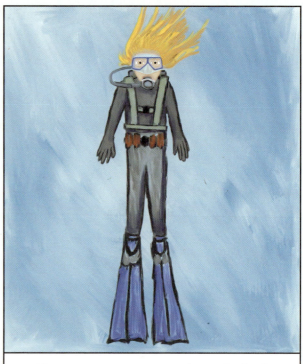

Human = **165 centimeters** (65 inches) tall

Blue Whale = **29 meters** (95 feet) long

Container Ship = **400 meters** (1,312 feet) long

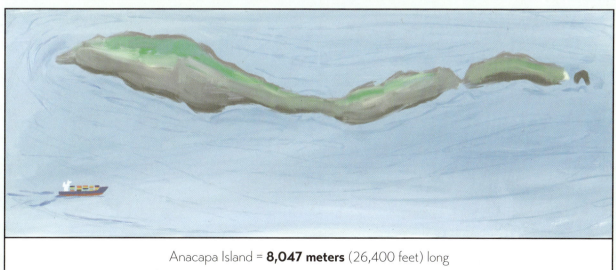

Anacapa Island = **8,047 meters** (26,400 feet) long

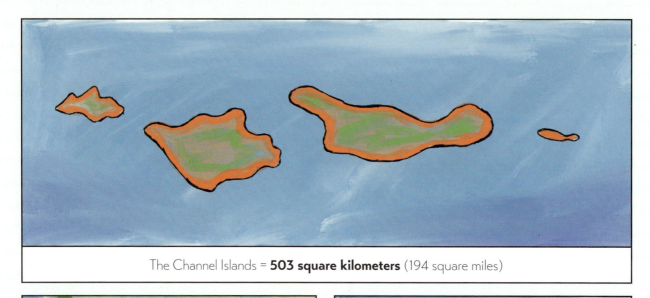

The Channel Islands = **503 square kilometers** (194 square miles)

California = **423,967 square kilometers**
(163,694 square miles)

Americas = **42,044,000 square kilometers**
(16,233,279 square miles)

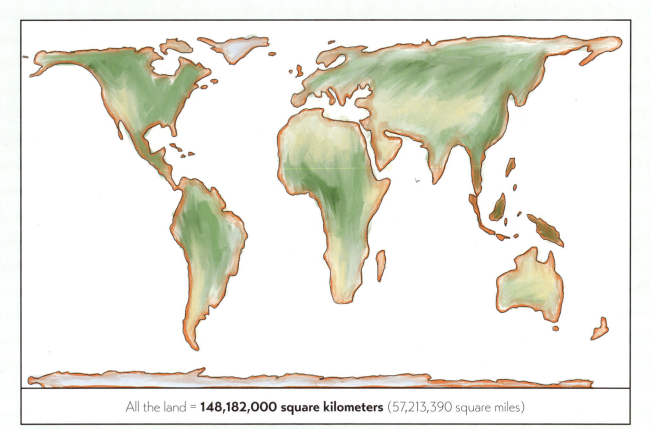

All the land = **148,182,000 square kilometers** (57,213,390 square miles)

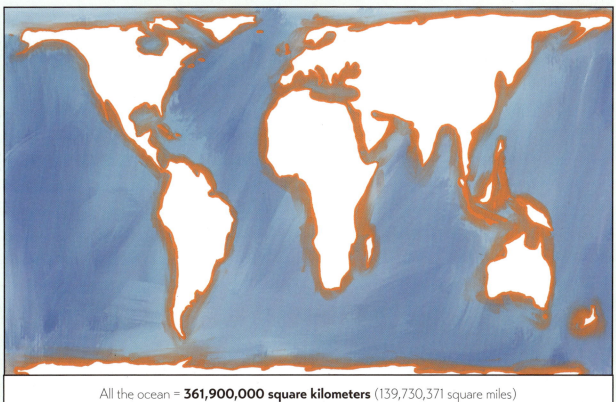

All the ocean = **361,900,000 square kilometers** (139,730,371 square miles)

This is Your Brain on Water

by Wallace J. Nichols – *Marine Scientist*

AGE 10 — Grew up with pet frogs and a revolving door of exchange students.

AGE 18 — In college, dived in nearly every lake, river, and quarry in Indiana.

AGE 30 — Helped Adelita, a sea turtle who swam across the entire Pacific.

AGE 47 — Published *Blue Mind*, a book about the impact of water on our brains.

I'm standing on a pier at the Outer Banks of North Carolina, 15 meters (50 feet) above the Atlantic. To the left and right, forward, back, and below, all I can see is ocean. I'm wearing a light blue hat that looks like a bejeweled swim cap, and a heavy black cable snakes down my back like a ponytail.

The cap is the nerve center of a mobile electroencephalogram (EEG) unit invented by Dr. Stephen Sands, a biomedical science expert. When groups of neurons are activated in the brain by any kind of stimulus—a picture, a sound, a smell, touch, taste, pain, pleasure, or emotion— a small electrical charge is generated, which indicates that brain functions such as memory, attention, language processing, and emotion are taking place. By examining where those electrical charges occur in the brain, Steve's machine can measure everything from overall engagement to attention, visual or auditory stimulation, whether the subject's motor skills are involved, and how well the recognition and memory circuits are being stimulated.

The ornamented swim cap on my head will sample these electrical charges 256 times per second. When amplified for analysis, these data will allow neuroscientists to see in real time which areas of my brain are being stimulated. Typically such data

are used to track shoppers' responses in stores like Walmart as they stop to look at new products on a shelf. In this case, however, the 68 electrodes plugged into the cap on my head are for measuring my every neurological up and down as I plunge into the ocean. It's the first time equipment like this has been considered for use at (or in) the water, and I'm a little anxious.

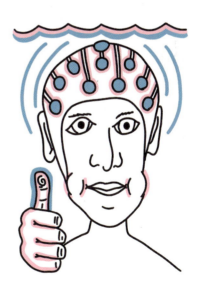

It's only recently that technology has enabled us to delve into the depths of the human brain and into the depths of the ocean. With those advancements, our ability to study and understand the human mind has expanded to include a stream of new ideas about perception, emotions, empathy, creativity, health and healing, and our relationship with water. Several years ago I came up with a name for this human–water connection: Blue Mind, a mildly meditative state characterized by calm, peacefulness, unity, and a sense of general happiness and satisfaction with life in the moment. It is inspired by water and elements associated with water, from the color blue to the words we use to describe the sensations associated with immersion.

BLUE

Whether it's logical or not, humans seem drawn to the color blue. It's overwhelmingly chosen as their favorite color by people around the world, beating its closest competing color by a factor of three or four. When marketers and psychologists have asked people what qualities they associate to blue, they use words like "credibility," "calming," "clean," "focused," "cleanliness," "openness," "depth," and "wisdom." Emotionally, blue is associated with trust, confidence, and dependable strength. Is it any wonder that companies such as Facebook, AT&T, Lowe's, American Express, HP, IBM, Walmart, Pfizer, and Vimeo use blue in their corporate logos? Blue even predominates on the packaging of black-and-white Oreo cookies.

FLOATING

Not long ago I found myself opening a hatch on a white, smooth, and rather modern-looking capsule. It was a very particular creation designed for a particular sort of quiet: a flotation tank. Inside the tank was warm, salty, 36-degree C (97-degree F) water—enough salt, 318 kilograms (700 pounds)—to keep my body afloat effortlessly at the water's surface. And it was dark—as in no light whatsoever.

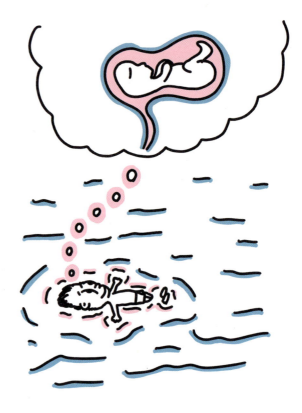

For about 30 minutes, floating in the dark, my brain looped the familiar patterns, schedules, urgencies, absurdities. Then, what I can best describe as a dissolving process began. Reference points, images, and ideas began to soften and erode like a tablet in water. My sense of location and time, my plans for the day, month, year, all slowly flaked away into nothingness.

The theory is that flotation tanks allow the brain to transition from the waking state, through the state of wakeful relaxation, and ultimately to the state of deep meditative consciousness akin to the moment between waking and sleeping. In this altered state the mind settles into nothingness, the inner voice is silent, and often a feeling of oneness and bliss occurs. I suddenly realized why "floaters" include everyone from software engineers, high-tech entrepreneurs, writers, actors, and other creative types, NFL players, and even (reportedly) U.S. Navy SEALs.

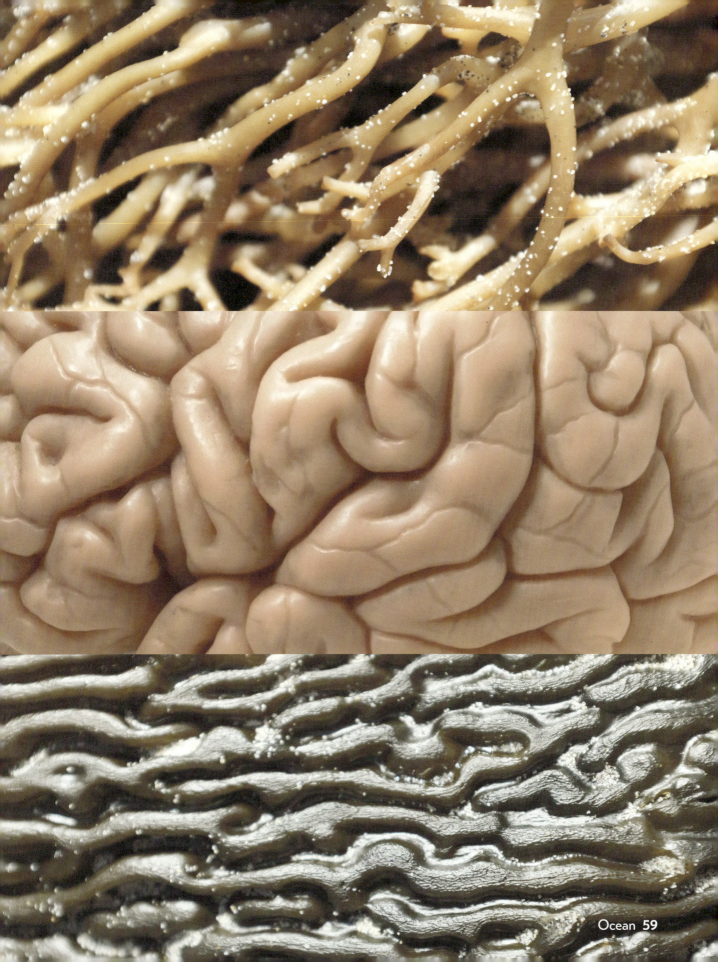

Keep Swimming

The resistance and pressure of water contribute to swimming's role as one of the best forms of both aerobic exercise and muscle toning. Because the pressure of water outside the body is greater than the pressure inside, explains Bruce E. Becker, director of the National Aquatics and Sports Medicine Institute at Washington State University, water forces blood away from the extremities and toward the heart and lungs. The heart responds by upping its effort, pushing this extra volume of blood more efficiently with each heartbeat, and thus circulating upwards of 30 percent more blood volume than normal throughout the body. To cope with this increased load, the arterial blood vessels relax and create less resistance to blood flow.

Here's the intriguing part: one of the hormones that regulates arterial function is catecholamine, and catecholamines are part of the body's response to stress. As Becker describes it, "During immersion, the body sends out a signal to alter the balance of catecholamines in a manner that is similar to the balance found during relaxation

or meditation." In other words, just being in the water can create a feeling of relaxation and a decrease in stress.

Like other forms of aerobic exercise, swimming can produce the release of endorphins and endocannabinoids (the brain's natural cannabis-like substances), which reduces the brain's response to stress and anxiety. The muscles are constantly stretching and relaxing in a rhythmic manner, and this movement is accompanied by deep, rhythmic breathing, all of which help to put swimmers into a quasi-meditative state. As one of the greatest competitive swimmers of our time, Michael Phelps, describes it, "I feel most at home in the water. I disappear. That's where I belong."

The Fishbowl

In one fascinating survey, people recovering from heart surgery looked at one of three scenes shown on panels at the foot of their beds. One showed an enclosed forest, another a view of open water, and a third an abstract design or blank white panel. Patients looking at nature scenes needed less pain medication. What is especially interesting, however, is that the anxiety levels of patients viewing the open-water scene were significantly lower than for those looking at the enclosed forest.

Viewing water and fish in aquariums also has been shown to help lower stress and promote a better mood. A study done at the National Marine Aquarium in Plymouth, England monitored the blood pressure, heart rate, and self-reported relaxation levels and moods of 112 people who spent a minimum of 10 minutes observing an aquarium tank with three different levels of biodiversity (no fish or shellfish, a few specimens, and a healthy variety of marine life). In all three

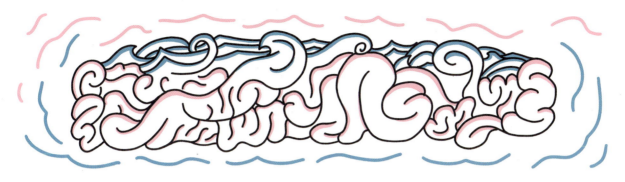

conditions, blood pressure dropped substantially during the first five minutes in front of the tank, while the most positive changes in heart rate, relaxation, and mood occurred with the greatest amount of biodiversity.

WOMB SOUNDS

As a Harvard Medical School Senior Research Fellow specializing in the effects of sound, Shelley Batts is supremely qualified to speak about sound and water. "We spend our first nine months underwater, hearing sound through water in the womb," she comments. "We hear the whooshing of our mother's heart, her breath going in and out, the gurgle of her digestion. These fluid, rhythmic sounds are very much like the ocean. Perhaps that's why the ocean often brings up feelings of relaxation and tranquility." From the womb onward, sounds have a profound effect on us physically, cognitively, and emotionally. And while prolonged exposure to loud noise causes the release of stress hormones and can lead to long-term damage, not just to our hearing but also to our general health, pleasant sounds at comfortable levels have been shown to improve mood, induce relaxation, and enhance concentration. According to Batts, sounds like that of water are inherently pleasant to our ears because they are not high frequency or harsh, and feature a regular wave pattern, harmonic pitch, and low volume.

The sound of water evokes some of the same sensations as meditation, and studies by Japanese researchers show that the sound of a creek in the forest produces changes in blood flow in the brain that indicate relaxation. In 2012 a group of dentists in Malaysia played the sounds of water fountains for patients between the ages of 12 and 16 prior to dental care. They found that the natural water sounds reduced the teenagers' worry and anxiety about treatment by nine percentage points compared to the control group.

BACK TO SEA

I look out from the pier at the vast Atlantic and imagine all the ways that the sight, sound, and smell of the water are influencing my brain. I take a moment to notice the feelings that are arising. For some, I know, the ocean creates fear and stress; but for me it produces awe and a profound, immersive, and invigorating peace. I take a deep breath and imagine the leap, cables trailing behind me as I plunge into the waves surging around the pier. The EEG readings would reflect both my fear and exhilaration as I hit the water feet first. I imagine Dr. Sands peering at a monitor as data come streaming in. Water fills the light, the sound, the air—and my mind.

Adapted from Blue Mind.

WITNESS THE OCEAN

by Morgan Maassen – *Photographer*

Dad pushed him on an ancient Doyle soft top into his first wave at Miramar.	Mowed lawns and walked dogs to pay for undersea camera housing.	Quit job as graphic designer to travel, camera and surfboard in hand.	First professional surf photography shoot in the water at Teahupo'o.

As the son of a Channel Islands urchin diver, Morgan Maassen grew up in the water. Now a photographer, he travels the world documenting the wonder and power of the ocean. By placing himself above, on, and in the waves, he has gained a unique perspective on this big blue expanse that covers much of our planet. Here is the ocean, in his images and words:

"Playing with water in-between waves while bodysurfing at Hendry's Beach."
(Santa Barbara, California)

"Exploring the Channel Islands feels like you're experiencing California centuries ago." (Santa Cruz Island, California)

"My dad, Jeff, emerging from the depths after diving for sea urchins near San Miguel Island. He counts his blessings to call them his office." (San Miguel Island, California)

"Watching winter storms pass by the Gold Coast of Australia, I caught this brief glimmer of light break through amongst the brooding clouds and rain squalls." (Gold Coast, Australia)

"Surfers watch the last of a winter storm roll by. While the waves were recuperating from the morning's wind, the ocean never disappoints for its beauty." (Rincon Point, California)

"Crossing the Santa Barbara Channel
frequently warrants running into a pod
of common dolphins. In this case, we
ran into a pod of well over a hundred
who gleefully joined us as we were
sailing back from Santa Cruz Island."
(Santa Barbara Channel, California)

"We saw the calf playing in the water. It was playful as a puppy, yet still clocking in at a solid 5 meters (16.5 feet) long. Suddenly it disappeared into the depths, only to return a minute later, ascending underneath its massive mother, who was 20 meters (67 feet) long. Not only was I dumbstruck, I literally couldn't breathe. They drifted silently towards the surface. Moments before the mother's pectoral fin was within touching distance, I found my composure to snap this one photograph. They surfaced, grabbed a breath of air, and were gone with the flick of a tail...but this photo lives with me forever, a postcard of the most profound moment of my life." (Tahiti)

"Evan Mock, upside in the crystalline water."
(Waimea Bay, Hawaii)

"A perfect wave breaks far out to sea, moments before a squall engulfed it in a veil of darkness and sent us running for the safety of our car." (Stradbroke Island, Australia)

"The vibrant channel off of Point Conception after a strong and beautiful winter storm." (Point Conception, California)

"Dane Peterson, dancing on a scorching hot day."
(Noosa Point, Australia)

Ocean Places

It is easy to think of the ocean as just one big pool. Dive below the surface, and another world opens up. Think of the seafloor as a continuation of dry land just beneath the waves. The ocean's mountain ranges, valleys, and forests dwarf those on land. To better understand the vastness of this seascape, scientists divide the ocean into zones. Organisms in each of these zones have adapted to radical differences in pressure, light, temperature, and nutrients. They have formed aquatic cities and suburbs that challenge any rainforest for diversity, complexity, and beauty.

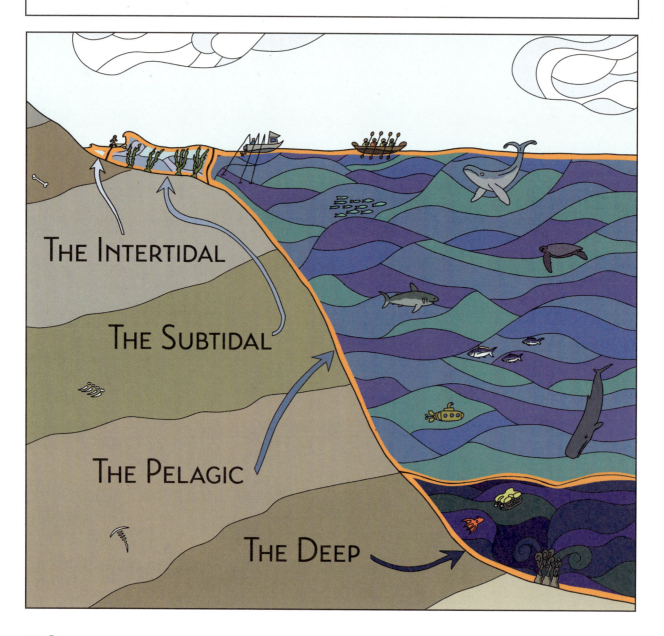

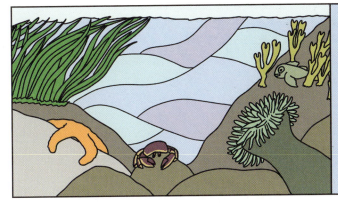

THE INTERTIDAL

You wade and splash in this zone at the beach. Located where the waves meet the shore, the intertidal is exposed to the air at low tides, and underwater at high tide. Organisms living here adapt to life in and out of the water—think bustling tidepools full of barnacles, anemones, mussels, sculpin, and hermit crabs.

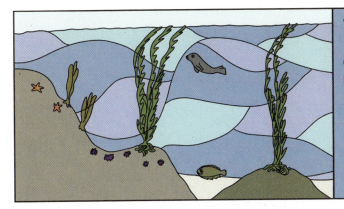

THE SUBTIDAL

Close to shore, this zone stretches from the low tide line to 30 meters (100 feet) below the surface. Light penetrates here, allowing for photosynthesis—where plants and algae convert sunlight to energy, and sustain life. The subtidal zone that surrounds the Channel Islands supports vast kelp forests full of countless residents.

THE PELAGIC

Meaning "open ocean" in ancient Greek, the pelagic makes up most of the sea on our planet. It is home to the blue whale, the great white shark, and schools of countless fish, from sardines to salmon. At the bottom of this zone, less light and oxygen is available. The creatures living at such depths must adapt to these harsher conditions.

THE DEEP

Hundreds of meters down, no light gets through. The pressure is immense. However, this icy water holds vast stores of oxygen and nutrients. As a result, the deep sea hosts a wide variety of fantastical life. Here there be blind fish with huge teeth, alien-like glowing creatures without skeletons, and fearsome-looking vampire squid.

EXPLORING THE DEEP

by Tommy Riparetti Brown – *Teacher*

AGE 10 — Uncle dared him to lick a sea anemone. Ouch, that stung.

AGE 14 — Took first high school science class. Liquid nitrogen demo was crazy!

AGE 22 — Got molecular biology degree. Learned to make glow-in-the dark bacteria.

AGE 29 — Taught high school physics. Used guitar to explain wave science.

"No one has ever seen this before!" I exclaim into my headset. At that moment, remotely operated vehicles (ROVs) *Hercules* and *Argus* shine their floodlights upon the muddy basin of Bodega Bay, 2,800 meters (9,186 feet) below the ocean's surface. It's true. Like the first astronauts on the moon, we are the first to lay eyes on this place. A bright red vampire squid shoots past. We can just make out the sharp spines that line the cape-like membrane that gives this Dracula-like creature its name. It is unlike anything that I have ever seen.

I'm 42 kilometers (26 miles) off the coast of California aboard exploration vessel (E/V) *Nautilus*, a 64-meter (210-foot) ship capable of traversing the ocean, tracing its coastlines, and probing its great depths. Right now I sit in the control van, a special room behind the ship's bridge. I can feel the surface conditions of the sea gently rocking the craft back and forth. Below me, I mean way below me, *Argus* and *Hercules* transmit images and data to E/V *Nautilus* by a long, armored cable.

"What is that?" the *Hercules* pilot says, craning his neck toward the monitor. The video engineer leans in, zooming the camera controls on a strange object sticking out of the mud. The moment the camera focuses on

NAUTILUS

the object in the mud, we all realize what it is. It's a plastic water bottle. Here, where the pressure is 280 times what it is at the surface, there is a piece of trash. You would implode at this depth, yet even on this unexplored sea floor there is evidence of humankind's presence on Earth. We know that the bottle traveled a long way to get here. Not just because we are more than a mile underwater, but because the words on it aren't in English.

Working on E/V *Nautilus* gives me a newfound respect for the connectedness the ocean provides. During training, I studied how the Arctic current moves cold water from Alaska and mixes it with warm currents from Mexico, creating conditions for vibrant life. I learned how the ocean absorbs gases in our atmosphere and "breathes" with our planet. Yet, at the same time, I'm now seeing first-hand how these currents can spread our trash to such seemingly remote places.

Down here, it isn't all trash though. Throughout the rest of our mission we will see how incredible this deep sea frontier truly is, from its teaming ecosystems of colorful coral gardens to bizarre fish and much more.

I'm off my watch in the dining cabin, eating pancakes with Dan, a scientist from the National Oceanic and Atmospheric Administration (NOAA). He's telling me stories about expeditions halted by high seas and strong winds. He explains how the ocean can be unpredictable, and how lucky we are that it is allowing us this great adventure.

The adventure came to be because scientists from NOAA sought to ask questions like "What organisms live in the depths in this part of the world?" Carina, a scientist from UC Davis, asks the question "What can the chemistry of the deep tell us about climate change?" Katelyn, a graduate student from the Harvard robotics program, wonders whether her robotic arm called "squishy fingers" can be an effective tool for picking up soft invertebrates in the deep-sea.

We know very little about the seafloor. Dr. Robert Ballard, the scientist who founded the non-profit Ocean Exploration Trust (OET), has been trying to change that. His curiosity led him to discover the wreck of the *Titanic* and, more importantly, the hydrothermal vents (openings in the sea floor from which heated mineral-rich waters flow) and incredible life which exists around this alien landscape.

The E/V *Nautilus*, my current home-at-sea, is owned and operated by OET. The *Nautilus* and its ROVs have made amazing deep sea discoveries, from whale carcasses teaming with hungry octopus to a never before seen purple orb creature found just off the Channel Islands. On this expedition, the *Nautilus* creates a 3D map of the seafloor to locate hard substrate—rocky areas that coral can grip onto. It's these unique targets that the team wants to explore with *Hercules* and *Argus* to get a better look.

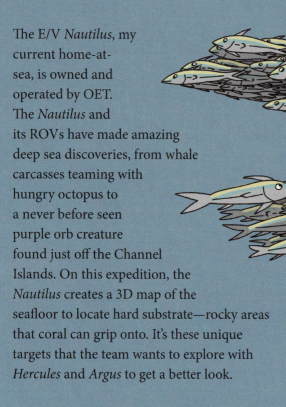

On my walk back up to the control van, I look west just in time to see a blue whale spout 46 meters (150 feet) starboard. These whales migrate through this area of the world because of those same mixing currents that may have transported that plastic bottle to its deep-sea resting place. I open the door, take my place next to the monitor, and adjust my microphone. The video feed from the ROVs will be broadcast live over the internet, so the world can explore alongside me.

Over the next few days I see marvelous things.

I see ctenophores (comb jellies) undulate in front of the camera, reflecting back all the colors of the rainbow.

I see a dumbo octopus, a mola mola, and many other cool animals.

I see pink polyps of coral filter marine snow.

We take some samples, and hope that one of them might be an undiscovered species! When E/V *Nautilus* turns back towards land and cruises underneath the Golden Gate Bridge, I wonder what I didn't see. More jaw-dropping and seemingly alien life forms—and probably more than a few more plastic bottles.

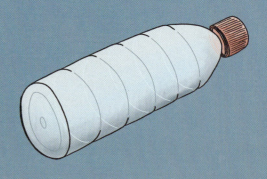

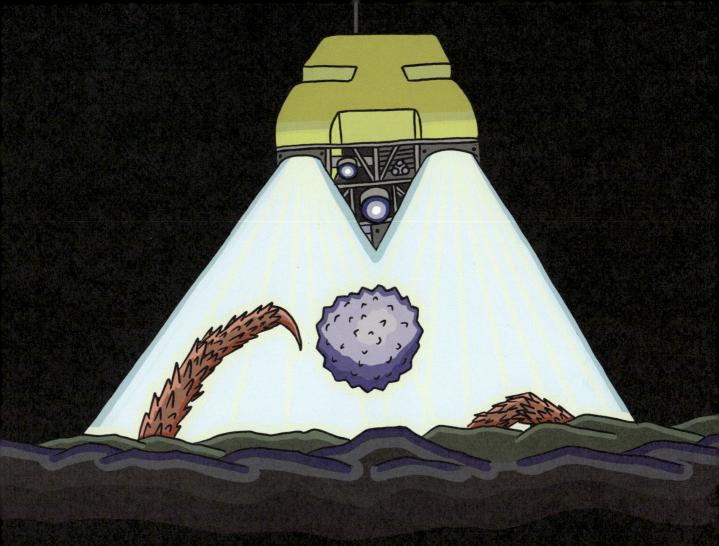

Island Depths

Deep in the ocean around the Channel Islands, life takes on unimaginable shapes. Some organisms, like the purple orb above, have been discovered only recently. Meet a few other residents of our local sea floor:

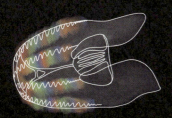

Comb Jelly: This jellyfish reflects light in rainbow patterns, just like a strand of holiday bulbs.

Deep Sea Octopus: Eight arms. Three hearts. Incredibly smart. Changes color at will. Beat that.

Lophelia pertusa: While it forms vibrant reefs, this coral is also very vulnerable to ocean acidification.

by Sylvia Earle – Oceanographer

AGE 7
Explored the woods around her home in Camden, New Jersey.

AGE 16
Attempted first dive using a copper helmet, before SCUBA was available.

AGE 35
Lived in an underwater laboratory for two weeks, studying the life in the sea.

AGE 55
Chief Scientist, National Oceanic & Atmospheric Administration.

"Suppose the oceans dried up tomorrow. Why should I care? I don't swim. I hate boats. I get seasick! I don't even like to eat fish. Who needs the ocean?"

The questions were fired at me without pause by an impish young Australian standing along the shore near Melbourne. I was a featured speaker at a 1976 conference about the oceans, and anticipated answering questions about what it was like to live underwater, meet sharks, dive on shipwrecks, or perhaps tell about exploring unknown depths, about going where no woman—or man—had gone before.

I glanced at the rippled edge of the vast, sparkling blueness that dominates the planet, embraces islands and continents, shapes the character of climate and weather, and, from the sunlit surface to the greatest, darkest depths seven miles down, is home for most of the life on Earth. Then I said, with a sweep of my arms:

"Right, dry up the oceans. Think of all the good stuff lost at sea that you could just scoop up. The trouble is, there wouldn't be anybody around to do that. Without an ocean, there would be no life—no people anyway."

"Well, how so?" she prodded. "People don't drink salt water."

"Okay," I began. "Get rid of the ocean, and Earth would be a lot like Mars. Cold, barren, inhospitable. Ask those who are trying to figure out how astronauts can live there. Or, how about the moon. There's a place with no bothersome ocean. And no life. It doesn't matter where on Earth you live, everyone is utterly dependent on the existence of that lovely, living salt water soup. There's plenty of water in the universe without life, but nowhere is there life without water."

I have tried to think of other responses to those simple-sounding questions about why oceans matter. Sometimes I try to imagine what intelligent aliens, viewing Earth from afar, might think about the sea. From their perch in the sky, they could immediately see what many earthlings never seem to grasp: that this is a planet dominated by salt water! In fact, the ocean is the cornerstone of the systems that sustain us: every breath we take is linked to the sea. Clouds of fresh water are moved from the sea surface to the atmosphere as vapor and return there, via land, as fog, rain, sleet, and snow. This vast, three-dimensional realm, accounting for 97 percent of Earth's water, also makes up more than 95 percent of the biosphere, the planet's "living space." NOAA biologist Nancy Foster says it succinctly: "Earth is a marine habitat."

Sometimes I try a poetic approach: describing how luminous, rainbow-colored jellies, starlike planktonic creatures, giant squid, translucent pink prawns, gray dolphins, brown lizards, spotted giraffes, emerald mosses, rustling grasses, every leaf on every tree and all people everywhere, even residents of the inland cities and deserts who may never see the sea, nonetheless depend on it.

The most likely places for life on Earth to begin and prosper may have been deep in the sea, perhaps in hot mineral-laden springs associated with volcanic activity. Another possibility is that life originated in warm, shallow lagoons. Whatever the actual place or places of origin, it appears that life started in the sea. Gradually, Earth became a vibrant and ever-changing living system. Billions of minute, active components drew energy from the sun, directly or indirectly, and through countless transformations, yielded oxygen, carbon dioxide, and water back to that system, slowly developing a protective atmospheric cocoon over land and sea.

It is tempting to hope that there is no need to be concerned about "life support systems" or grand Earth "processes," and to embrace the thinking of skeptics who point out that the planet is, after all, large, robust, resilient, and quite capable of taking care of itself. After all, life persisted through immense meteor-induced devastation, the impact of multiple mega-volcanoes, and more. Surely, the argument goes, life will continue to prosper no matter how much damage we inflict on the natural systems.

While it is possible to imagine that humankind could set in motion a chain of events causing Earth to become truly lifeless, like the moon or Mars, it is far more likely that human actions could modify the planetary systems in ways that might be unfriendly for, say, flowering plants and air-breathing vertebrates (like us), but still be acceptable for cockroaches, fungi bacteria, pond scum, and many sea creatures. There is no guarantee that humankind will be among the survivors of even subtle changes to the global environment, despite our technological cleverness and the widespread belief that our species enjoys unique status that somehow absolves us from responsibility.

Might the subtle changes we are causing in the chemistry of the sea now set into motion waves of extinction? Could certain microbes, now occupying highly-specialized, restricted niches, find the conditions we are creating more favorable—and enjoy population explosions that trigger other events inhospitable to us?

But there is hope. Savvy visitors from Chicago or San Juan or London or Moscow to an oceanic sanctuary such as the Florida Keys may see it as part of this nation's commitment to protect natural areas that contribute importantly to the basic ingredients of a hospitable planet. The oxygen produced and carbon dioxide absorbed in the protected seagrass meadows, like in the rainforests of Brazil, help offset oxygen consumed and carbon dioxide produced by automobiles, by industry, by people throughout the country—and the world. Billions of natural microorganisms in the sanctuary act on excess fertilizer, pesticides, herbicides, and other contaminants from air- and land-based sources, gradually breaking them down into less harmful components.

Even people who never venture within several thousand miles of the Florida Keys sanctuary might regard the sanctuary there—or the four in California (including the Channel Islands), the reefs offshore from Georgia, or even the little speck of reef in American Samoa—as a "priceless national asset," each area doing its part in maintaining planetary health vital to all people everywhere.

Sometimes I am asked what I believe to be the greatest threat to the oceans, and thus to human survival and well-being. Is it the huge amount of trash and toxic chemicals that are dumped into the sea? Pesticide-, herbicide-, and fertilizer-laden runoff from the fields and lawns of the land? Acid rain and other toxins falling from the sky? Dredging and filling of shoreline marshes and productive shallow seagrass meadows? Oil spills? Overfishing? The introduction of exotic species?

These are all problems, and all are contributing to the changing sea we are now witnessing—and causing. But if I had to name the single most frightening and dangerous threat to the health of the oceans, the one that stands alone yet is at the base of all the others, it is ignorance: lack of understanding, a failure to relate our destiny to that of the sea, or to make the connection between the health of coral reefs and our own health, between the fate of the great whales and the future of humankind. There is much to learn before it is possible to intelligently create a harmonious, viable place for ourselves on the planet. Changes in the sea in the past few decades should command our rapt attention—the sort of interest one might take in, say, the life-support system of a spacecraft housing all of the past, present, and future of humankind.

YOUR WEATHER

The ocean is responsible for our planet's weather patterns. Most of the sun's heat enters our atmosphere around the equator, where the ocean absorbs it. The ocean then spreads this warm water out across the planet. Some evaporates, forming clouds that then release water back onto land in the form of rain, hail, and snow. Most raindrops actually started their life in the ocean!

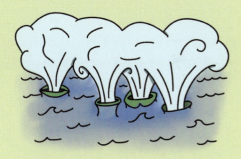

YOUR BREATH

While it may look empty, the ocean is packed with life. Countless microscopic plankton, along with towering forests of kelp, absorb much of the carbon dioxide in our atmosphere. These organisms transform carbon dioxide into oxygen, which makes its way back into the air. More than half of the oxygen that we breathe comes from this process. That is every other breath. No ocean, no island fox. No big blue, no us.

Storm clouds created by the sea return to the sea in Hossegor, France.
Photo by Morgan Maassen

by Hillary Hauser – *Activist*

AGE 10 — Spent hours at the beach getting lost in the solace of tidepools.

AGE 23 — Took first dive off of Santa Cruz Island, hooked on wonder of the place.

AGE 52 — Went to beach and saw "No Swimming" sign. Shocked.

AGE 54 — Started Heal The Ocean to help clean up the mess we have made in the sea.

The ocean always tells a different story, depending on where and how you experience it. There is the drama of the seashore, the activity and thunder of waves, the quiet beach that provides the place for a contemplative walk. From a hillside, the sun- or moon-sparkled expanse of sea points to the silent grandeur of unlimited space, the lure of unlimited possibilities. From the top of a very high mountain, the sea horizon appears to bend at the edges, and one gets the feeling of a door opening to the rest of the world—a hint of seaways and freighter lanes.

Pulling back even farther and higher, there is the astronaut's view—God's view, the Universe view. Earth is so much a water planet that someone once said it should never have been called Earth, but Sea.

There is another view of the ocean that is the best of all—the underwater world. And my perspective of ocean life began beneath the waves at the Channel Islands.

My first closeup view of the islands was at Profile Point, a rocky outpost on Santa Cruz Island. I was sitting on top of the wheelhouse of the old diving charter boat *Emerald*. It was fall. The sea was very still and the gulls were screeching loudly as they dipped and soared. From my perch on the roof I watched a dozen or so divers on the deck below suiting up for a morning plunge. I was in awe of the whole thing–of my surroundings and of what these black-suited people were doing. At this point, I'd never been diving in my life.

It was 1966 and I had just graduated from college. Like a lot of graduates, I had no idea of what I was going to do next. However, the day before this trip to Santa Cruz I'd bumped into Glenn Miller on Miramar beach. He told me he had a boat (*Emerald*), and that he took divers out to the Channel Islands. Did I want to come?

It was just that easy. An invitation to see something. Which is how I found myself on top of a wheelhouse of a dive boat the next day, looking over the side and down into the sea. I had to know this world!

It has been 50 years since my first dive at Profile Point on Santa Cruz Island. Since then I have taken many, many notes—not only about the Channel Islands but about the sea itself. Writing about science in the sea, fishermen, ocean politics, and other aspects of the Big Blue has given me a college education of another kind. I have learned how delicate the ocean is from the tiniest of teachers: microscopic plankton which create most of the air that we breathe. They have shown me how human activities such as dredging can have a profound impact on them, and thus on the health of our planet as a whole. At the same time, floating underwater amid the fishes, corals, sea lions, and sharks—more teachers—has shown me the beautiful pulse of the world that sustains our planet Earth. Without the ocean we would not be here.

I think my greatest appreciation of the sea was not at the bottom of an Australian sinkhole, or searching for a Spanish galleon in the Bahamas, or bodyboarding waves in Fiji—it was during mornings when I quietly got out of bed in my beach cottage, walked out to the sea, and simply went in. Just floating and looking up at the clouds, cool water swirling about me... my friend the ocean lifted my spirits to meet the day. I did this almost every morning of my life. When I failed to go swimming, the day was not right.

One morning in 1977 I went to a local beach, and there, like a horrendous monster out to scare everyone before eating them up, was a sign: "No Swimming." One of those red circles with a diagonal cut across the image of a swimmer.

I was stunned. I actually stood there and stared at that sign and couldn't move. What? Human beings have gone so far in our carelessness that we can no longer swim in the ocean? I looked out to the islands—and could only thank the heavens that humans' industrialization hasn't reached that far.

But how long would it take before the Do Not Swim issue stretched 32 kilometers (20 miles) off the mainland? The ocean pollution problem was at that time accelerating, with no checks and balances in place. This realization led me to start a citizens action group called Heal the Ocean. And among the first things we did was tackle the need to upgrade our mainland sewage technology–significantly–to treat human waste. No more ocean dumping! No more putting it into the ground and our groundwater, only to have it go out to sea unseen!

In the 20 years Heal the Ocean has been working, we've removed septic systems (machines that filter human waste underground, rather than at a sewage treatment plant) from seven miles of coastline. We've captured millions in State money to get wastewater plants on their way to becoming recycled water plants. It's been hard work, but worth it—because in the middle of it all there has been a paradigm shift. Today the sea is viewed as a precious resource, one that needs protection, not abuse.

The ocean off the mainland is still a long way off from matching the pristine sea that encircles the Channel Islands. However, the goal for all of us working in the sea—and all of us who love the sea—should be to return the entire ocean to this state. Such a return is possible.

To know the ocean and appreciate what it can be, hitch a boat ride to the Channel Islands. When you get there, go over the side, sink below the surface and look around. All you see is beauty and life—a silent grandeur of unlimited space, the lure of unlimited possibilities. You may be underwater in a tiny cove near an island cliff, swimming along a small reef, but you will feel a door opening to the rest of the world.

Ways To Heal

There are many different ways that one can help heal both the land and the sea. Here are a few to get you started.

Go into nature. Take a hike. Walk on the beach. Take someone else to your favorite outdoor spot. We value and protect only what we know, so get out there and connect with the natural world.

Volunteer for a local water conservation group. They monitor the water quality in local creeks and estuaries. These data help us make sure that no toxic chemicals are making their way into the ocean.

Learn more about the state of the sea. Take a marine biology course. Consider a career in environmental science or public policy. It is going to take people who understand the world to heal it.

Speak out against the pollution that you see in your community. Concerned citizens spur change. Contact your local congressperson. Go to a city council meeting. Make your voice heard.

Clean the beach. When you pick a piece of trash up off the sand you are preventing it from drifting out to sea. Many organizations put together regular beach cleanups on our local shores.

Ocean below me, ocean around,
On miles and miles of sea.
Sun rises, fish jump, and colors abound,
The only sign of our species is me.

A glorified dust speck sitting atop
A glorified hunk of driftwood,
A tapestry thriving as my backdrop,
A tapestry often misunderstood.

Through the eyes of the creatures that drift in the deep,
I can catch a quick glimpse of my soul.
Awake for a moment from societal sleep,
A fragmented piece of a much greater
whole.

I flow through these waters, totally free,
On miles and miles and miles of sea.

"Drift Would"
by Jayden Francis, Student

Photo by Morgan Maassen

CHAPTER 3

FIRST PEOPLE

LIMUW Santa Cruz Island

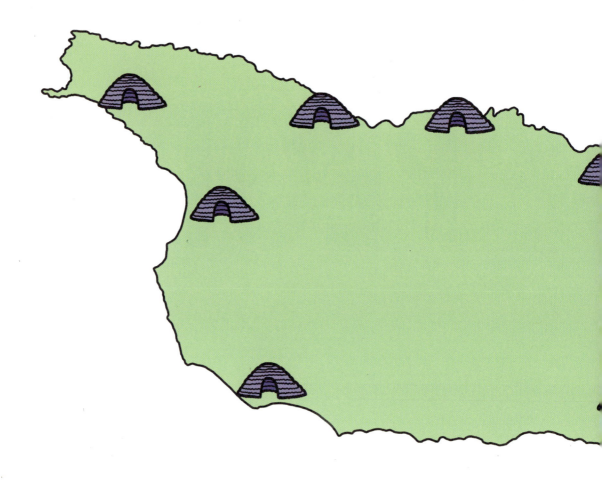

 = Proposed Chumash Village Site

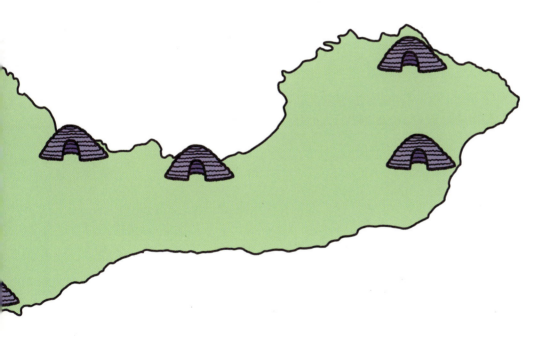

Photo by Pedal Born Pictures

WE ARE ALL FROM SOMEWHERE.

Somewhere that shapes the way you speak...the way you step...the way you dream. If you live there long enough, you might begin to see how connected you are to that somewhere. It is keeping you alive, and you might want to return the favor.

For thousands of years, a seagoing people known as the Chumash called the Channel Islands their somewhere. They crafted shell bead money found as far away as Arizona, chased swordfish from masterfully built redwood canoes, and tended an island garden that fed one of the largest village networks in western North America. Some might say that the land belonged to them. They would say that they belong to it. While they no longer live across the channel, to the Chumash these islands are still home.

Timeline

...No Humans...No Humans...

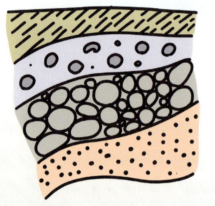 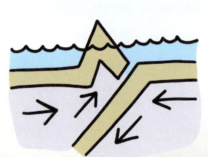 

18,000,000 Years Ago

Deep beneath Earth's crust, the long, slow process that will create the Channel Islands begins. Not a human to be seen.

5,000,000 Years Ago

Two tectonic plates start pushing what will become the island of Santarosae, ancestor of the Channel Islands, up from the ocean floor.

40,000 Years Ago

Giant wooly mammoths migrate out to Santarosae from mainland. They evolve to be smaller, eventually becoming pygmy mammoths.

...No Humans...Humans!

20,000
Years Ago

Sea level was 107 meters (350 feet) lower than today. Mammoths have been on Santarosae for 20,000 years. Still no humans on the island.

15,000
Years Ago

Species, including the flightless goose and giant deer mouse, continue to thrive undisturbed alongside the pygmy mammoth on Santarosae.

13,000
Years Ago

After following a "kelp highway" down the coast by boat, the first humans arrive on Santarosae. This changes everything.

Arlington Springs Man

by John R. Johnson – Curator, SB Museum of Natural History

AGE 9	AGE 14	AGE 17	AGE 26
Discovered his first arrowhead in sand dunes near Humboldt Bay.	Participated in his first supervised dig on Catalina Island.	Worked as scout camp counselor in archaeology in New Mexico.	Hired by Forest Service. Devoted life to study of indigenous past.

Back in 1959, Phil Orr was the Curator of Anthropology (study of humans and their cultures) and Paleontology (study of fossils) at the Santa Barbara Museum of Natural History. He got his vehicle stuck in the mud of one of the springs in Arlington Canyon on Santa Rosa Island. It turned out that what appeared to be a minor predicament led to the most consequential discovery of his career—a discovery that would forever change our understanding of the human history of North America.

Near his trapped vehicle, Phil noticed that a human femur was protruding from the side wall of the canyon in a layer of soil where he had also found bones of pygmy mammoths. Orr realized that this discovery was

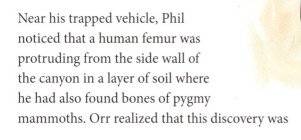

of great significance. It suggested that people had arrived on Santa Rosa Island by the end of the Pleistocene (the last Ice Age), and that they would have encountered the pygmy mammoths. This was much earlier than we had previously thought, and challenged long-held ideas of how humans arrived on the continent.

In the 1960s, radiocarbon dating (a test which measures the age of carbon-based materials such as bones) was still a new scientific tool, and it was not possible to obtain an accurate age for ancient bone. Phil Orr discovered a piece of charcoal buried nearby, which yielded an age of about 10,000 years. There was always a question about whether the charcoal was the same age as Arlington

Springs Man. New techniques for dating very small samples made it possible to find an answer.

In 1989 Don Morris, the first archaeologist employed by Channel Islands National Park, approached me about re-dating Arlington Springs Man. We carefully unwrapped the plaster jacket surrounding the femur, which was still in its earthen block. I contacted a leading expert in dating old bone, Dr. Thomas W. Stafford, Jr., who then had a lab in Boulder, Colorado. When Stafford dated the carbon from Arlington Man's femur, he made a remarkable finding. The bone appeared to date from 13,000 years ago, making it the oldest human skeletal element yet discovered in the Americas!

The presence of humans on an island off our coast at that early age shows that people then were using watercraft. This lends support to the hypothesis that the earliest human arrivals to North America could use watercraft in their journey southward from the Bering Land Bridge down the Pacific Coast. This discovery was quite incredible, as it brought into question the long-held theory that humans spread into North America via an ice-free corridor east of the Rocky Mountains, a journey that would have taken many decades.

To verify this exciting discovery, we needed more evidence from the field. We began a series of investigations at the location where the bones were originally discovered. Our purpose was to study the geological layers above and below where the bones were found, and thus confirm the age of the Arlington Springs Man. In 2001 we obtained a grant from the Santa Cruz Island Foundation to conduct detailed excavations.

Our plan was to obtain samples for radiocarbon dating, and to gather evidence that would allow us to get a better picture of the environment at the time that Arlington Springs Man lived. We assembled a team of archaeologists, geologists, photographers, mapping experts, and a licensed surveyor, and set off for our basecamp located at a National Parks Service facility on the island. After many hours of fieldwork and radiocarbon dating in the lab, we were able to verify that the layer that contained Arlington Springs Man's bones did indeed date to about 13,000 years ago.

Since 2001 we have launched three subsequent expeditions to the island, gathering additional evidence to better understand the story of Arlington Springs Man. In the same layer that once contained the human bones we found tiny chert flakes, providing evidence of stone tool sharpening near this location 13,000 years ago. We took samples from multiple locations that we later studied to reconstruct the geological history before, during, and after Arlington Springs Man lived. We have shown how the rapid buildup of soil that buried his bones was related to the rise in sea level that covered the former shoreline of Santa Rosa Island. As oceans worldwide rose from glaciers melting after the last Ice Age, the mega-island of Santarosae that existed during the Pleistocene began to break up into the separate northern Channel Islands that we know today.

The rise in sea level filled in canyons like the one in which the Arlington Springs Man was found. Only about 7,000 years ago did sea levels stabilize. By then, the 13,000-year-old bones had been deeply buried in soil that settled next to Arlington Springs, preserving the femur until the eroding side walls of the canyon exposed it enough to be encountered by Phil Orr in 1959.

With this heavy blanket of sediment still in place across many of the islands, one has to wonder: What similar unimagined discoveries still remain hidden for future generations of scientists? How will these discoveries further change our understanding of how the first humans spread across North America?

ASIA

ALASKA

CANADA

CALIFORNIA

CHANNEL ISLANDS

MEXICO

Thanks to Phil Orr's discovery of the Arlington Springs Man, scientists have a new theory about how humans originally traveled from Asia to North America.

These first humans followed a "kelp highway" down the coast, traveling by boat. The kelp forests that gave this route its name were full of tasty seafood, from tiny crabs to giant seabass. [Check out page 230 for an idea of all the menu options that these first human residents of North America had on their journey.]

Island Prosperity

Over a period of 13,000 years, the descendents of the Arlington Springs Man developed a vibrant and complex island culture on the Channel Islands. They traded up and down the coast using their state-of-the-art plank canoes, and established a currency system that was used across central and southern California.

By 1542, there were more than 3,000 people living in 21 villages spread across the islands. That was more people per square mile than anywhere else in California. The mainlanders called these island residents *Michumash*, meaning "makers of the shell bead money." European explorers would hear this as "Chumash" and use it to refer to both the island and mainland people of the region. While there are no longer Chumash living on the islands, descendants of both island and mainland Chumash are very much still here. Through organizations like the Wishtoyo Chumash Foundation, they are working to protect their homelands and educate their communities and youth, keeping their culture alive.

A traditional Chumash tule reed home is called an 'ap. Chumash village locations ('apanish) on the islands still retain the foundational impressions where these homes once stood in abundance. The Chumash community continues this traditional knowledge and practice to this day as seen here at Wishtoyo Chumash Village in Malibu. *Photo by Mati Waiya / Wishtoyo Chumash Village*

'Anchum

For more than 7,000 years, the Chumash used a form of **shell bead currency** that became known as 'anchum to trade between the islands and mainland, and with tribes across California. These shell beads have even been found as far north as Oregon, and as far east as Arizona.

Live on the islands and need a bundle of deer pelts? Folks on the mainland are selling them for three strands of 'anchum each. Need an island stone bowl for your mainland home? A craftsperson in *Swaxil*—the largest village on *Limuw*—is selling some beautiful ones for four strands apiece.

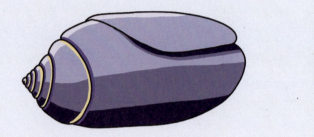

While the Chumash made beads from the shells of many different sea creatures over the centuries, they eventually settled on a tiny ocean snail as their money material of choice. The ***Olivella biplicata*** washed ashore in the winter, making them easy pickings.

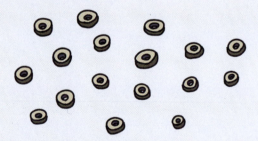

The island Chumash produced most of the 'anchum used across central and southern California. First, they broke each shell down into small discs. Then they used a stone drill to cut a hole almost all the way through the shell. To finish this hole, they used a finer drill made from the tip of a **sea lion whisker**. Just like a cat's whisker, these are quite sharp and rigid. Once completed, the Chumash strung the discs together into strands.

The Chumash measured the value of *'anchum* based on how many times a strand could be wrapped around one's hand. One no longer needed to lug around a heavy stone bowl or pile of deer pelts to trade; a simple **strand of beads** would do.

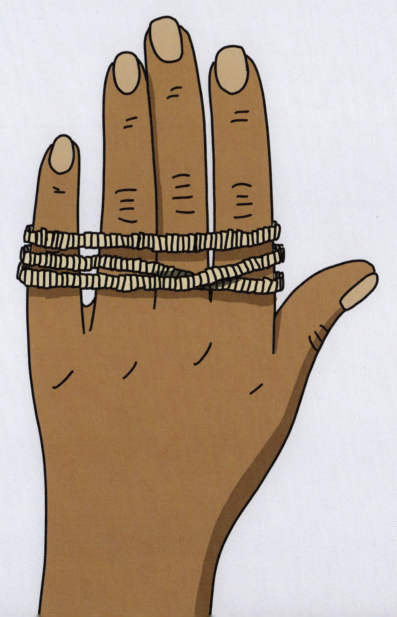

Giant coreopsis bloom on 'Anyapax (Anacapa Island).
In the spring, the blooms are so numerous that they
can sometimes be seen from the mainland.
Photo by Robert Schwemmer

by Georgiana Valoyce Sanchez – Professor, CSU Long Beach

AGE 4
Grew up without a television. Father was a great storyteller.

AGE 47
Became American Indian Studies Lecturer at CSU Long Beach.

AGE 54
One of her poems was put on a plaque on a San Francisco MUNI platform.

AGE 61
Witnessed the second *tomol* crossing of the Channel in more than 150 years.

There was a time, at night, when you were in the tomols *[plank canoes], it would be like a necklace of fires—where you would see all the villages up and down the whole coast.*

-Mati Waiya, Ceremonial Elder of the Santa Clara River Turtle Clan
Founder/Executive Director of Wishtoyo Chumash Foundation

The Channel Islands off the coast of Southern California are often shrouded in mist and cannot be seen from the mainland. After days of thick marine fog, it would be easy to believe the islands do not exist and that they are just a story made up by dreamers. Most people do not know the mythological, cultural, and historical meaning of the islands to the Original Peoples that inhabited them. We now know these Original Peoples as "Chumash."

The Chumash are part of a large coalition of Peoples who share a basic language and an extended territory in Southern California. The main groups are the *Tilhini* People (Obispeño); *Samala* (Inezeño); *Shmuwich* (Barbareño); *Micquanaqa'n* (Ventureño) and *Cruzeño* (named for Santa Cruz Island). The missions they were named for were instrumental in the devastation of the Chumash Peoples' ancient way of life.

The most prominent island, *Limuw* (known as Santa Cruz Island), is majestic and large, blooming like a miracle on clear days. The next largest island is *Wima* (Santa Rosa Island) and sits to the west, just behind *Limuw*. A little farther west, behind *Wima*, is *Tuqan* (San Miguel Island). The smallest island, *'Anyapax* (Anacapa Island) is at the eastern tip of the Big Island, *Limuw*; it was mostly used as a fishing camp and is now a bird sanctuary.

Ancient stories tell of a time when all Chumash Peoples lived only on the Channel Islands. The islands were alive with People working, laughing, speaking in the language given to them by *Hutash*, the Spirit of the Earth, and *Kakunupmawa*, The Mystery Behind the Sun.

Life on the islands was very good. The People were happy and healthy, and as time passed more people were born. Soon the islands became very crowded, and that was not healthy for the islands or the people. So, *Kakunupmawa* told the people that some would have to move to the big Land across the channel.

Kakunupmawa looked closely at the people and chose many young people, some with children and babies. The middle-aged grandparents of the children were also chosen, so the family would be together and help each other. Elders were chosen, especially those with wisdom and a special fire in their eyes.

One old woman asked how they were going to get to the big Land, reminding everyone that the channel could be very treacherous even for the best of swimmers. This was so long ago; they still had not invented the *tomol*, the famous sewn-plank canoes that the Spaniards were so impressed with when they explored the California coast in 1543.

"Don't worry," *Kakunupmawa* said. "A rainbow will be your bridge." And at that moment, a beautiful rainbow appeared from *Limuw* Island to the Big Land across the channel. The People were astonished, remarking on the brilliant colors of the rainbow. The Chosen Ones began to gather their belongings and baskets of acorn meal, dried fish, and berries.

"Wait," *Kakunupmawa* said. "When you get to the top of the rainbow do not look down or you will get dizzy and fall." Everyone agreed not to look down. The Chosen Ones said farewell to their loved ones and began the long walk across the Rainbow Bridge.

It was a beautiful day. The sky and ocean were so blue. The ocean sparkled as if someone had scattered millions of crystals across the water. They could see this even as they kept their eyes straight ahead. Higher and higher they climbed and, as some reached the top of the rainbow, they could not resist the sparkling, singing ocean. They looked down and fell.

They fell down and down, calling out and yelling as they fell, but those on the Rainbow Bridge kept their eyes straight ahead and prayed. The ones who fell hit the water hard and were stunned. They began to sink beneath the ocean. The stronger ones tried to swim up to the light but they too sank into the deep darkness.

Hutash felt the people dying and called to *Kakunupmawa* to save them. So, with the love and compassion of *Hutash* and the benevolent Power of *Kakunupmawa*, the people dying below began to change. Their bodies became sleek and smooth and they could swim toward the light. They jumped out of the water, twirling around, so happy to be alive. The Chumash Peoples tell this story to this day to remind us that the dolphins are our very close relatives.

On the first weekend of September in 2001, Chumash families crossed the channel and set up camp on the big island of *Limuw* at the ancient village site of *Swaxil*, which is now Scorpion Campground. They were there to await the arrival of *'Eleye'wun*, the latest traditional plank canoe of the Chumash. It was the first time since 1834 that Chumash paddlers would make the historic crossing to *Limuw*. While the people set up camp, everyone said it was "good to be home."

As they waited for the Paddlers, they told stories. In one story, Coyote, *'Ashk'a,'* and Lizard, *'Onok'ok,'* tell of island hillsides covered in golden poppies, island poppies found no place else on Earth,

flowers so beautiful that just the story of their beauty brought healing to the people. *'Ashk'a'* and *'Onok'ok'* said, at times, there were so many poppies that on a clear day, from the mainland, the big island of *Limuw* shimmered golden in the sun.

Later, with the paddlers resting *'Eleye'wun* safely on the beach, Elders were taken to a hilltop, with wind blowing through grasses and the sun setting in the west. The sky was streaked lavender and gold, the mainland sleepy and purple across the channel. The Elders gazed in hushed reverence.

Like the Elders on the hilltop, island oak and ironwood are being replanted throughout the islands. The unique golden poppies have never left, blooming, here and there, wherever they could, like Chumash Peoples. *Limuw*, the ancient homeland of The People, seemed to embrace the Elders that day, reminding all of the sacredness of life and our responsibilities as human beings to care for our wounded world, the earth and waters, all of creation...and each other.

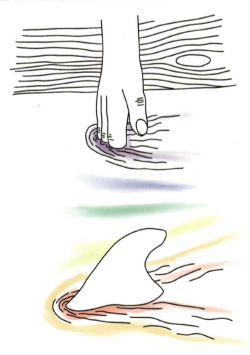

Tomols

Before the modern day kayak, sailboat, or yacht, the *tomol* plied the waters of the channel at the hands of the Chumash. Coming in at 2.5-9 meters (8-30 feet) long, it is the oldest ocean-going watercraft in North America and is still in use today. Unlike a heavy, hollowed-out log canoe or flimsy raft of reeds, the *tomol* is light, fast, and capable of hauling large amounts of cargo across the rough waters of the channel.

Food

The swift *tomol* was the perfect vessel for hunting swordfish. Chumash fishermen used cloth-wrapped bundles of bait to attract fish, then harpooned them from the bow. A braided fishing line attached to the harpoon allowed fishermen to pull in the catch once it got tired.

TRADE

While rich in food, the islands lacked some resources that could only be found on the mainland. The *tomol* allowed the island Chumash communities to exchange shell bead money and other manufactured island goods for mainland specialties like deer pelts and arrows.

TRANSPORTATION

The *tomol* allowed those on the islands to visit family and attend ceremonies on the mainland, and those on the mainland to do the same on the islands. Passengers could pay for their travel using the shell bead money that formed the cornerstone of the Chumash economy.

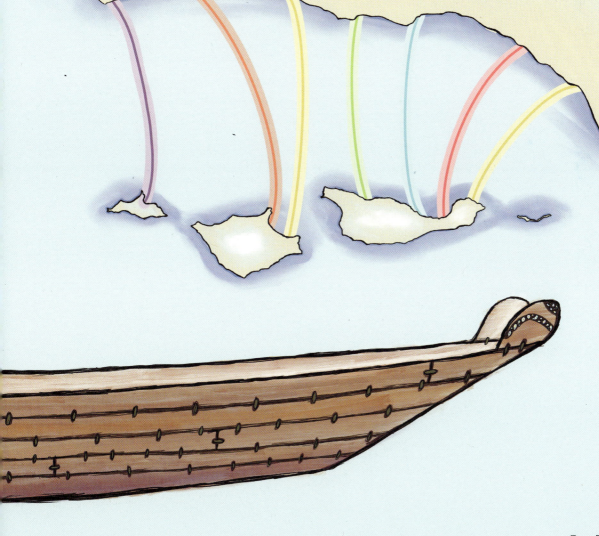

Chumash paddlers guide a *tomol* across the Santa
Barbara Channel to *Limuw* (Santa Cruz Island).
Photo by Robert Schwemmer

Just As Before

by Casmali Lopez – *Student*

Age 0 — Born the same year that the *tomol* 'Elye'wun crossed the channel.

Age 14 — Helped paddle *tomol* across the channel as part of annual crossing.

Age 17 — Helped get Ethnic Studies mandated for all Santa Barbara high schools.

Age 18 — Enrolled at Colorado College to continue his studies.

The *tomol* is at its core about relationships and movement. There is no *tomol* without the ocean. There is no *tomol* without the resources required to make it. Each of these resources represents a whole set of relationships to plant, animal, geological, and insect lives. There is also no *tomol* without the people who listen to the water, plants, fish, animals, rocks, and insects. Every piece requires the others to exist. Every piece requires the relationships to the others in order to exist. These are active relationships. They need movement and the changes of each other to continue to be. To become still is to stop listening to the new needs of each of these relationships.

I learned these lessons living my life always with a *tomol*. I am a part of a generation that can say, just as the ancients did, that they grew up not knowing what it is like to grow up without a *tomol*. This is both a new and a very old thing.

For many generations, *tomol* society was sleeping. With pride I can say it is now awake. In the year I was born, 2001, the *tomol* 'Elye'wun completed the crossing from the mainland to the island of *Limuw*, which some now call "Santa Cruz." 'Elye'wun was birthed by a community reviving a sea-going culture.

What does it mean to revive a culture? It is not a return to the past. The damage of colonization—and missionization—cannot be healed in a way that returns things to exactly how they used to be. In a way, colonization freezes things. To thaw a culture out is to adapt it to the realities of today. To revive a culture is to move forward with that culture. This is not done passively but actively, by us, to change our future.

The modern role of the *tomol* has been adapted to fit the way things are today. Now the currents sometimes are not the result of a storm, but of a tanker barreling through the Santa Barbara Channel. Now we cannot fish in some places because the exploitation of the kelp forests has devastated populations. Now some of the oil in the water is because of spills from platforms and pipelines, not natural seepage. Now there are few *tomols* out in the water. Now many of the Chumash have been killed in the process of colonization (the arrival of a foreign power that takes over a land and/or people).

Despite all of this, some things are as they always have been. Just as before, the *tomol* exists, flexing with the current of the ocean, filled with Chumash people. Just as before, we listen and learn the lessons the ocean has to offer—creating new traditions in the process of reviving the old traditions. Just as before, new and old songs ring out over the water. The waves resonate with stories of whales, dolphins, and floods—ancient floods that speak of creation, and new floods that destroy and redefine what life is.

The *tomol* is not simply a canoe. It is not simply a boat. It instead is a living craft—full of story and magic, ceremony and relationships. It is the song of the ocean echoing in our spirits for all of us to listen to. We should all listen, and listen closely. For this song speaks of the pain of colonization. It speaks of the pollution, violence, and terror of our so-called modern civilization. But equally important, it speaks about the possibility of something else. Not a dream, but what was before and what can be again: a different set of relationships and movement.

REDWOOD

Tomols are built out of planks fashioned from fallen redwood trees that drift down the coast. The planks are shaped with shark skin.

MILKWEED

Craftsmen drill holes in the redwood plank. They then stitch them together with a braided twine made out of milkweed.

YOP

The *tomol* is glued together and sealed with *yop*, a paste made of pine sap and asphaltum, the tar that you might see on the beach.

ABALONE

Abalone shells harvested from the sea are broken up into small chips. These chips are then used to decorate the bow of the *tomol*.

"Found"

1491 For more than 12,500 years the Chumash lived on the Channel Islands. At their peak, more than 3,000 Chumash called them home.

1542 Spanish explorer Juan Rodriguez Cabrillo sailed up the California coast and "discovered" the Channel Islands.

1769 Father Junipero Serra founded the first California mission to help "save" native tribes–by converting them to Christianity.

1786 Spanish built Mission Santa Barbara. Mainland Chumash were rapidly forced into missions, leaving the island Chumash without a key trading partner.

1806 A measles epidemic killed one in five island Chumash. They had no immunity to this European-brought disease.

1815 El Niño destroyed island food sources, forcing Chumash to the mainland, where missions controlled the only source of food.

1820 Spanish removed last island Chumash to the missions, ending their 13,000 year habitation of the Channel Islands.

2001 Chumash paddle *'Elye'wun* from the mainland to *Limuw* (Santa Cruz), celebrating a return to the islands.

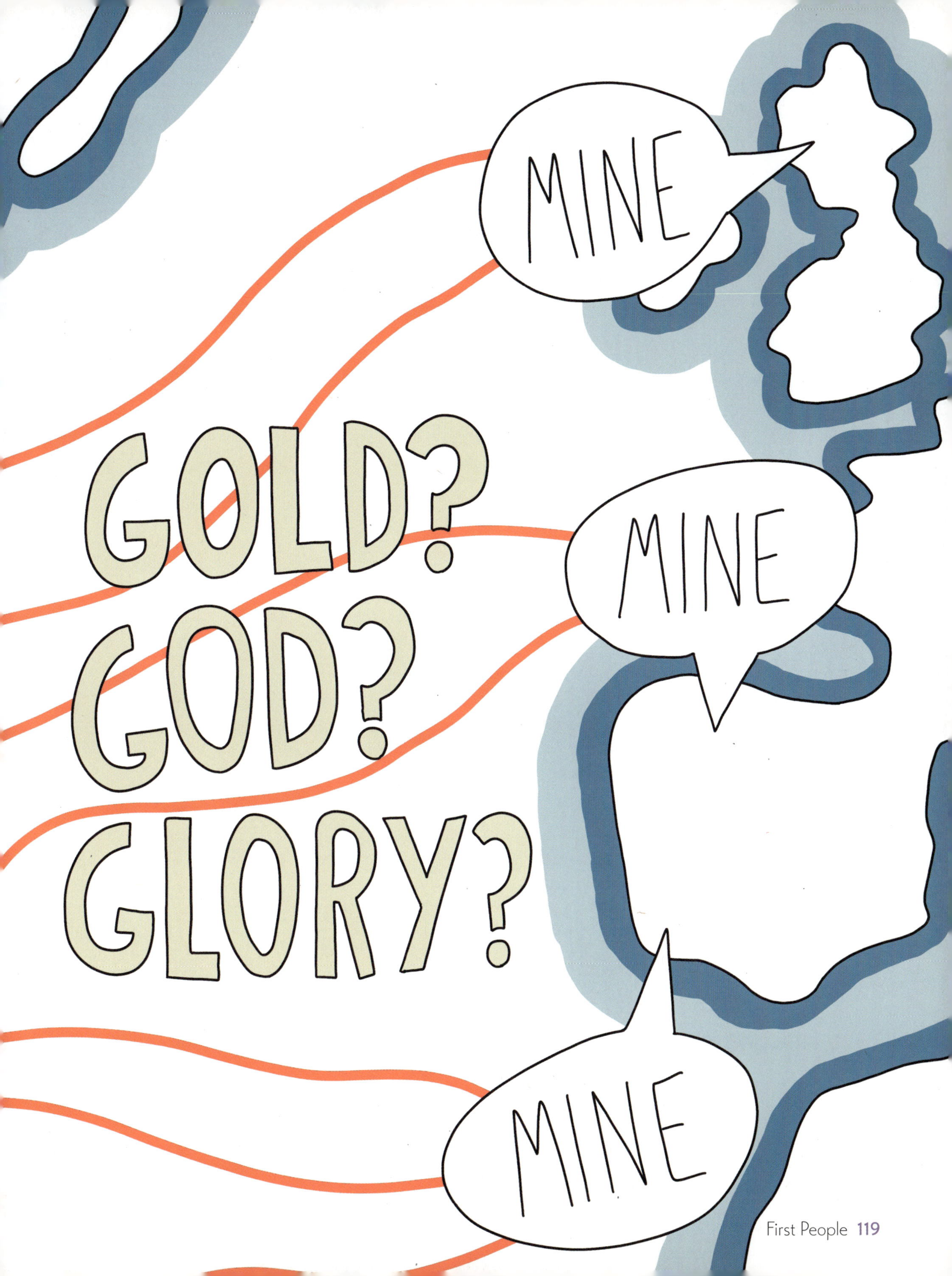
MINE
GOLD?
GOD?
GLORY?
MINE
MINE

DEAR SONORA

by Deborah A. Miranda – *Writer*

AGE 7
Wrote first story, about John Rabbit family. Hand cramped. Was hooked.

AGE 15
Story "Turquoise Blues" won contest. Maybe she's good at this writing thing?

AGE 35
First poetry book, *Indian Cartography*, published. Worth the wait.

AGE 49
Native American Lit Ph.D. and teaching job mean she gets paid to write.

Recently, the Ohlone-Costanoan-Esselen Nation received a request from a sharp fourth-grader asking about the Native experience in California missions. Here is that letter and our response, written by writer and professor Deborah Miranda, who is of both Costanoan Esselen and Chumash descent:

Dear Ms. Ramirez,

I am a fourth-grader and I am doing my report on Mission Nuestra Señora Dolorosisima de la Soledad. I discovered that Coastanoan and Essellen are some of the names of the tribes that went to the Soledad mission, and I was searching for some info on them when I stumbled across your email address on www.ohlonecostanoanesselennation.org. Me and my mom decided that maybe you could help us/me. Anyway, what I was searching for was the opinion of the Coastanoan and Esselen Native Americans. I want to know if the Native Americans liked the mission, which priests were their favorites...stuff like that, and I'm hoping you can help me. If you can help me, or even if you can't, thanks a ton!

Sincerely, Sonora

Dear Sonora (what a great name!),

I can tell you right away that writing to California tribes on your own is a smart move—many people don't think to ask us, or they think we are all dead. Still here! You wanted to know the Ohlone-Esselen-Costanoan opinion of the missions. That's a tough question. Some Indian people will tell you that the missions were great, and brought us Catholicism and agriculture; others will tell you that anything that kills about 80 percent of your people can't be good.

California Indians were actually doing fine before the Spanish, Mexicans, and Americans arrived. Our Ancestors had everything they needed, including Indian religions, leaders, music, languages, jobs, and education. But because our Ancestors' traditions were different from the way Europeans did those things, lots of Spanish people thought Indians needed "civilizing." Of course, Indians were curious about the Spanish, and about their religion, and often helped the Spaniards find food and water, or exchanged things in trade with them, but that did not mean our Ancestors wanted to become Spanish. People should be allowed to decide for themselves how they want to live.

Instead, the missionaries made that decision for our Ancestors. Sometimes the Spanish priests would "baptize" women and children who came to visit, and then refuse to let them go. The husbands and fathers would come to get them, and were told that they could not see their families unless they, too, allowed themselves to be baptized.

Of course, none of the Indians knew what baptism really meant, and when the priests then told them that, once baptized, they could not leave the mission, it was a big surprise. Remember, missionaries and soldiers thought of themselves as "civilized" so they figured they must be right, and the Indians were wrong. Civilized people don't hurt other people for being different, though. Many Indians today do not think the Spanish were very civilized.

The missionaries did a lot of things that hurt Indian people and families. For example, all little girls over the age of seven had to go sleep in the *monjerio*, a small building with no bathroom and small windows way up taller than anyone could reach. These rooms were dark, smelly, and dirty, and the young women and girls kept in there got sick from germs and lack of fresh air. They were also very homesick for their families. They didn't see their parents much, since during the day the parents were forced to work for the missionaries, doing all the work to build, maintain, and farm for the mission. Our Ancestors were also forced to attend the Catholic church, learn prayers in a new language, and take new names in Spanish. None of the Indian ways of living— religions, leaders, music, languages, jobs, and education—were allowed by the Spaniards.

Also, I'm sorry to say, Indians at the mission were whipped with a very heavy, painful leather whip if they broke any of the priests' rules—and since Indians didn't know Spanish, and missionaries didn't know Indian languages, there were a lot of misunderstandings about what the rules were. Plus, of course, sometimes the Indians (who had taken very good care of themselves for thousands of years) didn't think Spanish rules made sense in the first place, so they would do things that were against the rules like gather wild food, go hunting, leave the mission to visit their families elsewhere, marry who they wanted to marry, or

other things they considered part of their rights as human beings.

Over time, the European livestock and plants that the Spanish had brought with them to California took over the land, and many basic foods that Indians depended on were destroyed, so our Ancestors became very dependent on the European foods from the missions. Our bodies sometimes could not handle this change in diet, which made it harder for us to get over small illnesses like colds and flu, and big illnesses like European smallpox, measles, and tuberculosis.

So many Indians died in the missions that the padres had to keep sending Spanish soldiers out to capture more Indians to do the work of running cattle, farming, building, weaving, cooking, and all the chores a big mission requires.

You might be wondering, why would the Indians put up with all this? I suggest you look up things like "California mission rebellion" or "California mission revolt" on the internet. I think everyone, historians and Indians alike, agree that missionization was a disaster for the Indians: our estimated population numbers went from about one million to 15,000 in just under 200 years. We lost almost all of our land, all of our natural resources (which provided food and shelter); many

of us lost our language, religion, and communities. Can you imagine if eight out of every ten people you know died when another group of people showed up and took over your town?

An Indian baby born in a California mission only lived to be seven or eight years old; some disease or other would kill them before they could grow up. Also, because of a European strain of a disease called syphilis, many Indian men and women could no longer have babies, so there were no new kids to replace the people who died. Every time an old person died, it was like an entire library of knowledge, history, and stories burned down.

There were many bad consequences from the California missions for California Indians. Those bad consequences continued on through the Mexican Era and into the American Era. The hardest consequence was losing our homelands. The Spaniards made us move into the missions, but 65 years later when the missions closed down, all of our land had been taken by other non-Indian people. We had nowhere to go, no way to feed ourselves, no food, shelter, or clothing. Mexicans, who governed California after the Spanish, used Indians as free labor on their large ranches. For a meal and a place to sleep, Indians worked almost like slaves for the Mexicans, just to stay alive. Most mission Indian communities were broken up and it was even harder for tribal members to stay connected than in the missions.

But as bad as that was, after the Mexican government came the American government, with laws that were even worse—American laws

prevented Indians from owning land, voting, or taking a white person to court for even the worst crimes against Indians. The U.S. Congress passed a law giving millions of dollars to Americans to round up and kill Indians who were "in the way." In my family, we have stories about Ancestors who answered a knock at the door, opened the door, and were shot for the bounty money! As late as 1866, Indians could be bought and sold just like slaves in the American South—and thousands were, especially women and children. Even Indians like my great-great-great-great-great grandfather, Fructuoso Cholom Real, who received land in a Mexican land grant after the missions were closed down, ended up losing their land to Americans.

But some of us did survive, and in California our communities are slowly growing and working to recover from those bad consequences. Like several other California tribes, the Esselen are petitioning the U.S. government for recognition—that means we would be eligible to get back a small piece of government "surplus" land in our homeland that we could use as a center, apply for educational scholarships that are only available to federally recognized tribes, and receive some basic health benefits. It's funny, but even though I can prove my family history was Indian all the way back to 1770, when the Spaniards started keeping paper records, the government still considers me "non-Indian!"

Oh—I realize that I didn't actually answer your question about favorite priests. The Spanish priests, and later the Mexican priests, were human beings with the same gifts and flaws as anyone else. So like most people, some priests were considered "kind" and others were considered "mean." Father Serra, for instance, wrote in his letters about how much he loved the Indians, and how badly he felt when the Spanish soldiers hurt or killed Indians. But as kind as he seemed, Father Serra never questioned whether the missions should be built or maintained. He never thought to ask, as you did Sonora, what Indians thought of the missions or the priests. He believed that the Spaniards' way of living was the ONLY way of living. So Indians, who lived differently, must be made to change—even if it meant killing them, or spreading disease, or denying them human rights.

This way of thinking is called "colonization." Colonization, or in California what we call "missionization," is a cruel and unkind way to treat other people. It means, basically, that a colonizer doesn't think Indians or Native people are really human beings. It is a very strange, selfish way of seeing the world.

Good luck with your report,

Deborah A. Miranda

BUILT ON A PLANT

The history of the islands can be traced through the story of a wondrous little plant with an energy-packed root. Known by several names—*six'on* in Shmuwich, blue dick in English—this rich food source was both readily available and actively cultivated (grown) by the island Chumash. Combined with abundant fish, masterfully-built *tomols*, and a strong currency, this plant allowed them to build a vibrant island society. However, just as the Chumash presence on the islands has changed over time, so too has that of the *six'on*. By listening to this plant, we can better understand the past, present, and future of the Channel Islands.

Names: *Six'on* (Shmuwich), blue dick (English), *Dichelostemma capitatum* (Latin)

Description: Small plant with purple flowers and a dark purple stem. Grows out of an underground bulb-like structure called a corm.

Habitat: Found everywhere from Oregon to Mexico, California to Utah. Can thrive in a variety of ecosystems, from grasslands to chaparral to desert. They pop up frequently after fires and heavy rain.

Human Use: Everyone needs a reliable source of carbohydrates (think potatoes, pasta, and bread) to keep them going. The villagers on the mainland gathered acorns, and the island people specialized in *six'on*. Its corm is full of energy-giving goodness. Both foods are highly valued by modern Chumash people.

Grow Your Own

Six'on still grows across the islands, but they are not as common. Picking them yourself can damage the fragile ecosystems that they call home. However, you can grow *six'on* in your backyard.

1. Visit your local native plant nursery and purchase a packet of seeds. **Plant** in fall or late winter, ideally in a place that gets good sunlight all day.

2. Once your *six'on* have reached flowering size, you can **dig** them up with a sharp stick. Be careful not to damage the bulb-like corms at the end of the roots.

3. Separate the larger corms from the smaller corms. **Replant** the smaller corms 1-2 inches deep in the soil to ensure that your garden continues to grow.

4. Blanch the corms for 20-30 seconds in boiling water and dry. Gently **peel** away the outer layers. You will want to prepare at least a small handful of them.

5. Warm oil in a pan over medium heat. Gently **sauté** the corms for 10 minutes until they soften up. Salt and eat! Try adding to other recipes in place of onions.

SONG OF SIX'ON

by Julie Cordero-Lamb – *Ethnobotanist and Herbalist*

AGE 9	AGE 10	AGE 33	AGE 47
Stopped to wonder at lavender on way to school. Always late.	Knew the best places in her neighborhood to find honeybees.	Studied at Southwest School of Botanical Medicine.	Founded organization to preserve traditional Chumash food practices.

What the *six'on* plant saw:

Here they come,
our people,
quietly singing,
softly walking up the hill.

Our past season of thriving growth has left us crowded. Our young are tight around us. They need loosening into the soft soil. We itch for our peoples' nimble fingers, delicately pulling our young parts and burying them.

We wait for the feeling of their silky hard ironwood sticks, separating the layers between us. The ironwood tools sing with them, tapping, tapping, tapping us closer to their hands. We hear the great ironwood trees on the hills, standing straight, whispering, witnessing their people fulfilling promises made when they cut their branches.

"We will never waste you, relatives. We will only be what you need us to be for you. Thank you for your gifts. It will continue indefinitely, relatives." It is the promise we all taught them, in the days when the people listened and sang with us.

In this soil, all our peoples' things are here with us. Bits of shell, broken baskets for our food, wavy flakes of translucent stone, beads and seeds, both lost and offered, fluffy black depths of cooking ash from endless feasts, and all the laughing stories, all the deep-time stories. Here there are vast lenses of tears, and even deeper layers of geologic love. And to our great and lasting joy, the song they sing tells us that the deepest, oldest memory buried here has not been forgotten; that we taught them this song back in that original summer. Their first days here on our hill. This memory pulls from deep in the soil, grows through their stories and opens to this day's sun with their song, just as our brilliant blue flowers do. They listen closely as we sing together, and they smile.

All of this they bring to us, singing and stepping softly up the hill. And we have something for them. We give life to them, because they have listened to us, and because they respected what we told them. Since that very first day on our hill they have heard us.

We need our people to come. They know us as family. We love their names for us. Pretty names. Fond nicknames. Food names. *Six'on*, they call us.

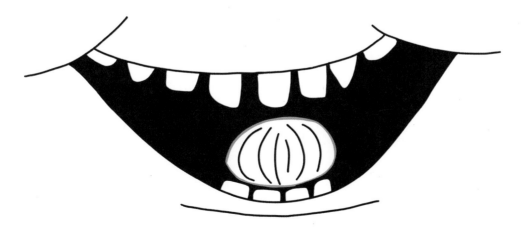

And then one day, they were gone. All at once. The foxes came and sat, their heads just above the blue sea of our flowers, looking across the blue sea of water, wondering. The tiny bees sing to us the song of going on, and it helps some. But still. Our people and their pretty names and gentle fingers and ancient honoring song for us, after tens of thousands of summers, they were gone.

The big-nosed animals came. They didn't know our songs, nor could they hear us telling them. They just ate. They rooted nearly every one of us away.

Those were the days that all the promises were broken. These are the days when violence and death is the only promise. These are days when strangers tell us things, and can't listen to the song.

We grew thin.
And then one day, from far across the water,
we heard a song.
We heard the song.
It came closer.
We heard the paddles dipping, each one a prayer.

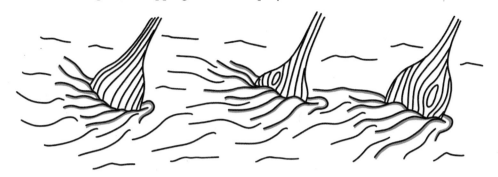

We heard the happy voices of our people gathered in the long-empty village place. And then came a small group of them, with strange tools. We heard many new things. We heard shots ring out from the sky. We heard the big-nosed animals squeal and drop where they stood. We heard the wires around us twanging open as our people cut them, with love for us in their eyes.

Their steps were heavy, and we could hear the sickness and sadness in their voices. They kneeled among our remnants and cried. They prayed for our health. Our people prayed for us to return to health, and for us to help them back to their health, their strength from their ancestors' times.

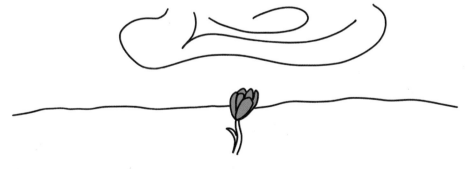

They sang the old song to us, and dug deep. Their soft fingers, filled with canoe-builders' redwood splinters, they found us deep in the soil's memory. They pulled our tight knots of young loose and buried them in the dark softness of our long times together. It was the deepest relief and a kind of love that the whole world sings. If only you listen.

And together again, we grow.

Sunrise off the east end of *Limuw* (Santa Cruz Island).
'Anyapax (Anacapa Island) lies in the background.
Photo by Robert Schwemmer

Our land is hurting.
We are hurting.
We need to heal.
Our land needs to heal.
We can't do it separately.
It has to be together.
We are here to help our land.
Our land is here to help us.

– Julie Cordero-Lamb
Founder, Syuxtun Plant Mentorship Collective
Enrolled Member, Coastal Band of the Chumash Nation
KCET Tending Nature Series

Photo by Robert Schwemmer

CHAPTER 4

NEW CLAIMS

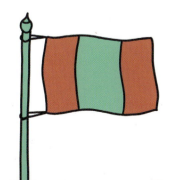
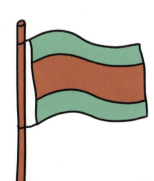

Who Manages Santa Cruz Island

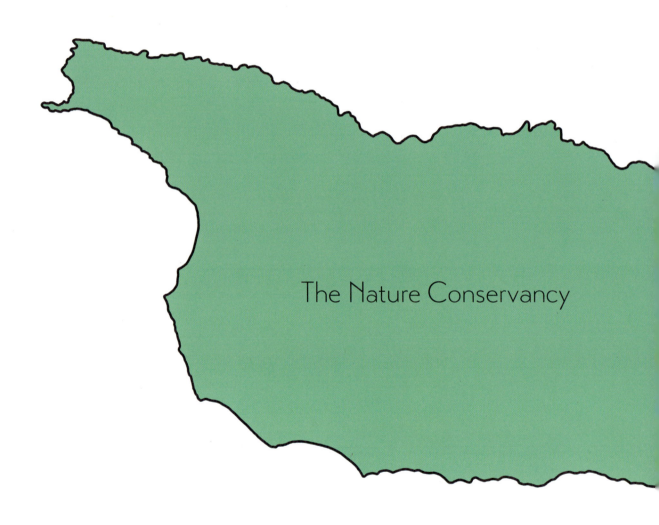

The Nature Conservancy

National Park Service

Photo by Robert Schwemmer

IN 1493, THE POPE DECLARED

"...all islands and mainlands found and to be found, discovered and to be discovered" by Christian countries were the property of those countries.

Everyone from Spanish explorers to the modern-day U.S. government has used this statement to claim ownership of lands like the Channel Islands. Nevermind that the Chumash had already lived there for thousands of years.

What makes a piece of land yours? People have claimed to "own" the Channel Islands for many different reasons. Some sought to "save" the natives. Some wanted to graze their cows. More recently, others have realized how these islands need protection. One thing is for certain: since the Pope's declaration, the islands have never been the same.

THIS LAND IS MY LAND, THIS LAND IS YOUR LAND

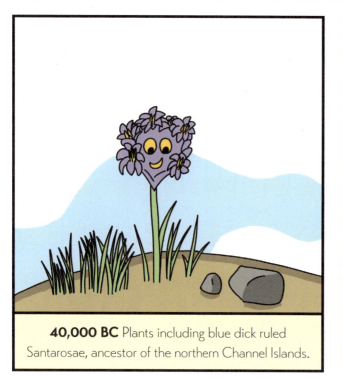

40,000 BC Plants including blue dick ruled Santarosae, ancestor of the northern Channel Islands.

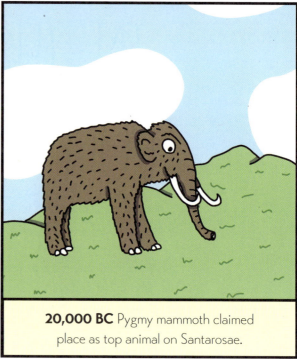

20,000 BC Pygmy mammoth claimed place as top animal on Santarosae.

5,000 BC Chumash thrived, living with the land on the now separated islands.

1493 Pope gave Spain the right to claim all lands that it discovered west of Europe.

1542 Juan Rodriguez Cabrillo sailed past the Channel Islands, claiming San Miguel for Spain.

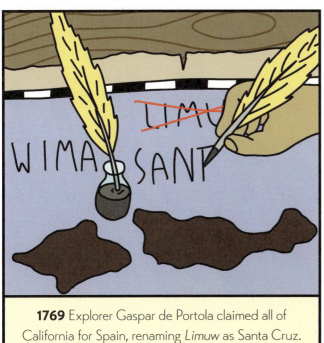

1769 Explorer Gaspar de Portola claimed all of California for Spain, renaming *Limuw* as Santa Cruz.

1800 Russians established sea otter hunting grounds around the islands.

1820 Spanish missionaries removed the last Chumash from the islands.

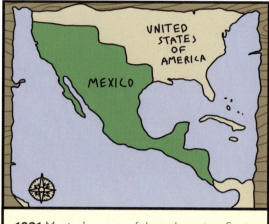

1821 Mexico's successful revolt against Spain allowed them to claim Alta & Baja California.

1848 U.S. got Channel Islands (and all of California) from Mexico as part of the Treaty of Guadalupe Hidalgo.

1853 Steamship *Winfield Scott* got lost in the fog, wrecking on Anacapa Island.

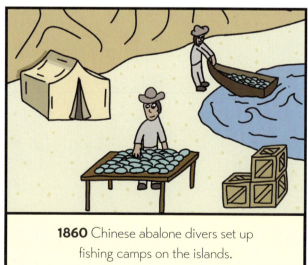

1860 Chinese abalone divers set up fishing camps on the islands.

1901 Walter Vail and J. V. Vickers ranched thousands of cattle on the hills of Santa Rosa Island.

1950 Navy used San Miguel as a bombing range.

2016 Island fox saved from extinction by a coalition of conservation organizations.

Present Hundreds of thousands of humans visit Channel Islands National Park every year.

Cowboys gather cattle at the Vail and Vickers ranch on *Wima* (Santa Rosa Island). *Photo by Bill Dewey*

Island Ranchers

Worried about the increasing numbers of Russian otter hunters coming down the coast, Mexico began giving out pieces of land (called land grants) to its citizens across California from 1938-1948. These grants brought the first ranchers to the Channel Islands. For the next 160 years, Mexican–and then American–ranchers built operations that covered much of the islands. At one point, more than 80,000 sheep grazed the hills of Santa Rosa Island alone. Despite their remote location and shortage of freshwater, the islands attracted enterprising businessmen and rugged adventurers alike. Here are a few of the men who sought to make their living ranching on these shores.

George Nidever

From: Tennessee   **Ranch Location:** San Miguel Island

Frontiersman George Nidever came to California in 1834 with the first American party to cross the Sierra Nevada. He made his way to Santa Barbara to ranch and hunt otters. In 1853, when he heard about the Lone Woman of San Nicolas Island (later made famous in *Island of the Blue Dolphins*), he sailed out and brought her back to live in his home. Nidever bought the rights to half of San Miguel Island in 1863, inheriting the sheep that the previous owner had ranched on the island.

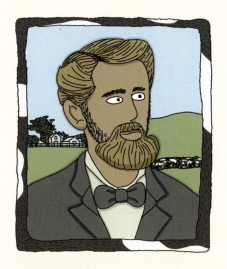

Walter Vail

From: Arizona   **Ranch Location:** Santa Rosa Island

Together with J.V. Vickers, Walter Vail built a business empire that included a mine and cattle ranch in Arizona, and a rail line to Los Angeles. In 1901 they bought the bulk of Santa Rosa Island. Vail removed the sheep and established a cattle ranching operation. His descendants ran the ranch right up until 1999, when the National Park Service removed the last of the cattle. You can still visit the ranch house in which the Vail family lived on Santa Rosa Island for nearly a century.

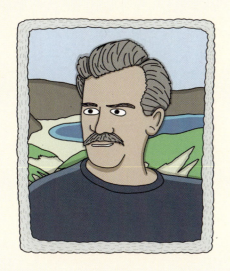

HERBERT LESTER

From: New York   **Ranch Location:** San Miguel Island

Known as the "King of San Miguel Island," Herbert Lester moved out to said island with his wife Elizabeth to manage a sheep ranch owned by a friend with whom he served during World War I. They had two daughters on the island, and were nicknamed "Swiss Family Lester" by newspapers across the country. The Lesters' compound had no electricity or running water, but included a tiny schoolhouse for the children and the famous "The Killer Whale Bar."

JUSTINIAN CAIRE

From: France   **Ranch Location:** Santa Cruz Island

Justinian Caire sailed to California in 1850 at the age of 23. He earned his fortune selling supplies to miners during the Gold Rush. In 1869 Caire helped found the Santa Cruz Island Company, eventually becoming the sole stockholder. Caire diversified the island's existing sheep ranching operation to include raising cattle. He also planted extensive vineyards and built a large winery. Caire died in 1897, and his family continued to manage Santa Cruz Island until 1937.

CAREY STANTON

From: Los Angeles   **Ranch Location:** Santa Cruz Island

In 1937 Carey's father Edwin Stanton purchased the majority of Santa Cruz Island from the Caire family. He removed the sheep and vineyards, transitioning the island to cattle ranching. After Edwin died, Carey took over, establishing a University of California research reserve on the island and founding the Santa Cruz Island Foundation to preserve the island's history. With Carey's death in 1987, the family's western 9/10ths of the island passed to The Nature Conservancy.

After The Cows

by Scot Pipkin – Director of Education, SB Botanic Garden

AGE 4 — Moved to subdivision on mountainside. Explored surrounding hills.

AGE 17 — Dad took him and brother on their first backpacking trip in the Sierras.

AGE 22 — First job as environmental educator in redwoods of San Mateo County.

AGE 35 — Hired as Dir. of Education and Engagement, SB Botanic Garden.

If you travel to the Channel Islands today, your experience may be a bit misleading. Upon stepping off the boat, you may be greeted by an island fox (*Urocyon littoralis*). Or perhaps you will see a peregrine falcon (*Falco peregrinus*) hunting for birds along the bluffs. More likely than not, you will get to see a variety of plants that exist nowhere else in the world. It might be tempting to think that these islands are an untouched paradise for native flora and fauna to survive.

Despite this seemingly stable and timeless landscape spread out before you, many of the Channel Islands' most iconic plants and animals were extremely rare until just a few years ago. This is largely due to the impacts that humans have had on the islands over the last 400 years. Our introduction of domestic livestock such as sheep, cattle, goats, and pigs, as well as deer for hunting, had a huge impact on the ecology of all eight Channel Islands.

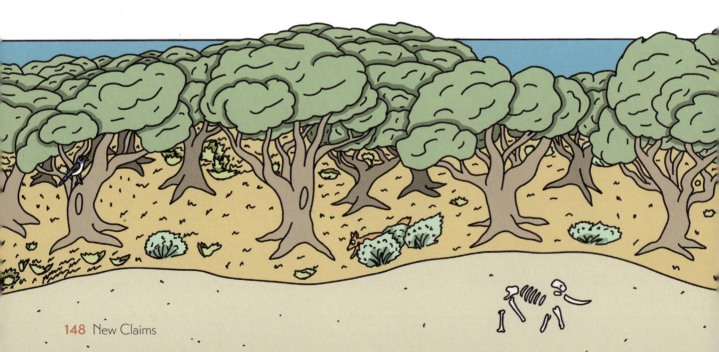

It's hard to identify a habitat on the Channel Islands that has not been affected by this ranching. Numerous early accounts all suggest that every one of the Channel Islands was more densely covered in plants before any of these plant-hungry animals were introduced. Santa Rosa is the perfect example: Ridge tops once covered in oak and pine cloud forests are now barren and eroded, struggling to recover to their pre-ranching state. Not exactly the scene that you thought you were looking at!

We know that humans have visited, inhabited, and interacted with the Channel Islands for approximately 13,000 years. For much of that time, the Chumash lived on the islands in relatively low population densities. Undoubtedly, these early settlements had substantial impacts on the islands. Archaeological evidence shows that inhabitants of the Channel Islands caught fish, harvested a variety of plants, and likely ignited fires to help maintain these resources. These island inhabitants may have also introduced domestic dogs and mainland plants to the islands. However, the total impacts of these actions over thousands of years don't even begin

to compare to the impacts of the massive-scale ranching over the last two centuries.

It wasn't until the middle of the 1800s that livestock, including cows, sheep, pigs, and goats, were introduced to the Channel Islands in significant numbers. While Mexican ranchers brought the first of these invasive animals to the islands, the worst was yet to come. Westward expansion in the United States–fueled by the Gold Rush, completion of the transcontinental railroad, and other factors–then brought even more people to California. Quickly, California's coastal communities became popular destinations for settlers, some of whom brought huge numbers of livestock across the channel to graze (eat plants close to the ground) and browse (eat bark and leaves higher up) unchecked.

The effects of ranching were particularly profound on plants of the islands. Having spent thousands of years living without the presence of browsing and grazing animals such as cows and pigs,

many plants on the Channel Islands have limited adaptations for dealing with these large herbivores (plant eaters). Take for example the Island ceanothus (*Ceanothus arborescens*). Most mainland species like this have small leaves that are filled with terpenes. Terpenes are chemical compounds found in many plants that tend to be not very tasty to herbivores. Because of these terpenes, mainland plants can protect their precious leaves from being eaten by insects, birds, reptiles, and mammals. In contrast, Island ceanothus has relatively large leaves that lack the terpenes of its mainland cousins, thus it never needed to protect itself from hungry herbivores. If you visit the Island View garden of the Santa Barbara Botanic Garden, which features plants from the Channel Islands, you may notice many plants are in netted enclosures and wire cages. This is because even native herbivores, such as mule deer, are capable of heavily impacting island plants that are not evolved for dealing with such hungry creatures.

Ranching effects on the plants of the Channel Islands don't end with Island ceanothus. In fact, that is just the beginning. One of the island habitats most heavily affected by ranching was oak woodlands. Oak seedlings were easy pickings for almost all grazing animals. Pigs were particularly devastating in oak woodlands, as they have a huge appetite for acorns. In the process of rooting for acorns, they disturbed the soil, making it easy for non-native grasses to take over the area and prevent future acorns from taking root. Cows and sheep also had a huge impact, browsing higher up, stripping oaks of their bark and leaves. Beyond oaks, they went after other fully-grown vegetation, as well as the seedlings and young plants of the next generation. Similar to the case of pigs eating acorns, the consumption of both young and full-grown shrub plants allowed non-native species of plants, particularly grasses, to take over.

Some individual plant species have even been pushed to the brink of extinction. This is true in the case of a low-growing member of the pea family, Santa Cruz Island birds-foot trefoil (*Acmispon argophyllus niveus*). On Santa Rosa Island, pigs alone significantly affected 16 species of plants. Half of those plants affected by pigs are federally listed as "threatened" or "endangered."

In addition to the hungry animals, competition from new plants also had a big impact on native

species. As ranching took off on the Channel Islands, seeds carried on mammal fur and clothes, stuck in wheels, and found in livestock feed took root in island soils. As with much of mainland California, these non-native, introduced plants did extremely well in the Mediterranean climate and quickly took root across the islands.

Livestock helped with the invasion. They cleared native plants, altered soils, and further spread non-native seeds through their droppings. This had devastating impacts on island vegetation communities. In many cases, whole ecosystems, such as oak woodland and shrub/chaparral communities, have been converted to non-native grassland.

It's tempting to think that if we want to promote the native beauty of the Channel Islands as they were before the mid-19th century, all land managers would have to do is remove the non-native animals. Removing sheep, goats, cattle, and pigs is an important step in the remarkable story of management and recovery on the Channel Islands, and has allowed species like the Santa Cruz Island birds-foot trefoil to begin remarkable recoveries. However, it is not the only step. On the islands where livestock have been removed, sometimes non-native plants are doing even better. For instance, on Santa Cruz Island after the removal of pigs, the non-native plant fennel (*Foeniculum vulgare*) took over. This was due to the removal of animals that eat fennel and the large amount of disturbed landscapes where non-native plants such as fennel tend to thrive.

Let's return to our hypothetical visit to the Channel Islands. As you look around and see the same island fox stalking the picnic benches, the same falcon hunting along the bluffs, and the same plants scattered along the trail, you might reflect on how resilient those ecosystems are to have survived centuries of ranching. You might also begin to think about the process of transition from native vegetation to disturbed rangeland to the ecosystems that are in recovery today. The story of how scientists, land managers, and volunteers are working to return the native flora and fauna to Channel Islands ecosystems is at the same time heartbreaking, uplifting, and empowering.

The *Vaquero* transporting cattle past the north side of *Limuw* (Santa Cruz Island). *Photo by Bill Dewey*

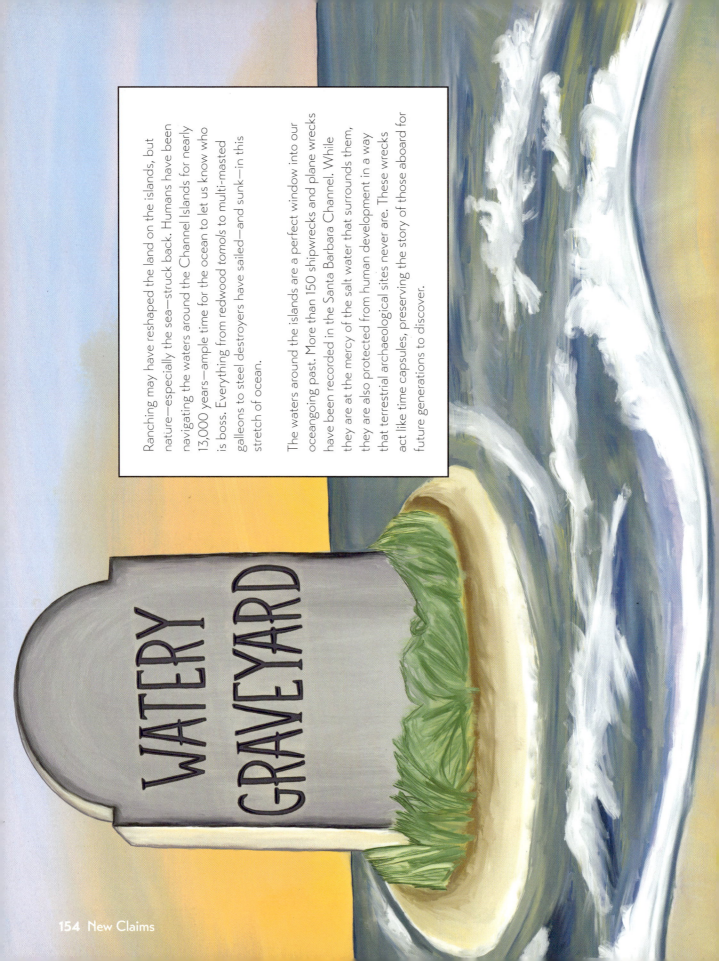

WATERY GRAVEYARD

Ranching may have reshaped the land on the islands, but nature—especially the sea—struck back. Humans have been navigating the waters around the Channel Islands for nearly 13,000 years—ample time for the ocean to let us know who is boss. Everything from redwood tomols to multi-masted galleons to steel destroyers have sailed—and sunk—in this stretch of ocean.

The waters around the islands are a perfect window into our oceangoing past. More than 150 shipwrecks and plane wrecks have been recorded in the Santa Barbara Channel. While they are at the mercy of the salt water that surrounds them, they are also protected from human development in a way that terrestrial archaeological sites never are. These wrecks act like time capsules, preserving the story of those aboard for future generations to discover.

Grumman Avenger - 1945

This bomber served in the South Pacific during WWII. While on a training exercise with four other planes, it collided with another in mid-air, crashing off Anacapa. Two crew members survived, but the third ejected in panic, and his parachute didn't deploy.

SS Cuba - 1923

This steamship was transporting 112 passengers and crew, along with a cargo of silver, when it wrecked on San Miguel due to a navigation error. Lifeboats full of passengers were rescued by the USS Reno, part of a squadron of destroyers traveling to San Diego. The squadron hit fog later that evening and crashed into the mainland. It was the worst peacetime loss of ships in U.S. Navy history. Some blame the crash on the distraction of the Cuba rescue effort.

Winfield Scott - 1853

This side-wheel steamer carried people and goods from the Panama Canal to San Francisco and back during the Gold Rush. Captains were notorious for racing to see who could complete the route fastest. This meant taking a shortcut that brought you close to the islands. In a thick fog, the Scott's captain miscalculated his location and crashed into Anacapa. The 500 passengers abandoned ship, which was also carrying $1 million in gold. They spent eight days stranded on the island before being rescued by the steamship California.

Goldenhorn - 1892

This iron-hull bark was sailing with coal from Australia to San Pedro for the Southern Pacific Railway. Lost in the fog around Santa Rosa, it hit a pinnacle. Some theorize that Chinese fishermen salvaged the coal for the fires they used to dry abalone at their island fishing camps.

DIVING THROUGH TIME

with Robert Schwemmer – *Maritime Historian, NOAA*

AGE 7 — AGE 20 — AGE 28 — AGE 57 ??!

Learned to skindive at YMCA Camp Fox on Catalina. In awe of the sea.

SCUBA-certified in the movie industry. Decided to dive at the Islands instead.

First shipwreck dive off San Clemente. Hooked on discovering wreck histories.

Helped discover the USS Conestoga, a top unsolved shipwreck mystery.

When did you first fall in love with shipwrecks?

I've always had a love for all things maritime (relating to the ocean). As a young child, my family traveled to ports and harbors along the California coast. I was fascinated watching the boats and ships pass through the waterways. Soon the walls of my bedroom were covered with posters of vessels that included both sail and steam. Also, I'm a descendent of the steamboat inventor Robert Fulton, so there's a bloodline connection. I got certified as a scuba diver in 1977. At first, I was just spear-fishing and taking pictures, but I always had the desire to dive on a shipwreck. Finally, in 1985, a wreck-diving class was offered through a local dive center.

Do you remember your first shipwreck dive?

My first shipwreck diving experience was on a small tugboat nicknamed "The No Name Tug," which sunk off San Clemente Island. I was hooked. I wanted to learn about the history of this vessel, what its real name was, why it sunk, where it was built, and who served on board. Thirty-two years later, I still have the same passion for solving mysteries and sharing my findings. I have developed a major research library to help me learn more about the ship and aircraft wrecks I have surveyed.

What is your favorite part about diving in and around a shipwreck?

I have been fortunate to be the first person to see shipwrecks since they were lost—sometimes a gap of more than 100 years. When you see the wreck for the first time, you are immediately taken back to that day in time when it was lost. You get to observe whether the ship was powered by sail or steam, in some cases what type of cargo it was carrying to a distant port, or the personal artifacts left behind by those onboard when the ship sank.

What can shipwrecks teach us about the history of the Islands, and the past as a whole?

We have an amazing underwater maritime museum in the Channel Islands National Marine Sanctuary and National Park. Each shipwreck has its own stories to be told: the story of the vessel itself, the stories of the people that served onboard, the stories of the passengers.

One particular shipwreck I have surveyed over the years is the California Gold Rush steamer *Winfield Scott*. It was enroute from San Francisco to Panama in 1853, when it got stranded on Anacapa Island with more than 500 passengers and crew. They were forced to live on the island for eight days

Island with a cargo of coal provided the Chinese abalone fishermen with a fuel source to boil the abalone on the island. These shipwrecks served as 19th century floating hardware stores.

How does a shipwreck compare to an archaeological site on land?

Shipwrecks at the Channel Islands reflect the diverse range of activities and nationalities that traversed the Santa Barbara Channel. I, along with other divers, have been fortunate to explore European sailing vessels and steam vessels, American coastal traders, vessels engaged in island commerce, and a Gold Rush-era steamer, but I'm still in search of a Chumash *tomol* and Chinese-built junk (the wooden ships used by Chinese fishermen).

Terrestrial archaeological sites often have layers of more modern events or artifacts on top of layers of earlier occupation, whereas shipwrecks tend to be isolated and provide a better time capsule that can be traced back to a given date of loss. On the other hand, the site integrity of submerged maritime archaeological sites continues to deteriorate due to the marine environment in which they are located. These sites should be surveyed as soon as possible so that their identities and human stories can be preserved for future generations long after they disappear.

What is the environmental impact of shipwrecks?

Most of the larger shipwrecks I have surveyed at the Channel Islands were a result of strandings in fog, and are found in the nearshore marine environments. Wreck sites in shallow as well as deep water environments are abundant with various species of marine life. The wreckage is typically covered with marine growth, in many

before being rescued, but there was no loss of life. Through the first-person accounts of the survivors, we learned how they got by on this small island that they called a "rock." Crew and passengers survived by salvaging what provisions they could from the wreck, as well as taking advantage of the sea as a source for food. They shared some accounts of meeting a 19th century fisherman named Captain George Nidever, who provided fishing hooks so they could fish from the shore of the island and from the salvaged lifeboats.

We also know that shipwreck strandings at San Miguel Island spilled cargoes of lumber. This lost cargo was then used as building material for island ranch houses. Similarly, a wreck off Santa Rosa cases camouflaging the wreckage. As a trained maritime archaeologist, I look for man-made shapes or symmetrical artifacts to pick these wrecks out from the natural environment.

Shipwrecks can also cause damage to the marine environment, either from the impact striking reefs, from spilled fuel oil, or hazardous cargoes onboard. At the Channel Islands National Marine Sanctuary and National Park, research suggests there are no potentially polluting shipwrecks.

Why is it important to preserve shipwrecks?

Shipwreck discoveries not only help archaeologists and historians studying these sites to have a better understanding of our maritime past, but they are also a great opportunity to share human stories with the American public and international communities–stories they can relate to. Stories of the ship's builders, crew, passengers, and the brave people who came to rescue them. They connect the public to the ocean. I have countless stories of people contacting me after some of my shipwreck discoveries. Maybe one of their family members was on board, in some cases lost, and they bring to life these important human stories.

What advice would you give to someone on their first dive into a wreck?

Before diving on a shipwreck, make sure you have proper training. Some shipwrecks may contain commercial fishing nets or fishing line, so know how to deal with possible entanglement. Never enter an enclosed shipwreck without proper training. If the wreck is in a region impacted by swells or surge, take caution to give yourself plenty of space between you and structures which can be razor-sharp. To enhance the dive experience, it's best to seek out information on the ship or aircraft wreck's history. Obtain a dive slate if it's available for the wreck site. These explain what you might see during your dive experience. Local knowledge through other experienced divers or dive charters is always useful. Do have fun diving into history, take lots of pictures or video, but only leave bubbles.

SS Cuba
Shipwreck
Site Map

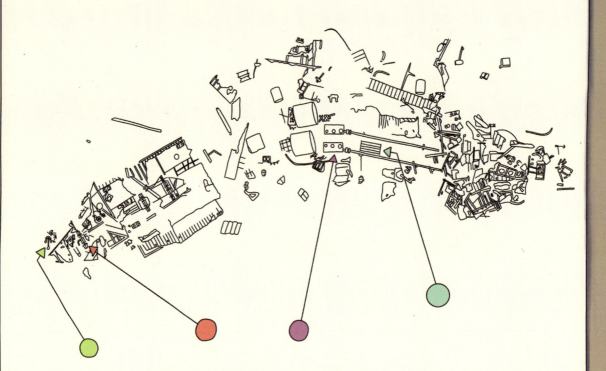

This wreck lies just off Point Bennett on the west end of San Miguel Island.
Photos courtesy of Robert Schwemmer

North

0   25   50 feet

- WINDLASS

- TRIPLE EXPANSION ENGINES

- CONDENSER

- ANCHOR

CREATING A PARK

In 1980 the U.S. government passed Public Law 96-199, which expanded Channel Islands National Monument (created in 1938 around Anacapa and Santa Barbara Islands) into Channel Islands National Park:

In order to protect the nationally significant natural, scenic, wildlife, marine, ecological, archaeological, cultural, and scientific values of the Channel Islands in the State of California, including, but not limited to, the following:

(1) the brown pelican nesting area;

(2) the undisturbed tide pools providing species diversity unique to the eastern Pacific coast;

(3) the pinnipeds which breed and pup almost exclusively on the Channel Islands, including the

only breeding colony for northern fur seals south of Alaska;

(4) the Eolian landforms and caliche;

(5) the presumed burial place of Juan Rodriquez Cabrillo;

(6) the archaeological evidence of substantial populations of Native Americans;

there is hereby established the Channel Islands National Park, the boundaries of which shall include San Miguel and Prince Islands, Santa Rosa, Santa Cruz, Anacapa, and Santa Barbara Islands, including the rocks, islets, submerged lands, and waters within one nautical mile of each island.

Safe Passage

by Jessica Morten and Sean Hastings – *NOAA*

JESSICA AGE 11	SEAN AGE 12	JESSICA AGE 29 SEAN AGE 29
Spotted humpback whales on a class trip off of Connecticut.	Caught waves with a pod of bottlenose dolphins in Del Mar, California.	Both started work at the National Oceanic and Atmospheric Administration (NOAA), helping to protect creatures that inspired their love for the ocean.

It's summer in the Santa Barbara Channel and we're on the hunt. Despite being the largest known animal ever to have existed on this planet, blue whales can be surprisingly tough to find. These marine giants can hold their breath for over 20 minutes at a time, and spend hours each day under the surface. On top of that, they cruise at speeds of 32 kilometers (20 miles) per hour and journey thousands of miles a year, meaning you need to cover some serious ground if you're somebody hoping to find them.

To add to the task, there just aren't as many of these blues left as there once were, with a local population estimated at 1,800 individuals off the west coast of the United States. Once numbering around 400,000 in total, blue whales were found in all the world's oceans, but commercial whaling targeting their baleen, blubber, and meat took a major toll, making our job of finding them all the more challenging.

But there's reason for optimism. The Santa Barbara Channel region is considered one of the best places in the world to catch a glimpse of these endangered goliaths. The whales come to these beautiful and rich waters in the summer and fall on a simple mission: to feed on krill and copepods. Using their large baleen plates, they filter feed their bellies with up to 1,000 kilograms (2,200 pounds) of these small invertebrates per day. Cumulatively, this means that these hungry giants have a big impact on the communities around them and play an important role in the local food web.

It's hard to believe that less than 50 short years ago, blue whales were hunted off these coasts by whaling ships. Today, as resource managers of Channel Islands National Marine Sanctuary, we scan the seas from a small twin-engine plane for signs of these whales, for a starkly different reason: to protect them from a man-made threat known as "ship strikes."

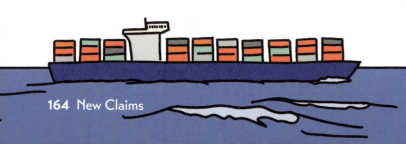

Around the globe, ports continue to report baleen whales strewn across the bows of incoming enormous vessels. These 27-meter-long (90-foot-long) creatures are being run over by the even larger cargo ships—the same ships we humans depend on to deliver 90 percent of our products and goods. Here in the Santa Barbara Channel, our local blue whales share these summer and fall feeding grounds with thousands of massive and fast-moving vessels, and it is our job at the sanctuary to find ways to protect them from ships.

For the past decade, our team and many partners have employed a range of tactics to help. We've adjusted internationally designated shipping lanes—essentially marine highways for these 397 meter (1,300 foot) ships—to areas away from where we know the whales like to go. We work alongside the shipping companies to slow their ships down in areas where we know whales are likely to be. We research new technologies that allow us to detect or sight whales from farther away, hoping to provide ships with more time to avoid whales. And we continue to conduct and support ongoing research—like these aerial surveys—to understand where these animals go and why. This crucial information will help us lessen our impacts and protect these endangered populations of majestic and mysterious blue whales for decades to come.

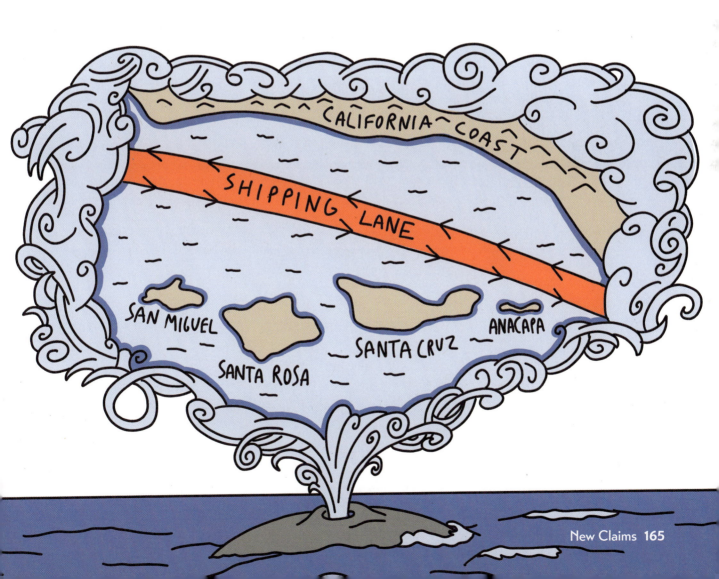

WHO OWNS WHAT

With the creation of Channel Islands National Park and Channel Islands National Marine Sanctuary in 1980, the federal government took ownership of much of the islands and the surrounding ocean. Two federal agencies now manage these public lands and waters. A private conservation organization owns and manages part of Santa Cruz Island.

Each of these groups has its own mission and perspective on what it means to be in charge of land and sea. These different philosophies shape how they manage different parts of the islands.

Tuqan
"San Miguel Island"

Wima
"Santa Rosa Island"

Limuw
"Santa Cruz Island"

'Anyapax
"Anacapa Island"

NATIONAL PARK SERVICE

Who: Government agency within the Department of the Interior

What they manage: San Miguel, Santa Rosa, Anacapa, Santa Barbara, and part of Santa Cruz islands, plus 1.8 kilometers (1 nautical mile) off each islands' shores

Objectives: "Protect park resources, both terrestrial and marine, and provide for the enjoyment of these resources in such a manner that will leave them unimpaired for future generations."

How to visit: Entrance is free to the public, but you must purchase a ferry ticket from Island Packers.

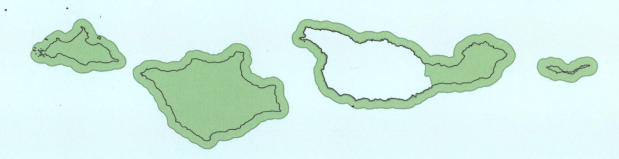

National Oceanic and Atmospheric Administration

Who: Government agency within the Department of Commerce

What they manage: The ocean from mean high tide to 10.8 kilometers (6 nautical miles) off the shores of San Miguel, Santa Rosa, Anacapa, Santa Barbara, and Santa Cruz islands

Objectives: "Understand and predict changes in climate, weather, oceans, and coasts, to share that knowledge and information with others, and to conserve and manage coastal and marine ecosystems and resources."

How to visit: Anyone can sail, fish, kayak, or snorkel–just be mindful of fishing restrictions in some areas.

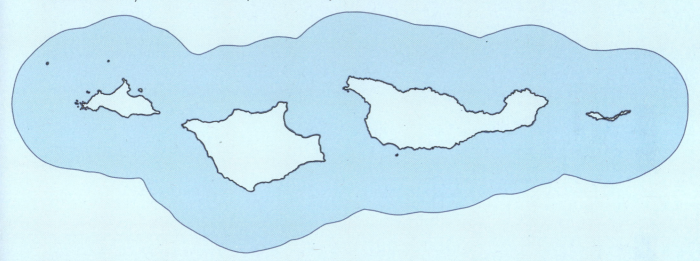

The Nature Conservancy

Who: Privately-run conservation organization that helps restore ecosystems around the world

What they manage and own: Western portion of Santa Cruz Island

Objectives: Work with partners to preserve "the island's unique plants and animals and sharing lessons learned in island restoration with other island conservation projects around the world."

How to visit: You must apply for a permit or be accompanied by an Island Packers guide.

A MODEL

by Rocío Lozano-Knowlton – *Founder, MERITO Foundation*

AGE 4 — Walked out into waves in Acapulco. Rescued by uncle. Loved it.

AGE 11 — Dad took her to Yucatan. Saw divers. Decided to be an oceanographer.

AGE 22 — Worked as a dive, kayak, and naturalist guide in Mexico and Japan.

AGE 36 — Developed a bilingual education program about the Channel Islands.

My very first experience at the Channel Islands was on a dive trip to San Miguel Island in 2000. San Miguel is surrounded by the cooler, nutrient-rich California Current, with water temperatures much colder than the Gulf of California, where I had been diving for the past nine years. At first, I was very concerned about the cold water and reduced visibility. To my surprise, I found an underwater paradise: beautiful, colorful, and abundant with marine life unique to the Santa Barbara Channel region. For the first time, I saw fish such as wolf eels, halibut, cabezon, and lingcod. The majestic kelp forest was a golden cathedral, with penetrating sunbeams surrounded by sea life. I was hooked on the islands.

Inspired by these wonders, I started working for NOAA Channel Islands National Marine Sanctuary, adapting an education program called MERITO to the Channel Islands. The goal was to engage multicultural youth and their communities in ocean protection.

Since then, the Channel Islands have been my muse, helping me to inspire and educate the next generation, as well as teach others around the world how to protect their own island wonders.

OUTDOOR CLASSROOM

The Channel Islands are a living laboratory—the perfect place for youth and adults alike to explore, discover, and learn about the delicate relationships between species and the habitats in which they live. In the National Park and National Marine Sanctuary waters around the islands, you can find rocky shores, sandy beaches, sandy seafloors, kelp forests, underwater canyons, open-ocean, and deep seas. These diverse habitats are full of life, including 27 cetacean species, 6 pinnipeds, 60 seabirds, more than 400 species of fish, including 23 shark species, and numerous species of invertebrates, algae, and seagrasses. The kelp forest alone, a major habitat within the park and sanctuary, is second only to coral reefs when it comes to biodiversity (the amount of different types of organisms that live within an ecosystem).

On land, Channel Islands National Park is home to a diverse collection of native and endemic plants and animals that are found nowhere else on Earth. These include the island fox, the island scrub-jay, the Santa Cruz Island ironwood and the Channel Islands slender salamander. Each of these species found their way out to the islands, where they evolved into something that looks different from their mainland ancestors.

FOOTPRINTS IN THE SAND

The islands and their waters are a window into not only the wonders of the natural world but also our human footprints on this planet. From the islands, students learn how excessive human burning of fossil fuels produces carbon dioxide that is trapped in the atmosphere and eventually makes its way into the sea. This changes our climate and the chemistry of our oceans. [See pages 250-255 for more on these impacts.]

Excessive carbon dioxide in the air is responsible for ocean warming and for the die-off of kelp beds at Channel Islands, home to hundreds of marine species. It also alters the amount of rain that island plants receive. Carbon dioxide in the air dissolves into the sea, making oceans more acidic, and thinning the shells of tiny plankton that feed many of the filter-feeding whales that migrate through the Channel each year. The runoff pollution washed into the ocean by rain, from Point Conception to Los Angeles, affects Sanctuary and Park waters. Oils, plastics, trash, fertilizers, and pesticides cause toxic algae blooms, reduce oxygen for sea life, and poison or entangle sea birds, fish, and marine mammals who mistakenly eat trash in their search for food.

At this moment in history, youth around the world are demanding environmental protection. They have the passion, care, and understanding of what is at stake, and are the main activists pushing for positive change. Learning about these impacts through the stories of the islands can teach students at an early age how critical these issues are. Local examples of global issues show the importance of both individual and collective actions in solving these problems.

MODEL FOR CONSERVATION

The Channel Islands are not only a living laboratory for students. They are also a great example of how we can best preserve island and marine ecosystems around the world. The network of state and marine protected areas (MPAs) established within the Channel Islands National Park and National Marine Sanctuary slow the loss of endangered marine species, restore depleted fisheries and damaged ecosystems, and allow

habitats and species to stay connected. [Learn more about MPAs around the Channel Islands on page 296.]

Over the past six years, I have had the privilege to work for the NOAA International Capacity Building Program, leading workshops with foreign countries that want to learn how to establish or better manage their own MPA networks. Very often, we teach them about the Channel Islands, and the practices that various State and Federal agencies use to manage this incredible place alongside other groups like research institutions, non-profit conservation organizations, and fishermen. These strategies range from getting everyone who values a place—called "stakeholders"—around the same table, to establishing sustainable tourism programs, to properly monitoring and enforcing MPA rules.

For example, CONANP, the Mexican government agency that manages the islands in the Gulf of

California, has adopted several of the best practices used by Channel Islands National Park and National Marine Sanctuary regarding visitors and tourism operators. Camping, kayaking, or diving operators need to apply for permits and comply with many usage requirements. Tourists are allowed to hike only in designated areas to avoid disturbance to wildlife or cultural resources. Fishing within marine reserves is prohibited. Tourists and operators need to remove their own garbage and secure their food away from wildlife. Feeding or disturbing the wildlife is not permitted. Boats must use mooring buoys instead of anchoring, or anchor on sand instead of rocky reefs if moors are not available. These are all practices that have helped make the Channel Islands what they are today.

The Republic of Korea has 27 MPAs. Prior to 2016, Korea did not have an MPA advisory council to represent the various stakeholders in these protected waters. In 2017 Korea adopted the Channel Islands Advisory Council model to establish their own MPA advisory council. This MPA advisory council is very similar to that of the Channel Islands, with seats for people representing commercial and recreational fisherman, research and education institutions, tourism, other government agencies, NGOs, and the public at large. This helped connect South Korea's MPAs to their communities and give people a voice in the management of their local waters—much like what we have accomplished around the Channel Islands.

I hope the Channel Islands continue to inspire all generations. The more people are exposed to their bounty and beauty, the better they understand our planet as a whole. The more people learn about how we have successfully managed these islands, the better our chances of protecting other special ocean areas and islands around the world.

San Miguel Island – 1955

Decades of sheep ranching stripped much of the native plant life (dark grey on the island), leaving sandy soil bare and vulnerable to erosion.

Army Map Service image courtesy of U.S. Geological Survey

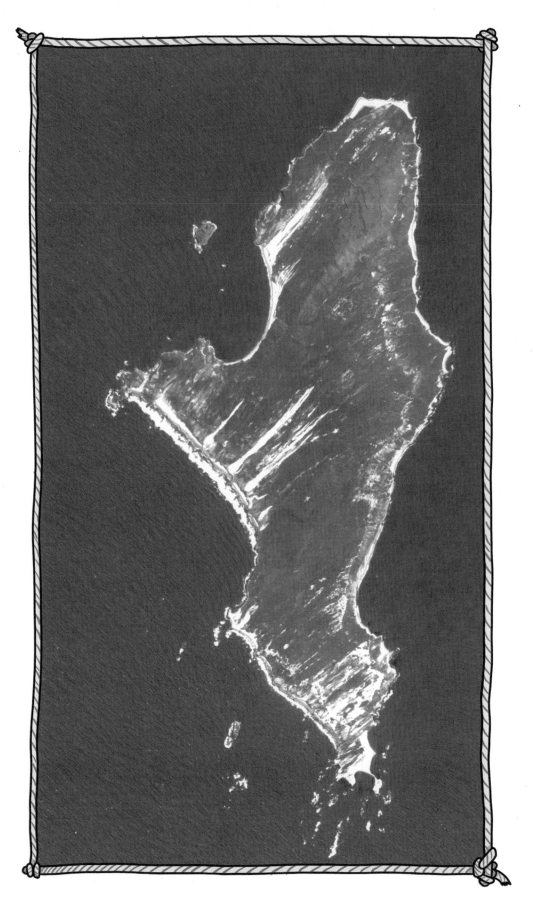

San Miguel Island – 2020

Forty years after ranching stopped, much of the native plant life (darker grey on the island) has regrown, holding the soil together and preventing more erosion.

Sentinel-2 image courtesy of U.S. Geological Survey, contains modified Copernicus Sentinel data 2020

By including humans in the picture,
we can most empower our strongest advocates for conservation.

When local communities everywhere understand
the value that nature provides,
see themselves as part of nature, and
see protecting nature as important
as protecting their home,
we will win the war for nature.

– M. Sanjayan, Conservation Scientist

Photo by Pedal Born Pictures

CHAPTER 5

ISLAND FOX

Fox M1092's Day: March 10th 2019

Limuw (Santa Cruz Island)

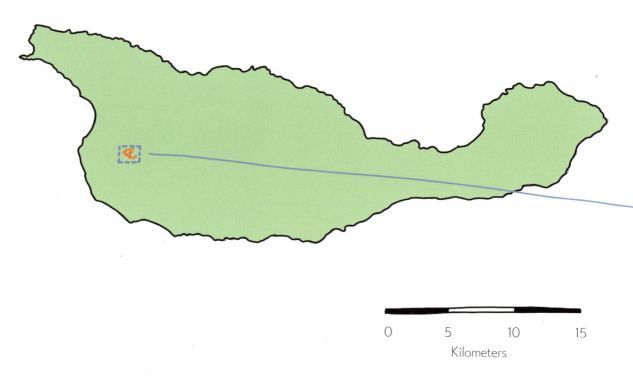

0   5   10   15

Kilometers

Fox tracking data courtesy of Northern Arizona University and The Nature Conservancy

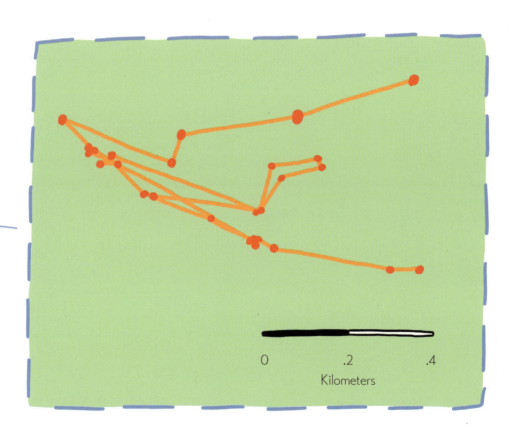

Approximate route fox traveled

Radio collar signals recorded approximately every 30 minutes

0   .2   .4
Kilometers

Photo by Greg Boreham

IT STARTS LIKE ANY OTHER DAY.

Catch a deer mouse for breakfast. Nap it off. Start looking for dinner.
But something seems off. The other island foxes haven't shown up for
the evening hunt. This island fox heads out anyway. He doesn't notice
the golden eagle swooping in from above until it's too late.

Turns out the golden eagle came to the islands because of us humans.
We triggered a chain reaction on the mainland, disrupting the
delicate habitat that the island fox called home. As a result, we nearly
caused this tiny Channel Islands native to go extinct. Every one of
our actions has consequences for our furry and feathered neighbors.
When we break a system, no one is going to fix it but us.

Meet the Fox

Known in the Chumash Shmuwich language as *knuy*, the island fox's Latin name translates to Tailed Dog (*Urocyon*) of the Sea Shore (*littoralis*). This tiny shore dog is **endemic** to the Channel Islands, meaning that you can't find it anywhere else on the planet. Each island has its own subspecies that has evolved with slight genetic differences.

Evolved

Over thousands of years on the islands, the mainland gray fox evolved into a new species, the island fox. We call this shrinking of a species over time **dwarfism**. It's hard to say for sure exactly what made the fox grow smaller. It could have been the fact that there was less food on the islands, or simply that the islands got too crowded for larger foxes.

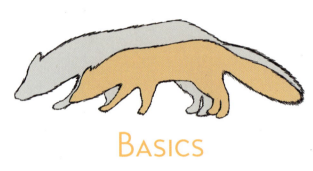

Basics

The island fox is two-thirds the size of the mainland fox, or a bit smaller than an average house cat.

Lifespan: up to 15 years
Weight: 1-3 kilograms (2.5-6 pounds)
Length: 58-69 centimeters (23-27 inches)
Height: 31-33 centimeters (12-13 inches)

Diet

This little critter is an **omnivore**, meaning it chows down on both animals and plants:

- Deer mice
- Jerusalem crickets
- Beetles
- Earwigs
- Cactus fruit
- Manzanita berries
- Saltbushes
- Marine invertebrates

Island Days

Gray foxes on the mainland are primarily **nocturnal**, hunting during the night to avoid predators spotting them on the landscape. On the islands, these smaller foxes have no natural predators and can be seen roaming around during the day. The lack of other animals looking to eat them also makes island foxes relatively unafraid of humans.

ISLAND FOX MYSTERY

by Courtney Hofman – *Archaeologist, U. of Oklahoma*

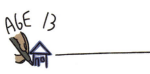

AGE 13 — AGE 18 — AGE 20 — AGE 22

Wanted to be an architect. Three years later, decided not to be an architect.

Started as a biology major, fell in love with anthropology.

Studied abroad in Cairo, Egypt. Began to pursue archaeology as a career.

Interned at the Smithsonian, first exposure to the Channel Islands.

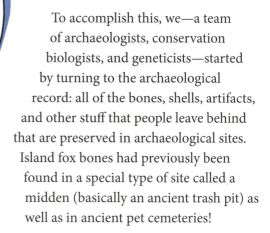

I became interested in the island fox while working as an intern at the Smithsonian National Museum of Natural History. I wanted to study the human past, but I also was really excited about a new research field that used DNA from old bones, teeth, and other archaeological material to study the human past in a new way: using genetics, the study of how traits are passed on from generation to generation.

By working together, archaeologists and geneticists could produce new ideas about the past, changing our understanding of human history. I liked the sound of this, and decided to become a molecular anthropologist by studying the origins and history of the island fox. I was intrigued by not just the origins of the fox, but also how people—both ancient and modern—impacted the biology of this unique creature.

To accomplish this, we—a team of archaeologists, conservation biologists, and geneticists—started by turning to the archaeological record: all of the bones, shells, artifacts, and other stuff that people leave behind that are preserved in archaeological sites. Island fox bones had previously been found in a special type of site called a midden (basically an ancient trash pit) as well as in ancient pet cemeteries!

I traveled to museums across California, as well as the Smithsonian in Washington, D.C., to find these fox bones. I took pictures of each fox bone, then cut the bone to take a sample. I performed the following analyses on the samples: genetic—to figure out how old the bones were; chemical—to figure out what the foxes ate; and radiocarbon—to figure out how old the bones were.

We also had to compare these ancient bones to those of living animals, as we wanted to know how the island fox's genetic diversity has changed over its history. We collaborated with wildlife managers who gave us blood samples that they collect each year to make sure that island fox populations are healthy. We compared DNA from these samples, and found that island foxes have very little genetic diversity. Diversity is important because it allows animals and plants to adapt when their environments change.

We also explored when island foxes first appeared on the Channel Islands. We analyzed the age of any fox bone in an archaeological site...and found the oldest fox bone to be about 7,300 years old! Native Americans first arrived on the Channel Islands roughly 13,000 years ago. That means foxes arrived on the islands well after people did. By identifying the oldest fox bone on each of the six islands where foxes live today, we developed a model of how foxes arrived on the islands. Based on these data, we think that foxes first arrived on the northern Channel Islands (San Miguel, Santa Rosa, Santa Cruz, and Anacapa) and were subsequently moved to the southern Channel Islands (San

Nicolas, San Clemente, and Santa Catalina, but not Santa Barbara, which was too small) by Native Americans. We cannot say for sure how foxes first got to the northern Channel Islands, but it could be due to a natural rafting event (a fox traveling on a piece of debris such as a floating log) or by a human introduction (fox on a boat!).

We tested these two hypotheses by comparing chemical signatures in island foxes, dogs, and humans through time. We found that island foxes for the most part ate terrestrial foods (insects, fruit, etc.). There were a couple of individual foxes—especially on San Nicolas Island—that were eating lots of marine foods (shellfish, fish, etc.). This diet was similar to that of people living on the island and the dogs they kept as pets. Perhaps these foxes were being kept as pets too? At this time we cannot know for sure. However, future research will help uncover the different types of relationships that island foxes had with people since they arrived on the islands. We hope this information can be used to protect this unique creature.

Keystone Species

As the largest terrestrial (land-based) predators on the islands, these pint-sized hunters are a crucial piece of the island ecosystem. If the fox ceased to exist, this loss could impact many species both on the islands and in the surrounding waters. We call organisms like these **keystone species**.

Foxes love the fruits of plants such as the Catalina cherry and manzanita. Fox **scat** (poop) helps transport these plants' seeds across the islands. Without this process, many native plants would have trouble surviving.

Without these plants to hold the soil together, rain and wind would wash away the top layer of dirt, a process known as **erosion**. This dirt would get carried into the ocean, where it could damage the kelp forests that are home to countless marine creatures.

As a predator of island deer mice, the fox is a key part of a complex island **food web**. Without the fox, mouse populations would skyrocket and bird populations would fall, as mice love to eat bird eggs. This island fox is more than just a cute miniature version of its mainland cousin. It is a keystone species that is crucial to maintaining the balance in ecosystems both above and below the waves of the Channel Islands.

by Jennifer Boyce – Restoration Manager, NOAA

AGE 10	AGE 2	AGE 30	AGE 35
Ran elementary school bake sale to help protect turtles from shrimping nets.	Got bachelors degree in Wildlife Management from University of Maine.	Lived as a field researcher in a puffin colony on Eastern Egg Rock Island.	Worked with NOAA to bring bald eagles back to Santa Cruz Island.

It is still dark and chilly out as we depart California's Ventura Harbor and head for Santa Cruz Island. It is the spring of 2002, and I do not mind the extra early wake-up. In fact, I could barely sleep the night before! We are embarking on a historic day. After many years of hard work, planning, and dedication, we are releasing the bald eagles back onto Santa Cruz Island with the hope that we will eventually have breeding eagles there for the first time in 50 years. This is a moment that will have a far-reaching impact on the other residents of the islands, especially the critically endangered island fox.

After the two-hour boat trip, navigating windy roads and hiking up a steep trail, we reach the hack towers (elevated artificial nests) where young eagles brought to the island from Alaska and the San Francisco Zoo have been acclimatizing to their new home. After making sure that all the birds are healthy and fit, we open the doors to the towers. After a brief hesitation, the first majestic bird takes flight over our heads.

Bald eagles once bred on all eight of the California Channel Islands. By the 1960s, the entire population was wiped out. This was likely due to a combination of eagle hunting by ranchers, removal of eggs by collectors, and finally, the introduction of the pesticide DDT into the ocean off Southern California. DDT is a chemical that bioaccumulates and is very slow to break down. Bioaccumulation works like this: Animals at the top of the food web, such as bald eagles, often feed on lots of smaller animals that are contaminated with DDT. Because they consume many of these smaller animals, larger predators build up large quantities of this dangerous substance in their bodies. This accumulation causes many bird species, including bald eagles, to lay thin-shelled eggs that dry out or break during incubation.

In 1972 Congress banned the use of DDT. Across the U.S. bald eagle populations started to recover, but continued to struggle in southern California. The Institute for Wildlife Studies (IWS) began bald eagle restoration efforts on Santa Catalina Island in 1980, nearly 20 years after bald eagles had disappeared from the Channel Islands. Unfortunately, some DDT remained and continued to impact the birds.

So where does the island fox come in? Four island fox subspecies underwent catastrophic declines in the 1990s. On San Miguel, Santa Rosa, and Santa Cruz Islands, the decline was linked to invasive golden eagles. For centuries the fox had lived without a major predator. Bald eagles eat mostly fish. They had ruled the islands, preventing golden

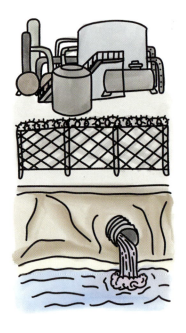

eagles—which prey on mammals like the fox—from coming out from the mainland. Unfortunately, the decline of bald eagles, combined with the human introduction of pigs and deer (favorite snacks of the goldens), allowed golden eagles to thrive on the islands. The fox, unused to threats from above, was an easy target. By the year 2000, goldens had reduced the fox populations to just 15 individuals on San Miguel and Santa Rosa Islands, and fewer than 80 on Santa Cruz Island. In 2004, all four island fox subspecies were on the U.S. Endangered Species List.

When I assumed my current position with the National Oceanic and Atmospheric Administration (NOAA) Restoration Center in 2001, NOAA and our fellow State and Federal Natural Resource Trustees had just reached a settlement in the lengthy lawsuit over the releases of DDT that had contributed to this ecosystem collapse. The hard-fought legal case was brought against several factories who, from the late 1940s to the early 1970s, had produced hundreds of millions of pounds of DDT and other chemicals and released them into the sea through a wastewater pipe located off shore of Palos Verdes.

Studies by the U.S. Geological Survey (USGS) and other independent organizations showed that more than 100 metric tons of DDT remained in the sand on the sea floor off of Southern California. These studies also showed that this dangerous chemical continued to contaminate marine life and birds long after it was banned in 1972. The settlement that had been reached forced polluters to pay $140.2 million, approximately $38 million of which would be used to restore natural resources harmed by DDT and other chemicals. My first assignment was to lead the Montrose Settlements Restoration Program (MSRP) which was in charge of using these funds to help restore these damaged resources. It was an exciting but intimidating task.

One of our first actions was to partner with the Institute for Wildlife Studies, the National Park Service, and The Nature Conservancy on an ambitious five-year bald eagle restoration study on Santa Cruz Island. We were optimistic that eagles would be able to reproduce successfully if located farther from the primary DDT source off the Palos Verdes Peninsula. Our goal was to re-establish a self-sustaining population of bald eagles on the Channel Islands.

This is where the island fox came back into the picture. It was thought that the reintroduction of territorial bald eagles would help keep golden eagles from breeding on the islands, and thus from preying on foxes. This would allow the island fox populations to rebound.

Sixty-one bald eagles were released from hack towers on Santa Cruz Island from 2002 to 2006. The chicks were held in the towers until they were 12-weeks-old. The birds were closely monitored following their release to track their survival. Chicks were outfitted with blue wing markers that had unique numbers and satellite transmitters. The satellite transmitters embedded in the wing markers allowed the project to track the movements of the released birds. One of the birds traveled as far as Yellowstone National Park in Wyoming before returning to Santa Cruz Island.

In the spring of 2006, elated biologists, program staff, and dedicated web camera viewers were thrilled to see a tiny bald eagle chick appear in a large nest that was built in the top of a 30-foot tree near Pelican Harbor on Santa Cruz Island.

This groundbreaking milestone marked the first successful nesting of bald eagles on the northern Channel Islands in more than 50 years.

The hope that the reestablishment of breeding bald eagles on the islands would prevent the establishment of golden eagles also proved to be true. Following the capture and relocation of breeding golden eagles, no breeding goldens have returned. Thanks to these efforts, along with a strong captive breeding program [see page 196], island fox populations have returned to healthy levels. In 2016, the U.S Fish and Wildlife Service removed three subspecies of island fox from the endangered species list, recognizing their comeback as the fastest recovery of any mammal listed under the Endangered Species Act. This entire effort, from the DDT to the eagle to the fox, has been a perfect example of how easily we humans can disrupt interconnected ecosystems—and how collective action by all of us can begin to right these wrongs.

CONSEQUENCES

In hindsight, it seems easy to see how industrial chemical dumping could create a chain of events that disrupts an entire ecosystem. But how did we humans let DDT get out there in the first place? Which of our day-to-day actions have similar ripple effects, and what can we do about these unforeseen consequences?

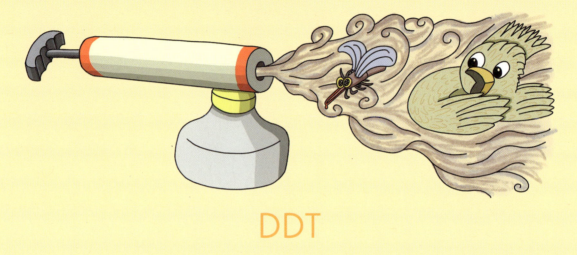

DDT

Mosquitoes spread diseases such as malaria in humans. Bugs eat our crops. To help kill these pests we invented DDT (Dichlorodiphenyltrichloroethane), a powerful pesticide.

The problem: DDT is very toxic to all forms of life, not just the insects that we target. It stays in the environment for decades and travels up the food chain via bioaccumulation, eventually poisoning entire ecosystems. DDT weakens bird shells and can cause cancer in many mammals, including us.

The solution: Recognizing the threats of this dangerous chemical, the U.S. banned DDT in 1972. However some countries still use it to kill mosquitoes that transmit malaria. These countries have decided that the consequences of using DDT are less severe than the spread of malaria which kills more than one million people each year.

Our impact on the planet isn't limited to chemical pollution and oil spills. Individual actions that we take on a daily basis can have small ripple effects that impact ecosystems around the globe. Here are a few to think about:

Fleece

Burger

Sunscreen

The problem: Warm and cozy fleece turns into a nightmare in the washing machine. Each time you wash it that jacket sheds hundreds of tiny fibers called microfibers. These make their way into the guts of everything from oysters to tuna—and then into our stomachs when we consume these tasty seafoods.

The problem: That tasty patty is a big contributor to climate change. Cows burp a lot, releasing tons of methane. Add this to the carbon dioxide burned in transporting them to slaughter, and you have a perfect recipe for climate change. Extreme weather, rising sea levels, more forest fires...a steep price per patty.

The problem: Many types of sunscreen contain the chemical oxybenzone. Waves wash this chemical off your skin and into the ocean. It disrupts the reproductive cycle of corals, leading to massive die-offs called "coral bleaching." Not good for the thousands of species that call the reefs home.

The solution: Wash your fleece less and install a filter on your washer that catches microplastics.

The solution: Think about what you eat. Burgers don't need to have cows in them.

The solution: Look for sunscreens without oxybenzone, such as those with zinc.

An island fox pauses in the grass on Santa Cruz Island to scratch an itch.
Photo by Greg Boreham

THE FOX RECOVERY

by Tim Coonan – Biologist, National Park Service

AGE 10 — Saw the Grand Canyon. Like walking into Dodger Stadium for the first time.

AGE 18 — Studied to be a doctor. Struggled in some classes, switched to biology.

AGE 27 — Caught bighorn sheep by helicopter in Death Valley. Hands still have scars.

AGE 39 — Brought last San Miguel island foxes into captivity. Saw a long road ahead.

In the mid-1990s I was working as a biologist with the National Park Service. We saw annual monitoring data that showed the island fox population declining, but we didn't know why. We began conducting research to figure out what was going on. We took blood samples from all six fox subspecies, but none showed any evidence of diseases such as rabies or distemper. Finally, in 1998, we put radio collars on San Miguel island foxes to determine directly what was killing them. Within two months we had our answer: Golden eagles were preying on the foxes, which had evolved without the presence of an airborne predator.

By 1999, there were only 15 foxes left on San Miguel and just a few on Santa Rosa. A team of experts agreed that several emergency actions needed to be taken to save them. Island foxes would have to be brought into captivity, and golden eagles needed to be captured and relocated far away. Additionally, we had to change the balance of power on the islands to favor foxes by removing pigs and deer and bringing back bald eagles.

Captive breeding was a journey into the unknown for us. No one had ever raised island foxes in captivity before. We constructed breeding pens on the islands and worked with local zoos to develop a diet, veterinary program, and breeding system. The captive populations grew quickly, and we were able to start releasing foxes back into the wild in 2003. Reintroduced foxes survived and reproduced well.

Raptor (bird of prey) biologists captured more than 40 golden eagles and relocated them to northwestern California. They caught the adults using remote-controlled traps set with bait, and removed the chicks by hand from their nests. None of the captured golden eagles came back to the islands. There were plenty of jackrabbits and squirrels—their natural prey— in the mountains.

To ensure that golden eagles never came back, the National Park Service and its partners undertook two major actions. With The Nature Conservancy we removed more than 6,000 wild pigs from Santa Cruz, ridding the island of its unnatural prey for golden eagles. The Institute for Wildlife Studies successfully reintroduced bald eagles to the islands.

With golden eagles gone, reintroduced foxes bred rapidly. They reproduced so well that we were able to cease captive breeding by 2007/2008. Island fox populations on San Miguel, Santa Rosa, and Santa Cruz all approached or exceeded their numbers before the population crash. Because of this multi-agency effort, the fox was removed from the endangered species list in 2016. While their numbers have recovered, we still watch them closely. [Read more about the present-day fox monitoring efforts on page 204.]

By The Numbers

The island fox recovery program took more than a decade and a half, bringing together dozens of government and private agencies.

Estimated cost of island fox recovery between 1999 and 2013

While humans have been keeping pets for centuries, the amount that we spend today on our animal friends is quite astonishing.

$563,000,000,000

Estimated total Americans spent on pets between 1999 and 2013

PLAY YOUR PART

with Wilson Sherman – *Volunteer, Santa Barbara Zoo*

AGE 16	AGE 17	AGE 18	AGE 19
Volunteered with parrots, sea lions, and leopards. Cleaned a lot of poop.	Participated in summer internship with cheetahs in Namibia.	Went to Berkeley to study wildlife conservation and communication.	Worked with chimpanzees and studied environmental education in West Africa.

What first drew you to working with animals?

I have always been interested in animals, but I started to see working with them as a possible career after my internship at the Santa Barbara Zoo during 7th grade career study week. I got to see how a variety of departments at the zoo worked, and thought it was super interesting. I started volunteering as a Zoo Camp counselor-in-training that summer, and continued to volunteer with the Zoo in a variety of capacities, including washing dishes in the animal kitchen, participating in awareness days and then educating the public as a docent.

What was your first exposure to the island fox restoration project at the Santa Barbara Zoo?

During that 7th grade internship at the zoo I got the chance to work with the island fox keepers. They told me a bit about how the zoo had played a critical role in saving the wild population from extinction. I then learned more extensively about the conservation efforts in classes the zoo offers its volunteers.

What do you see as the role of zoos in conservation efforts such as the fox restoration project?

Zoos play a critical role in conservation efforts, as they safeguard captive populations that can bolster wild populations in critical situations. Like a modern day "Noah's Ark," accredited zoos preserve genetically-viable captive populations.

Research done in zoos can help conservation efforts as well. The Santa Barbara Zoo was the first institution to breed foxes on the mainland, and the husbandry techniques the keeper learned were shared with other zoos, contributing to the captive breeding portion of the program. They also inspire young people to care about wildlife.

As a docent at the zoo, I saw children getting excited about the animals they saw, and then being motivated to make a positive change here on our planet. Accredited zoos also donate a cumulative average of more than $160,000,000 of their revenues towards conservation projects. Efforts like the fox restoration project require a huge amount of resources and manpower.

Why do you think these projects are so important?

While it can seem crazy to put so many resources into protecting something as simple as a fox, what projects like this really focus on is protecting ecosystems. As an apex predator, the foxes play a critical role in maintaining balance on the islands, which are home to a variety of plant and animal species found nowhere else on this planet.

Personally, I value these ecosystems because of their aesthetic and recreational value—I love hiking and kayaking around the islands because they are beautiful. Seeing wild foxes running around the islands reminds me that some places are still wild. I think we owe it to our future generations to protect as much of the natural world as possible, and the species that come with this planet are an essential part of this.

Zoos are sometimes seen as places to go to see exotic animals. Why do you think it is important for them to also have local species like the island fox?

While species like the island fox or the California condor are technically local species, surprisingly few people get the opportunity to see one in the wild, or even know that they exist. Making these species more accessible to the general public can inspire people to protect our local environment. At the Santa Barbara

Zoo, people are often blown away by the athletic prowess of the Amur leopards, but unaware that a big cat with a similar niche—mountain lions—could be walking through their own backyards. Introducing people to the wildlife that they have a direct impact on can make them value their own surroundings in a different way.

How has working at the Santa Barbara Zoo influenced your dreams and goals for the future?

Learning more about the issues that endangered animals face on our planet has absolutely made me want to pursue a career protecting them. The Santa Barbara Zoo has provided me with opportunities to get to know people with different careers in the animal industry. These mentors have given me valuable advice, which will absolutely influence my future. Their guidance is what inspired me to pursue a degree in wildlife conservation at UC Berkeley.

While I am not sure exactly what I want to do when I graduate, I know that I want to be teaching people to appreciate wildlife and wild spaces, and helping humans find ways to coexist with the natural world. At the moment, I imagine going to grad school to do research in conservation education, and maybe someday working in zoo and aquarium education.

WITH TIME

Over the course of 23 years, the island fox population went from stable, to near zero, to almost fully recovered. Without millions of dollars of work from multiple agencies and organizations this rebound never would have happened.

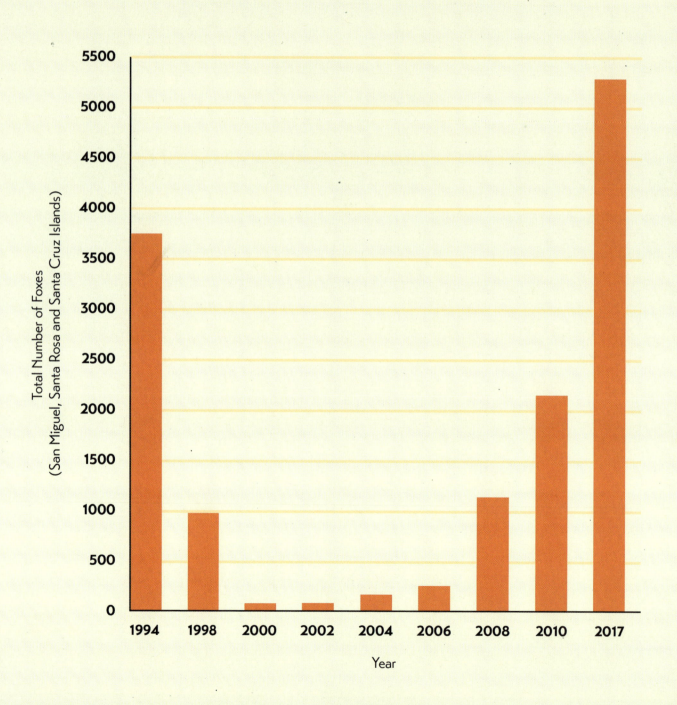

Total Number of Foxes
(San Miguel, Santa Rosa and Santa Cruz Islands)

Year

NOT OUT OF THE WOODS

by Christina Boser – *Ecologist, The Nature Conservancy*

AGE 8 — Heard about Alaska oil spill. Mom helped her realize world needed help.

AGE 10 — Started reading about the environment. Got involved in Earth Day.

AGE 19 — In college, realized career outdoors saving wild animals was possible.

AGE 27 — Got job with The Nature Conservancy protecting all people and animals.

Since the island fox was de-listed as an endangered species, we spend only about two months out of the year trapping and checking the foxes for radio collars. During fox recovery this was a nearly year-round process. We maintain about 50 foxes with live radio collars and still check on their survival every week. We can also monitor these radio collar signals via plane, which takes only about 45 minutes rather than the six hours it used to take us to drive around the island listening for active collars. For much of the year, the other researchers of the island help out with looking for foxes if a fox collar goes to "mortality mode" (shows that the fox may be dead). Here is what a day in the life of an island fox researcher looks like:

Out on Santa Cruz Island, I wake up an hour before sunrise. I have about two dozen traps that I need to check this morning. I'll need to hike about two miles today to get to these traps.

I prep microchips, which let us identify each animal we tag. I grab a few radio collars too. They send out beeps so we can figure out where the animal is located. If the animal were to stop moving because it died, then the beeps would double in pace.

This first trap has a fox, and it's sleeping on leaves on the floor of the cage—a little mattress that we left so that it can easily curl up and go to sleep. Most foxes have been trapped before, so they know they'll be released and are calm when I approach.

I put on my field gloves so I can safely handle the fox. I put a little blindfold over its eyes to calm it down. Then I assess how much muscle and fat the animal has on it. Generally, our animals are in good health.

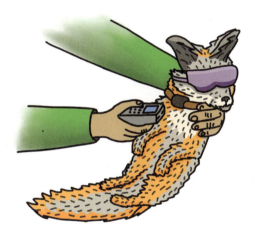

After the body condition check, I scan the animal with a tag reader. I run the handheld scanner over the back of the neck of the fox, looking for the microchip. If we have caught the animal before, it will have a microchip which allows us to identify it. With this identifier, we can figure out how many individuals are in the population. After several years of decline, the fox numbers are on the rise. On Santa Cruz there are now several thousand!

In the last trap I find a fox that was vaccinated the last time it was caught. Island foxes evolved without exposure to mainland diseases and have very little resistance to them. I give this fox a booster shot. When I release, it the fox runs forward a few paces and then turns to look at me. It shakes its head as if wondering why I'd go to so much trouble to catch it, then trots away. I pack up my gear and walk back to the truck to head home.

Animal / Human

We humans have been domesticating, worshipping, hunting, and eating animals since day one. But the way that we interact with our furry, feathered, and flippered neighbors varies dramatically across cultures. One person's sacred animal might be another's favorite snack. Our society deeply shapes which animals we decide to kill, and which we decide to protect.

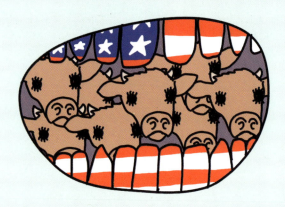

Whole Cow

While we might see cows as cute, we also sure love to eat them. The average American consumes four times as much beef as the global average. That is a lot of adorable calves that grow up to be hamburgers.

Holy Cow

Visit McDonald's in India and you will notice something missing: hamburgers. The cow is sacred to the Hindu majority. Instead of ending up on menus they wander free, often causing traffic jams.

Dogs so Hot

The strange little Corgi has taken America by storm. Memes. Instagram. There is even a Corgi expo, complete with races, costume contests, and a University of Corgifornia class photo.

Hot Dogs

In Vietnam, dog meat is a delicacy. While killing a dog for food might sound cruel, consider this: Who has it worse, the stray dog who can run free, or the factory-farmed cow living in a pen?

Insecticide

Entire business empires in America have been built on wiping insects off the map. Insecticides are chemicals that are used by everyone from home gardeners to industrial farmers to kill bugs that eat crops.

Insect Inside

In Japan, insects such as crickets and stag beetles have been kept as pets for centuries. Easy to catch, and even easier to care for, these tiny critters are said to bring good luck to their owners.

WHY SAVE THEM

by Peter Dratch – *Biologist, National Wildlife Refuge System*

AGE 9	AGE 18	AGE 23	AGE 33
Saw first moose and bald eagle on family rafting trip in Grand Teton NP.	Interviewed Senator Gaylord Nelson, the founder of Earth Day.	Studied reintroduction of wolves to Olympic National Park.	Started National Wildlife Forensics Lab to solve crimes against wildlife.

In 2004, I received a call from Tim Coonan, the biologist of Channel Islands National Park. The island fox was in steep decline. At the time, I was doing Endangered Species Act work for the National Park Service. I had previously spent 10 years with the Fish and Wildlife Service and done the genetics research for my thesis in a National Marine Fisheries lab. The recovery of the fox would be about preserving not just the fox on each island, but the genetic diversity of the entire population, so I was all in for the long haul.

It was hard to believe just how rapidly the foxes on Santa Rosa, San Miguel, and Santa Cruz were disappearing. But everything, from evolution to extinction, can happen so much faster on islands. For me the island foxes would become a great example, not only of professional courage and cooperation, but of how the Endangered Species Act (ESA) should work and why the ESA is considered among our most important environmental laws.

The 100th United States Congress made it clear why we needed such a law when they wrote in 1973 that "various species of fish, wildlife, and plants in the United States have been rendered extinct as a consequence of economic growth and development untempered by adequate concern and conservation." This law said that sometimes there needed to be a limit on our actions.

The ESA is visionary in another way: it connects species' survival to ecosystem health. "The purposes of this Act are to provide a means whereby the ecosystems upon which endangered species and threatened species depend may be conserved." So while the law focuses on individual species, those species are reminders that warn us of a much larger systemic problem.

There are five reasons why a species or a population can be listed under the ESA. Habitat loss or alteration is the most common one, and that relates back to an organism's role in the ecosystem. The others are over-consumption, disease or predation, lack of regulation, and other natural or man-made causes.

Several of these were considered in listing the island fox. Most immediate was predation by golden eagles. Then there was habitat alteration with the loss of bald eagles and the arrival of feral pigs and non-native deer. Finally, there was lack of regulation on DDT prior to the 1972 ban, which resulted in the eggshell-thinning in the bald eagles.

Over the next decade, scientists and managers from the Park Service and several other federal and state agencies, with dedicated partners at universities and non-government agencies, worked countless hours to recover the island fox. It was officially removed from the Endangered Species list in 2016, the fastest on-and-off in the history of the law.

The question that some have asked me when the story of this success is told, is why would Tim Coonan and so many others take so many chances and spend so much money to save a species that most people can't tell from their common mainland cousins? One reason is that the Channel Islands are a national park, and the Organic Act of 1916 which created the National Park Service carries with it the charge "to conserve the scenery and the natural and historic objects and the wild life therein…for the enjoyment of future generations." So the fox was saved from extinction not just to comply with the ESA. For a hundred years Park Service employees have been preserving the natural and historic, so that, another hundred years from now, people will be able to go to those places and appreciate them.

That is what we as a people want, and for that we are willing to make some sacrifices. A study of more than 10,000 citizens titled "The Nature of Americans" came out in 2016. It made clear just how closely our well-being is linked to the richness of the environment in which we live. One of its crucial conclusions was that "the conservation of species, the protection and restoration of habitats, and the provision of healthy streams and clean air are closely linked to human flourishing. A thriving natural environment helps Americans live happier, healthier lives."

We understand that a country where only the common species—those animals and plants that are well adapted to human habitats and have become tame and overabundant—survive, is a much diminished place. This is not only a matter of appreciation or even morality. When more of the planet's habitats lose their species, Earth as an ecosystem is less stable. This was already apparent half a century ago, and the rationale for why our lawmakers wrote the Endangered Species Act.

If you go for a hike on one of the Channel Islands today, there is a good chance you will see foxes, an experience unlike any other. The ESA worked not only in preventing the extinction of one species, but in restoring an ecosystem and preserving the quality of human life for generations to come.

A solitary island fox patrols the grassland on Santa Cruz Island. *Photo by Greg Boreham*

by Edward O. Wilson – *Professor, Harvard University*

AGE 9 — Started collecting butterflies in Washington D.C.

AGE 16 — Moved on from butterflies, began to study ants.

AGE 17 — Entered University of Alabama to become an entomologist.

AGE 32 — Won second Pulitzer Prize for his book *The Ants*.

Biodiversity is the totality of all inherited variation in the life forms of Earth, of which we are one species. We study and save it to our great benefit. We ignore and degrade it to our great peril.

But why should we care? What difference does it make if some species are extinguished, if even half of all the species on earth disappear?

Let me count the ways. New sources of scientific information will be lost. Vast potential biological wealth will be destroyed. Still undeveloped medicines, crops, pharmaceuticals, timber fibers, pulp, soil-restoring vegetation, petroleum substitutes, and other products and amenities will never come to light.

It is fashionable in some quarters to wave aside the small and obscure, the bugs and weeds, forgetting that an obscure moth from Latin America saved Australia's pastureland from overgrowth by cactus, that the rosy periwinkle provided the cure for Hodgkin's disease and childhood lymphocytic leukemia, that the bark of the Pacific yew offers hope for victims of ovarian and breast cancer, that a chemical from the saliva of leeches dissolves blood clots during surgery, and so on down a roster already grown long and illustrious despite the limited research addressed to it.

Humanity coevolved with the rest of life on this particular planet; other worlds are not in our genes. Because scientists have yet to put names on most kinds of organisms, and because they entertain only a vague idea of how ecosystems work, it is reckless to suppose that biodiversity can be diminished indefinitely without threatening humanity itself.

Field studies show that as biodiversity is reduced, so is the quality of the services provided by ecosystems. Records of stressed ecosystems also demonstrate that the descent can be unpredictably abrupt. As extinction spreads, some of the lost forms prove to be keystone species, whose disappearance brings down other species and triggers a ripple effect. The loss of a keystone species is like a drill accidentally striking a power line. It causes lights to go out all over.

Adapted from *The Diversity of Life* and www.eowilsonfoundation.org.

Am I cute?

Am I loved?

I don't have the fur,
I don't have the eyes.

To you I'm a blob,
I'm a brown patch of slime.

I'm a beetle that stinks,
I'm a bird that's gone bald.

I don't smell of roses,
I can't fetch you a ball.
I'll never be your pup,
in me there is no pet at all.

We may all seem pointless,
ugly and different and small.

We'd love you to love us,
please consider us all.

by the crucial but less "cute" creatures

Photo by Robert Schwemmer

CHAPTER 6

KELP FORESTS

Santa Cruz Island Kelp Forests

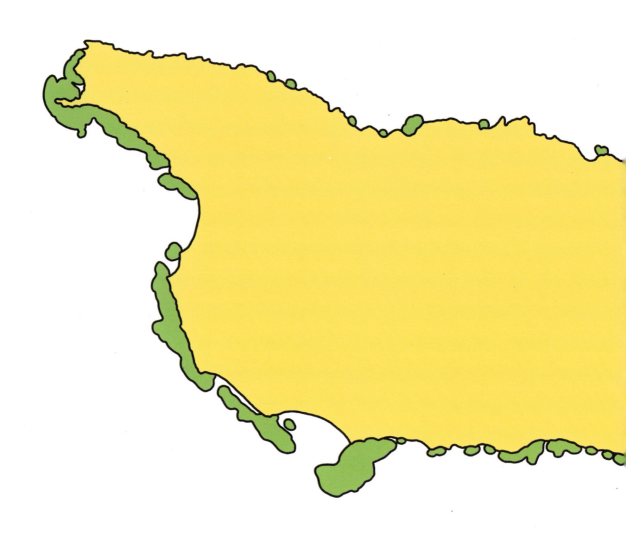

= Potential giant kelp forests

Photo by Douglas Klug

LOOKING ACROSS THE SURFACE, THE OCEAN CAN SEEM EMPTY.

Dive beneath the waves at the Channel Islands, and a whole world opens up. Towering forests of kelp rival any forest or jungle on land. Giant sea bass swallow other fish whole. Armies of urchins prowl the sea floor. These underwater cities are not so different from our own.

As humans have explored kelp forests, we have begun to see connections between the creatures of the sea and us, creatures of the land. Our aquatic neighbors literally keep us alive, yet we return the favor by trashing their homes, and thus our own. Only by seeing ourselves in these majestic forests can we hope to turn the tide.

Now you see me, now you don't.
A giant kelpfish hides in a mass of kelp.
Photo by Douglas Klug

GIANT KELP

Imagine a giant redwood tree growing hundreds of feet up from the forest floor. Now imagine that tree underwater, gently swaying back and forth in the current, fish swimming through its leaves and seals playing on its branches. This is giant kelp.

In Latin, it is called *Macrocystis pyrifera*.

Macro = Big   *Cystis* = Bladder   *Pyri* = Fire   *Fera* = Bearing

ANATOMY

While it may form forests that rival those on land, giant kelp is uniquely adapted to tower over the undersea world that it calls home.

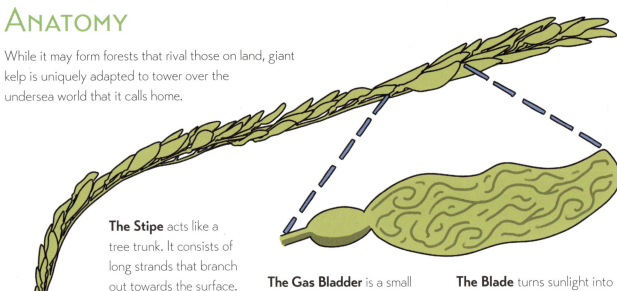

The Stipe acts like a tree trunk. It consists of long strands that branch out towards the surface. It is strong yet flexible and allows kelp to bend with the current.

The Gas Bladder is a small sack of gas attached to the blade. It helps kelp float, lifting it towards the energy of the sun.

The Blade turns sunlight into energy via photosynthesis. Its flame-like shape is what gives giant kelp its Latin name.

The Holdfast latches onto rocks with tiny arms. Think of it like a root system. Without the holdfast giant kelp would get carried out to sea.

SIZE

Giant kelp can grow up to **60 meters (200 feet) tall**. That's as tall as a 17-story building.

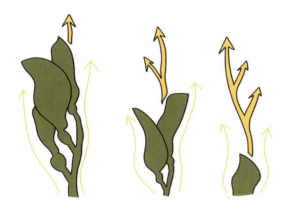

GROWTH

Giant kelp can grow up to **61 centimeters (2 feet) per day**, making it one of the fastest growing organisms on Earth. For comparison, an oak tree grows 30-60 centimeters (1-2 feet) in a year. Even as youngsters we humans grow only a few inches each year.

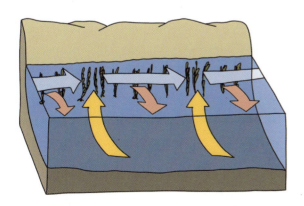

FOOD

Giant kelp thrives in coastal areas. Here, **upwelling** provides the nutrients that kelp needs to support its incredible growth rate. Winds blowing parallel to the coast combine with the earth's rotational forces, carrying warm surface water out to sea. Nutrient-rich deep water then "upwells" to fill this space, creating the perfect growing conditions for giant kelp.

Giant sea bass are quite the attraction for the divers.
I love diving alongside these 300 pound fish.
Photo by Douglas Klug

SWIMMING WITH GIANTS

by Kathy deWet-Oleson – *Photographer*

AGE 5 — Took photos on family trip up the California coast. Fell in love with the ocean.

AGE 18 — Studied art at Cal Poly, Pomona. Also learned to scuba dive.

AGE 24 — Taught scuba diving while earning Masters degree in Exercise Science.

AGE 36 — Started working in the diving industry on the Channel Islands.

The day began like most others. My husband and I arrived at the docks before daylight to prepare our charter dive boat. We started up the coffee and homemade soup that would warm divers later in the day. With passengers aboard, I cast off the dock lines.

After an hour-long crossing, we arrived at Anacapa Island. I helped set the anchor and gave a dive-briefing. After the guests entered the water, I did a final check of my dive and photo gear and slipped into the cool water, equipped and ready to photograph brittle stars, nudibranchs, and other small creatures.

Drifting down, the water was tinted green with plankton from a typical spring upwelling. I could see only about 6 meters (20 feet) in all directions.

Hearing only the sound of exhaled bubbles, I swam slowly past golden fronds of kelp, entering this vibrant forest. Brightly-colored juvenile fish with patterns very different from their grown-up counterparts darted in and out of the canopy. I scanned the reef as it began to come into view, not wanting to miss anything amidst the rainbow of brittle stars, nudibranchs, and anemones that clung to the holdfasts anchoring these massive underwater "trees" of kelp.

Visibility was muted by the kelp canopy above, but suddenly my eyes came to focus on a dozen large dark fish. As they came closer, I realized that each fish was almost as large as the other divers in the water. Giant sea bass. Though formerly common in this habitat, I had seen this species only once before, back in 1982. Even then, I had never experienced being surrounded by these giants.

As each fish swam near me, I could see their large brown eyes observing me just as I did them. Many had faces covered with small parasites that made it look as if they had whiskers surrounding big thick lips. Small fish gathered around the giants to feed on these whisker-like parasites—a behavior known as cleaning. They swam slowly around me as I settled to the seafloor and watched them in awe.

Some of the giants changed their color patterns like chameleons, blending in with different backgrounds. They had huge mouths, perfect for sucking up everything from spiny lobster to stingrays to small sharks. No wonder many call them the "kings of the kelp forest."

Back on deck, divers shared their stories of swimming with these giants…stories that prompted questions.

"How big can those things grow?"

"They look ancient. How old are they?"

"Some were different colors. Does that mean that they were male or female?"

I could identify the species and knew they had protected status in California due to overfishing, but there were many questions that I couldn't answer.

Since that dive in 1997, these kelp forest giants have been making a comeback. More and more divers are catching sight of these wondrous fish around the Channel Islands. NOAA scientists with the Channel Islands National Marine Sanctuary are hard at work studying whether these increased sightings are indeed evidence of a recovery.

As a diver, one has only a small window of time underwater to witness short snippets of the lifestyle and behavior of these mysterious creatures. On every dive into the kelp, I continue to look for their silhouettes in the water below, hoping to learn more about these majestic beings and their role at the top of the kelp forest ecosystem.

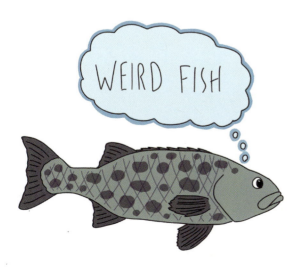

Underwater Skyscraper

Think of a kelp forest as an underwater Manhattan. Huge "seascrapers" of giant kelp are home to more than 770 diverse organisms, many of which rely on each other for survival—or dinner. These underwater highrises are made up of three distinct levels:

Canopy

The thick mat of giant kelp blades in the upper reaches of the forest provide lots of real estate and protection, making this the perfect place to raise a family. For many, it is also a great place to hide from the thing in 4B that wants to eat you for lunch. Just watch for seagulls.

California sheepshead munch on sea urchins, keeping kelp healthy

kelp crabs blend in

grey whales hide from killer whales

señoritas are the kelp forest

western gulls try to snack on critters

turban snails munch on kelp

opaleyes travel in schools and feed on kelp

fish use canopy as a nursery

UNDERSTORY

Underneath the thick canopy, kelp blades thin out as towering stipes anchor the forest to the seafloor. This makes room for vibrant schools of fish that use the level above as a nursery. It also serves as the favorite sushi bar for the larger predators in the building. Here you can find other species of kelp such as feather boa.

HOLDFAST

On a budget? Don't mind using your living room as a kitchen? These units are for you. The root-like tangle that makes up the holdfast has tons of nooks and crannies, with room for thousands of individual organisms from more than 150 different species. Time to brush up on your sea urchinese.

kelp bass usually live alone

sea stars eat urchins, also they chill

doctors; they clean parasites off other fish

sea lions eat almost everything on this level

great white sharks wander in, looking for a seal to snack on

giant sea BASS

PHISH

sea cucumber

red octopuses search for food

urchins are kelp's #1 predator

1 square meter can contain 300 brittle stars

nudibranchs come in many colors

California spiny lobsters don't have claws

The red rock shrimp is the star of this shot as the eel makes his presence known from the background.
Photo by Douglas Klug

A red sea urchin sits amongst the myriad of life that calls the kelp forest home.
Photo by Douglas Klug

TAKING THE HOUSE

What do Russian fur traders, sushi chefs, sea otters, and urchins all have in common? They are all players in the same complex kelp forest food web. Otters eat sea urchins. Urchins eat giant kelp. When the population of one of these organisms rises or falls, it can impact the entire web. Throw urchin-eating, kelp-harvesting, otter-hunting humans into the mix and the web will never be the same.

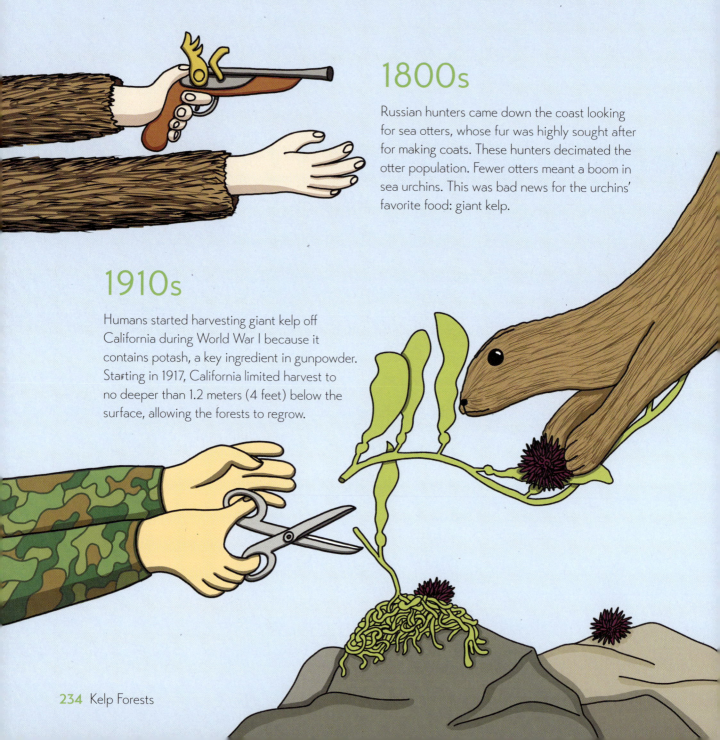

1800s

Russian hunters came down the coast looking for sea otters, whose fur was highly sought after for making coats. These hunters decimated the otter population. Fewer otters meant a boom in sea urchins. This was bad news for the urchins' favorite food: giant kelp.

1910s

Humans started harvesting giant kelp off California during World War I because it contains potash, a key ingredient in gunpowder. Starting in 1917, California limited harvest to no deeper than 1.2 meters (4 feet) below the surface, allowing the forests to regrow.

1970s

Commercial urchin diving was introduced as a way to bring urchin populations under control. This created a whole industry that is now one of the top fisheries in the region.

1980s

Sea otter conservation efforts have attempted to restore the species to its previous numbers. Unfortunately, populations have not yet reached pre-trapping levels. This is likely because of pollution and diseases spread by domestic house pets.

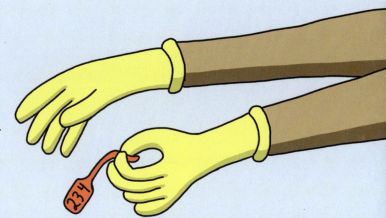

NOW

Sea otters have made a slow recovery on the California coast. A small population was reintroduced to San Nicolas Island but otters have yet to return to the northern Channel Islands. Without the otter, commercial urchin diving plays an important role in reducing the numbers of this kelp predator. We must continue to listen and learn from our actions in order to restore balance to this fragile food web.

DIVING FOR GOLD

with Bruce Steele – *Urchin Diver*

AGE 9

AGE 16

AGE 19

AGE 21

Grandfather took him on first trip to the islands. Caught a barracuda.

Learned to scuba dive. Bitten by moray eel at Catalina Island.

Began diving commercially for sea urchins.

Became captain of his own boat. Has been diving for over 45 years since.

When did you decide to become an urchin diver?

When I was in high school, I got into an advanced placement marine biology class at Moorpark College. Back then, in the late '60s and early '70s, there was a perceived problem with sea urchins eating the kelp. Marine biologists and commercial divers came to talk to us about the problem. That was what got me hooked. I realized that I could go out and pick sea urchins, do something good for the kelp beds and the environment, and earn a living in the process. I never ended up going to college.

What is your favorite part about diving?

As humans we live our lives on land. All 7.5 billion of us. The part of the world that we know about is terrestrial life. When you get in the ocean as a diver you are in a different world. There are things that are similar to those on land…like we have spring and fall underwater. But pretty quickly it becomes much different. The current moves you around. You are never really sitting in one place. You are always moving. Everything is in flux. You get a chance to live life in a place that very few of the billions on Earth ever see.

Can you walk us through a day in the life of an urchin diver?

A normal day would be: wake up in the dark, drive to the islands, dive in. Urchin divers breathe through a hose that runs up to an air compressor on the boat. The hose also helps keep you from drifting away. You pick urchins for four or five hours, and take a break in the middle of the day. If you are diving really deep, maybe take a few breaks so that you don't get the bends (a condition that you get from coming up so fast that air bubbles form in your blood). At the end of the day, put the urchins on the boat and drive back to the harbor. It can be a pretty long day. If you head out to San Miguel, you can spend the day driving the boat 140 kilometers (100 miles), plus four or five hours diving. You get home at dark, and the next day you start over.

What makes the Santa Barbara Channel so good for urchin diving?

The Channel Islands are a great place for urchin diving because of the kelp beds and high concentration of nutrients that help the kelp grow. Urchins feed on kelp, so lots of kelp means more urchins—higher quality urchins. Up in my head, I have this little map. If you took me out in the ocean and we were sitting in a kelp bed, I could draw you a good picture of what the rocks on the bottom of the ocean look like, which way the reefs run, and where the sand channels are.

How have you seen urchin populations change since you started diving?

When I started, there was a pretty high concentration of them in many places. They were seen as a problem. We did our best to thin them out. After a while, it became obvious that we were having to go farther and farther out to get good urchins. But the Park Service has been collecting data for quite a while, and the number of urchins per square meter has been very consistent for quite a while. The main difference now is that the urchins used to be bigger. So we put a size limit in place so that the small urchins can survive and grow.

Also, there are still lots of big urchins down deep. Urchins can live as deep as 91 meters (300 feet). So there is a reserve of urchins that nobody has ever touched. And, for the most part, sea otters don't even touch them. Biologically, we think that the sea urchin stock is pretty robust.

Urchin diving initially took off in California as a way to help restore kelp forests. Did that work?

I think people got a bit carried away. They thought, "If we just control the sea urchins, then the kelp will be happy." In reality, El Niño brought along a big storm surge and did its damage to the kelp, ripping a lot of it out. In the next few years we might see that happen again. It will look like there are sea urchins everywhere, but ultimately the predators come back and eat the urchins, and things balance back out. I think people place too much value on what we can do to control and manipulate environments. You have to take a step back and look at where you are in the cycle.

What is the importance of involving fishermen in science?

Fishermen spend an enormous amount of time out there—a lot more than most researchers are going to get the opportunity to have. I have been out there for 40 years. Some have been out there for 50 or 60 years. We have this sort of long perspective on what's happening. If a fisherman sees something going wrong, they can put it in context of what they think should be happening given what they have seen over time. We are eyes on the ground when we are out there.

What advice would you give to a kid who might be interested in trying out urchin diving?

Take a scuba diving course. You can do that when you are in high school. Learn how to be a diver. Go put eyes in the ocean.

EATING IN THE FOREST

Sea urchins are one of giant kelp's top predators, capable of mowing down entire forests. They are also prized by chefs around the world. Inside their shells are bright yellow reproductive organs called uni, which make tasty toppings for everything from pasta to sushi. You can find these spiny delicacies for sale at many fish markets.

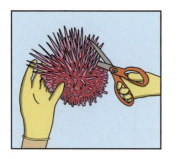

1. Wearing gloves, use kitchen scissors to **trim** the spines. Find the mouth and cut a hole in the bottom.

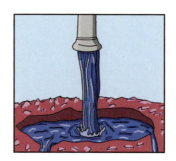

2. **Flush** water through the shell to rinse out the nasty bits while preserving the golden uni.

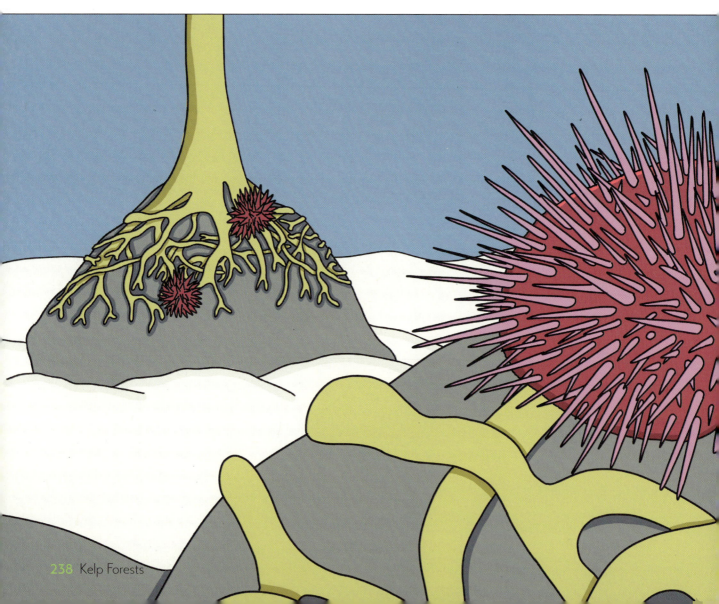

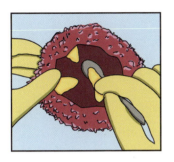

3. Use a spoon to **scoop** out the golden goodness. Rinse any remaining dark bits off of the golden part.

4. **Enjoy** with a squeeze of lemon, add to sushi, or toss it with pasta for a delicious "ocean" finish.

Reading the Forest

by Dan Reed – Research Ecologist, UCSB

AGE 0

Lucky to be born two blocks from the ocean in Santa Barbara.

AGE 12

Camped in the wilds of Los Padres National Forest.

AGE 15

Scuba dived in the kelp at Forney's Cove, Santa Cruz Island.

AGE 34

Completed PhD at UCSB and was hired as a research biologist.

Growing up in Santa Barbara, I was naturally attracted to both the ocean and the mountains. It did not take me long to realize that diving in kelp forests allowed me to experience the ocean and the forest at the same time.

After graduating from high school, I decided to enroll in the local community college to study marine biology. My dream: to someday find a job that allowed me to dive in these undersea forests for a living. One thing led to another, and I have been studying the ecology of kelp forests for more than 40 years since.

As an ecologist there are many reasons to study kelp forests beyond their natural beauty. There is the ecological and economic importance that many living things have for us humans. There is, also importantly, the fact that giant kelp grows at almost 4 percent per day. This makes kelp forests one of the most productive ecosystems on Earth, rivaling tropical rain forests.

However, unlike trees that can live for centuries, giant kelp lives for only a few years. Entire forests are regularly destroyed by natural disturbances. Fortunately, because they grow back so fast, kelp forests can rapidly recover from such disturbances.

Ecology

Ecologists study not only living organisms themselves but how these organisms interact with their environments. They regularly measure and collect data in order to better understand the relationships within complex habitats such as kelp forests.

EL NIÑO

In regular years, strong winds called trade winds blow west across the Pacific, pushing warm water to Asia. Cold water upwells from the ocean floor on our coast to replace this warm water.

Every few years, these trade winds weaken and warm water drifts back across the Pacific. This creates an El Niño effect: more storms in the western U.S. and abnormally high ocean temperatures for several months.

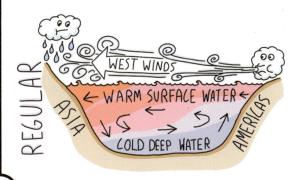

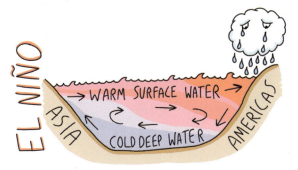

This makes them perfect places to study ecological processes that would take decades or centuries to study in slower-growing, longer-living terrestrial forests.

People often ask whether kelp forests have changed since I began studying them. The simple answer to this question is a strong "yes." Kelp forests change greatly over time. Most kelp forests in southern California live an average of three years or fewer before being destroyed by natural disturbances.

Kelp loss can be even greater when different disturbances happen at the same time. During El Niños, large waves occur at the same time as periods of warm, nutrient-poor water. This warm water weakens holdfasts, and the strong waves then easily tear up the kelp.

After a large loss of kelp from storms or poor growing conditions, sea urchins can leave their crevices in search of food, eating much of the remaining attached kelp. This creates large empty areas known as "urchin barrens."

Amazingly, kelp forests usually recover from these types of destruction within two years!

But what about climate change, ocean acidification, pollution, and overfishing? Saying that "kelp forests are constantly changing" is not a very satisfying answer to these questions. Because kelp forests are constantly dying and regrowing naturally, it has been difficult to measure our long-term impact on them. However, remote observation technologies, long-term observations by divers, and sensors attached to the ocean floor are starting to change the picture.

These tools are giving us clues into the causes of long-term change in kelp forests—clues that will be crucial to successfully managing this incredible ecosystem, preserving it for the next generation of young hikers-turned-divers-turned-scientists to learn from and explore.

TIDE POOLS

If kelp forests are the thriving undersea metropolises of the channel, think of tide pools as the vibrant frontier towns. You can find these pools both on the islands and the mainland shore. Existing right between the ocean and the land, they provide a home to many of the same creatures that live in kelp forests.

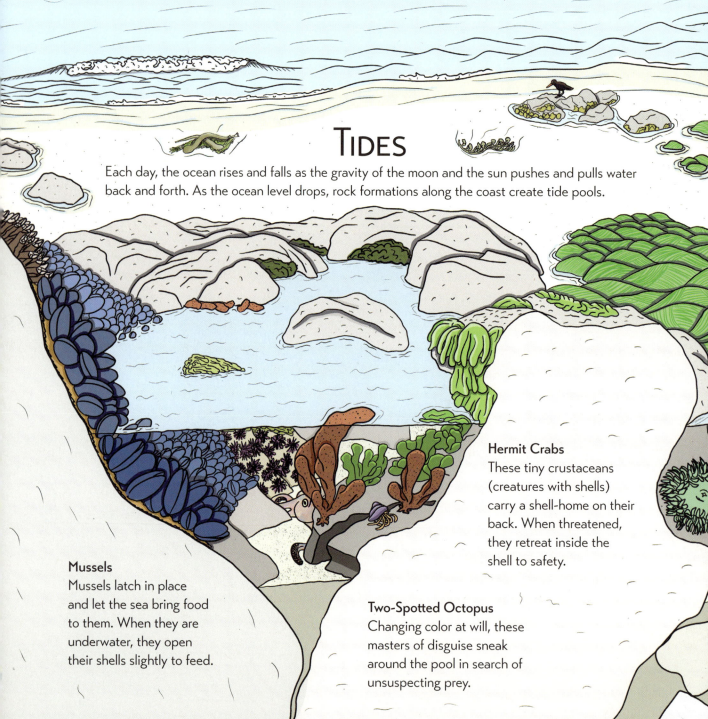

TIDES

Each day, the ocean rises and falls as the gravity of the moon and the sun pushes and pulls water back and forth. As the ocean level drops, rock formations along the coast create tide pools.

Hermit Crabs
These tiny crustaceans (creatures with shells) carry a shell-home on their back. When threatened, they retreat inside the shell to safety.

Mussels
Mussels latch in place and let the sea bring food to them. When they are underwater, they open their shells slightly to feed.

Two-Spotted Octopus
Changing color at will, these masters of disguise sneak around the pool in search of unsuspecting prey.

Giant Kelp
Look out beyond the waves for patches on the surface. These mark the tops of kelp forests.

WHERE AND WHEN

Every day has at least one high and one low tide. The times of these tides change each day, but we know when they will occur based on the rotation of our planet. Tide pools form at low tide. Search for a local tide chart to find the next one, and head to a beach with lots of rocks.

Starfish
Though they don't do well out of water, starfish can regrow any arms that are eaten by predators.

Rockweed
Many types of kelp, such as the rockweed, thrive in the ocean and tide pools alike.

Giant Green Anemone
These invertebrates use stinging tentacles to catch prey. Above water, they curl up for protection.

Tidepool Sculpin
Unlike their ocean-going cousins, these fish can breathe air, a big help when the tide gets low.

KELP IS NOT A PLANT

All life forms can be categorized as either plant or animal, right? Not so fast. Kelp fits into a third category: algae (singular: alga). Algae have existed on this planet for millions of years and are actually the ancestors of many modern plants. There might be family resemblance, but this is definitely a different crew.

Plants attach to the ground by roots that absorb nutrients. They transport these nutrients to other parts of their bodies using a vascular system (a network of veins like what we use to move blood through our bodies).

Algae can either float freely in water or anchor to the sea floor using a holdfast (a root-like structure that doesn't absorb nutrients). Because of this, each cell in an alga must absorb its own nutrients.

ALGAE IN YOUR LIFE

You can find giant kelp and its algal relatives in our fields, our food, and our bathrooms. Creepy, but true.

Ice Cream - Agar and carrageenan, two compounds that we harvest from kelp, keep your ice cream nice and smooth.

Toothpaste - Some of those same compounds are used to thicken toothpaste into a paste.

Fish - Kelp forests serve as a nursery for many species of fish. This helps keep fish populations—and nearby fishermen's catches—high.

Fertilizer - High levels of key nutrients such as nitrogen make ground or liquified kelp a huge boost to your garden or farm.

Soap and Shampoo - The slimy, gooey texture of many cosmetic products comes from compounds found in algae.

Sushi - Several types of edible green kelp are used to produce nori, the dark green crunchy wrapper that holds sushi together.

Underwater Plants & Algae

Brown Algae

Often called kelp, this olive green to dark brown category of organisms contains the largest forms of algae.

Elk Kelp
Second largest type of brown algae after giant kelp.

Bull Kelp
Part of the subfamily *Nereocystis* ("mermaid's bladder" in Greek).

Feather Boa
Can survive on rocky coasts where it moves with the surf.

Giant Kelp
The redwood of the sea and largest form of kelp.

Red Algae

Thrives in deeper, colder water. Its red coloring absorbs blue light, the only kind at lower depths.

Turkish Towel
Some people use its rough, bumpy, towel-like surface to remove dead skin!!

Green Algae

The oldest living ancestors of modern plants. Look more like plants than do any other type of algae.

Sea Lettuce
A high protein and iron snack. Loved by both humans and manatees world-wide.

Phytoplankton

A microscopic food source for countless organisms. Absorb huge amounts of carbon dioxide from the atmosphere, creating more than half of the oxygen that we breathe every day!

Dinoflagellets
Use their whip-like tails to propel them through the sea.

Diatoms
Tough shell but no tail. Can be found hitching a ride on currents.

Underwater Plants

While they may look similar to some species of algae, the organisms below are actually underwater plants.

Surf Grass
Unlike new surfers, this plant thrives in the "impact zone" where the waves break.

Eel Grass
Forms underwater meadows that filter runoff and serve as nurseries for young fish.

Phytoplanktonland

by Jessica Vega – Aquatic Biology Student, UCSB

AGE 4
Amazed by dad's fishing stories: shining squid, giant sailfish, and more.

AGE 9
Thought she could be a mermaid if she spent enough time in the sea.

AGE 17
Took AP Environmental Science. Learned about the threats to the ocean.

AGE 22
Worked at UCSB with K-12 students to share the wonder of the sea.

4,100,000,000,000, or 4.1 trillion. That is the number of plankton estimated in just the top 25 centimeters (about 10 inches) of water in Pelican Bay on Santa Cruz Island. If this amount of tiny creatures is found in just the surface waters, imagine how many plankton might be in the Santa Barbara Channel!

So what are plankton again? Plankton are any living organism in the water that is unable to swim against a current. The word plankton comes from the Greek word *planktos*, which means wanderer or drifter, so think of plankton as all the stuff just wandering about, carried by wind and currents in the water. When most people think of plankton, they think of microscopic creatures that get eaten up by whales. While some whales do eat plankton, not all plankton are super-small. Some, like the moon jelly (*Aurelia aurelia*) that sometimes wanders through the Santa Barbara Channel, can easily be seen with the naked eye. There are other ways plankton can be categorized,

besides size. We can group plankton based on what role they play in an ecosystem. Viewed this way, we have two basic categories: phytoplankton and zooplankton.

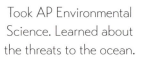

Phytoplankton are the microscopic primary producers of the ocean. In science-speak, they are "photoautotrophic," which means they make their own food through photosynthesis. Phytoplankton are usually only one to a few cells big, and can be a type of algae like dinoflagellates or diatoms. They are the same type of organism as giant kelp, only much, much smaller.

Phytoplankton make up the basis of the ocean food web by providing a vast majority of the energy available for higher consumers through photosynthesis. Besides making all that food, phytoplankton also produce oxygen as a byproduct of photosynthesis. Actually, more than half of the oxygen in our atmosphere is produced by algae such as phytoplankton and giant kelp. You can thank these organisms for every other breath you take.

Zooplankton are the animal plankton. They can be small, as small as phytoplankton, or they can be big, like the jellyfish we mentioned earlier. Zooplankton are primary consumers, which means they eat primary producers, in this case phytoplankton. They are also super-important for the ocean's ecosystems, as they are a food source for everything from tiny sardines to the majestic blue whale. Many marine organisms start off their lives as tiny zooplankton before growing and changing into their adult, non-planktonic forms. We call this kind of zooplankton "meroplankton." There are also "holoplankton," such as krill—zooplankton that stay planktonic for their whole life cycle.

How do you collect plankton? Just like catching butterflies or fish you use a net—one with very tiny holes, so the water flows through but not the plankton. Then comes the awesome part: You pour your sample into a bowl. You won't see the phytoplankton, but they're there. Those little white dots darting around are the zooplankton.

Now comes the most amazing part: checkin' 'em out under the microscope. All of a sudden there they are monsters and mandalas—inspiring and horrifying at the same time! Things straight out of a sci-fi movie. Predators! Aliens! And the phytoplankton—like celestial images of outer space. But this is inner space. This is life in a drop of sea water from an ocean planet.

Many fish—and a lot of invertebrates such as abalone and lobsters—start out life as zooplankton like this critter below. *Photo by Scott E. Simon*

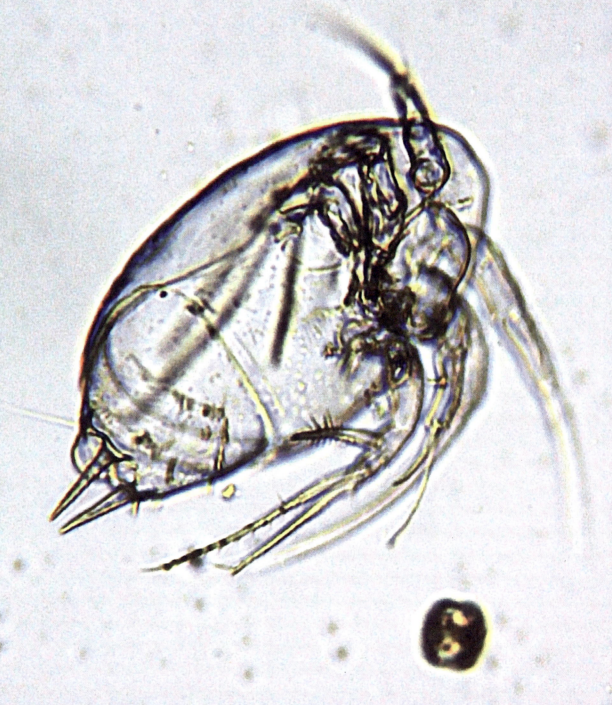

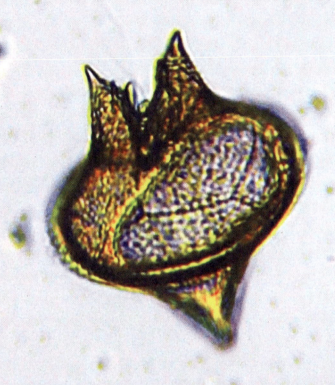

Dinoflagellates can be smaller than the tip of a human hair. At night, high concentrations of these phytoplankton glow in the dark.
Photo by Scott E. Simon

ALGAE PLANET

Our planet is full of cycles that allow life to exist. Algae like giant kelp are at the center of one of the most important ones: the carbon cycle.

1. PHOTOSYNTHESIS

Photosynthesis is the process that algae and plants use to get their energy. Instead of eating food and breathing oxygen like us humans, they consume water, carbon dioxide (CO_2), and sunlight. From this they create energy, which they use, and oxygen, which they breathe out.

WATER + SUN + CARBON DIOXIDE = ENERGY + OXYGEN

2. THEIR BREATH

Look at all these little algae and plant cells doing photosynthesis! This magic process isn't just done by trees and grasses on land. From giant kelp to tiny phytoplankton, the entire ocean teems with organisms hard at work turning carbon dioxide into oxygen. Think of this like their breath. In goes sunlight, carbon dioxide, and water; out goes oxygen. And guess where that oxygen goes?

3. YOUR BREATH

When you breathe, you bring the air of our planet into your body. You take oxygen out of the atmosphere and release carbon dioxide. Your body uses this oxygen to make energy. But where does this life-giving oxygen come from? Look to the sea. The algae of the ocean, including kelp and phytoplankton, are responsible for creating more than half of the oxygen that we breathe.

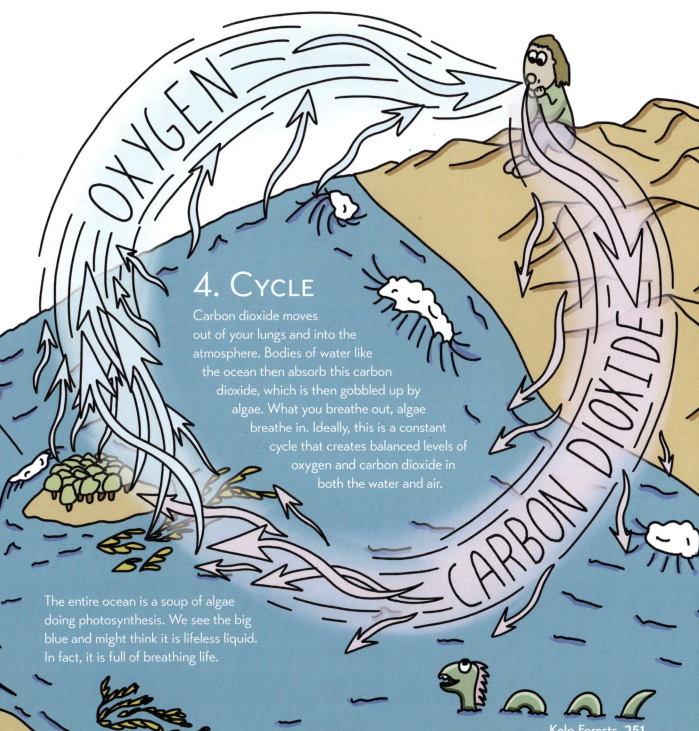

OXYGEN

4. CYCLE

Carbon dioxide moves out of your lungs and into the atmosphere. Bodies of water like the ocean then absorb this carbon dioxide, which is then gobbled up by algae. What you breathe out, algae breathe in. Ideally, this is a constant cycle that creates balanced levels of oxygen and carbon dioxide in both the water and air.

CARBON DIOXIDE

The entire ocean is a soup of algae doing photosynthesis. We see the big blue and might think it is lifeless liquid. In fact, it is full of breathing life.

1. TOO MUCH CARBON

The carbon dioxide in our air and water doesn't come just from our breath. Many human inventions, from factories to vehicles to power plants, create carbon dioxide by burning fossil fuels. This additional human-created carbon dioxide disrupts the planet-wide cycle that algae help maintain.

2. ACID OCEAN

In the ocean, this extra carbon dioxide bonds with water (H_2O) to create carbonic acid (H_2CO_3). We call this "ocean acidification." All this extra carbon dioxide is more than algae and plants can absorb and transform via photosynthesis. This has led to an unnaturally large buildup of carbon dioxide in both the ocean and the atmosphere.

3. Less Shells

Carbonic acid breaks down calcium carbonate ($CaCO_3$), a compound that many ocean creatures such as pteropods rely on to build strong shells. Pteropods are tiny plankton that serve as a food source for many kelp forest residents such as fish and krill, which are in turn food for bigger species, including the blue whale. As acidification eats away at pteropod shells, their population could drop, causing entire ocean ecosystems to suffer.

MORE ACIDIC

4. Changing Climate

The carbon dioxide that we release doesn't go just into the ocean. It fills the atmosphere, creating a gassy blanket that surrounds our planet. This blanket traps more heat from the sun, causing temperatures to rise and weather to grow more unpredictable across the globe. As with ocean acidification, this changes climate.

SUNLIGHT

TRAPPED

REFLECTED

5. Our Job

What makes climate change so scary is that we don't fully understand how it will impact our planet. What we do know for sure is that if we keep pumping carbon dioxide into the atmosphere as we do now, our big blue life support will never be the same.

CARBON FOOTPRINT

Every breath you take releases carbon dioxide (CO_2) into the atmosphere. This is okay! You've got to be alive to be sitting there reading this. Please don't stop breathing. Giant kelp needs at least some CO_2. That said, each molecule of carbon dioxide that you create is part of your carbon footprint on the planet. Sometimes this carbon footprint can come from not-so-obvious sources. Take buying a gallon of milk, for example:

First, a **truck** releases CO_2 when it burns gasoline while bringing cattle feed to the dairy farm.

Second, **cows** burp up a lot of methane. Like CO_2, this greenhouse gas blankets the planet, contributing to climate change.

Third, **another truck** releases more CO_2 when burning gasoline to transport the milk to the market.

Lastly, **you** release a blast of CO_2 when burning gasoline on the way to and from the grocery store.

BEYOND $

Every product you buy has a hidden cost beyond what you pay for it. Harvesting raw materials has a carbon footprint. Manufacturing goods has a carbon footprint. Moving products around the globe has a carbon footprint. Just recognizing the impact of the everyday things you eat, drink, or purchase is the first step towards decreasing your own carbon footprint.

WE ARE THE ONES

For the sake of the kelp forests, the islands, the planet, and, importantly, yourself, it's good to be aware of this invisible pollution that is a consequence of most of our actions. To reduce our impact, we must both take action as individual consumers and recognize when a community, country, and world-wide effort is needed.

Consider how you **go** places. Both making and driving a car creates CO_2. Biking, walking, and using public transportation substantially reduces your footprint.

Use a clothesline. The power in your house often comes from power plants that create more CO_2. A dryer is one of the most power-hungry appliances.

Fly **less**. Airplanes have by far the largest carbon footprint of any form of transportation. Traveling high in the sky across such big distances comes at a cost.

Buy **local**. The energy it takes moving goods around our planet creates lots of CO_2. The shorter the distance that a product travels to you, the smaller the footprint.

Eat more **vegetables**. Producing meat creates a lot of CO_2. Beef is the worst offender. Consider replacing the meat in your diet with protein-rich alternatives such as beans and lentils.

MULTIPLIER EFFECT

Each time you walk instead of drive, you are making a small difference. Day after day, these differences start to add up. Now, imagine if entire communities took action by building better public transportation or clean solar and wind power plants. Restoring the balance between us, algae, our atmosphere, and the ocean is going to take everyone. Remember that you are not alone. We humans made this mess. Together, we can fix it.

With the clear water and sunny skies, I spent some dives just enjoying the spectacular cathedrals of kelp that still surround Anacapa Island.
Photo by Douglas Klug

Harbor seals often swim playfully through kelp forests. This time I came prepared with my wide-angle lens. *Photo by Douglas Klug*

BUILDING A REEF

by Scott E. Simon – *Educator, UCSB*

AGE 5 — Grandparent taught him to snorkel off Santa Catalina Island.

AGE 7 — Helped save seabirds covered by oil from the '69 spill in the Channel.

AGE 12 — Watched "The Undersea World of Jacques Cousteau" every Sunday.

AGE 15 — Took his first breath underwater using SCUBA gear.

How precious is the ocean? Ninety-seven percent of this planet's water is in the ocean. Eighty percent of life is found in the ocean. Fifty percent of the oxygen in the air we breathe is produced by ocean organisms, many of which can be found in the kelp forest, one of the most productive environments on the planet. These forests provide us with food and oxygen and, ironically, they're breathtaking to explore!

Einstein said, "We cannot solve our problems with the same thinking we used when we created them." We've only explored 5 percent of the ocean. That means there's still 95 percent to explore. What mysteries, wonders, and solutions wait for us in the sea? My goal is to inspire others to think "deeper!"

I run the Research Experience & Education Facility, a.k.a. the REEF, a teaching aquarium at

UCSB's Marine Science Institute. The REEF is a magical place full of giant glass tanks that bring visitors face-to-face with our aquatic neighbors. From kelp forests to tide pools to rocky reefs, we have it all.

Whether they be a surfer headed out for a sunset session, or a kid on a field trip, people love the two-way communication that happens around our touch tanks. While we love to share our "Ocean View of the World" (the REEF motto), we also learn a lot from our visitors. Whether it's locals, scientists, students, moms, dads, little nerds, or others from around the planet, we gain new knowledge and insight from these curious minds. Through this sharing, we have found that there are quite a few interesting ideas about the ocean out there—ideas from geniuses of all kinds.

In my 15 years as director at the REEF, I've had several visitors share with me that their experiences here were the catalyst that inspired them to pursue a career in marine science. Sometimes, an entire family gets their wonder for the ocean sparked here. Sisters Ashley, Lexi, and Lauren have all participated in the high school mentorship program that we run at the REEF. Ashley went on to get her B.S. and M.S. in Earth Systems at Stanford. Lexi got her B.S. in Environmental Science from the University of Washington. Two years ago Lauren, the youngest sister, came through the REEF mentorship program. She just finished high school and was accepted to UCSB. This summer, during her tour of campus, she texted me the following, "Scott!! It's Lauren! After visiting UCSB today I decided that it is where I want to go, and I am going to commit!!!??? Isn't that exciting!!!??? I can't wait to spend the next 4 years bugging you at the REEF!" The ripples from the REEF experiences keep spreading.

We have often asked visitors to the REEF, "What is a reef?" Most people respond with something like, "Oh, it is made of coral!" While that is what a coral reef is made of, they are amazed when they learn that there are so many different kinds of reefs. We'll usually get an, "Ah, of course!" when we mention man-made reefs created by shipwrecks, but many still perceive these as a tropical feature. Looking out from REEF at oil platform Holly, we then share and explore the wonders of marine biodiversity these structures have created.

Decommissioned platforms have become incredible artificial reefs that are home to thousands of fish.

That leads us to what I believe are the most magnificent reefs ever: the temperate rocky reefs. If not for those gorgeous rocks, kelp would have nothing to hold fast to! These reefs are the literal foundation of these undersea forests. A reef is really nothing more than complexity added to the undersea world. Life loves complexity. Add some rocks, and kelp grows. Lobsters, abalone, sea stars, and more arrive. Then, finally, fish show up!

Just take a gander at Goleta Bay right out our front door. A menagerie of marine complexity: the pier, with all kinds of life on its pilings; the sewage pipeline, buried in a massive jumble of rocks and boulders, paralleling the pier and swarming with kelp, garibaldi, and rockfish. There's even an old, single-engine plane wreck reef out there with, amongst other things, a whole slew of swell sharks hangin' out up in the engine block! These are all reefs—all foundations for kelp forests.

If you wander back up to the end of the bay at Campus Point, there's our REEF. This is more than just a collection of touch tanks and ocean lovers. It is rocks and sand, kelp and red algae, sea stars and rockfish and sharks—the wonder of the macrocystis forest brought to land for all to see. It is a reminder of the importance and vulnerability of the underwater cities of our neighbors…a place for us people to explore, share, learn, and care.

The roots of the kelp
Ever so frail, so thin,
Cling onto the rock.
Holding on for its life against the raging waters,
Yet so beautiful, so calm in the sea.
The blades, so slimy above water seem so
Normal down here.
They seem so, at home,
Happy to be in place for all animals.
Roaring through, the water around mutes
All other noise leaving pure silence.
Pure beauty.

"Kelp Forests"
by Jake Feinstein, Student

CHAPTER 7

HARVESTING THE SEA

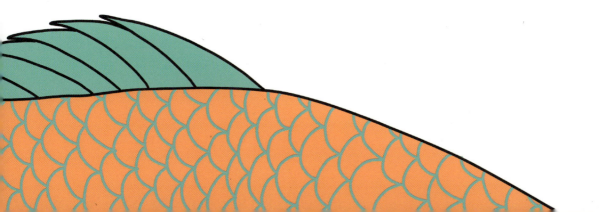

WHO MANAGES THE WATER

= CHANNEL ISLANDS NATIONAL PARK
from high tide to 1 nautical mile off shore

= STATE WATERS
from high tide to 3 nautical miles off shore

= CHANNEL ISLANDS NATIONAL MARINE SANCTUARY
from high tide to 6 nautical miles off shore

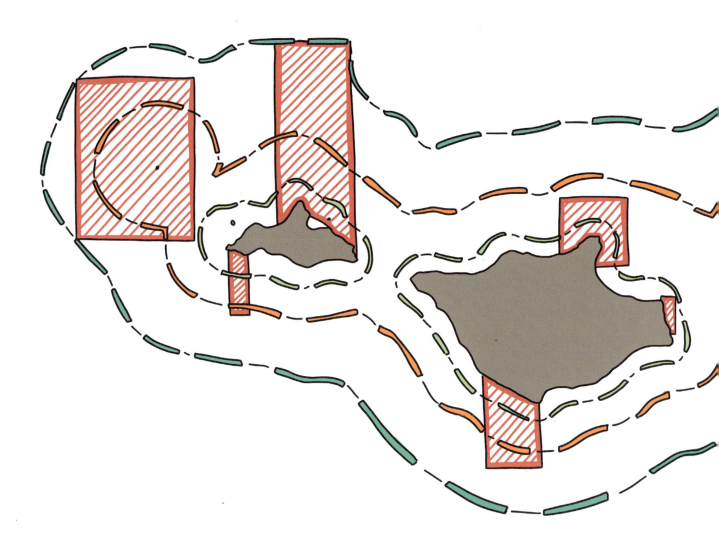

= MARINE RESERVE
no commercial or recreational fishing allowed

= MARINE CONSERVATION AREA
some commercial or recreational fishing allowed

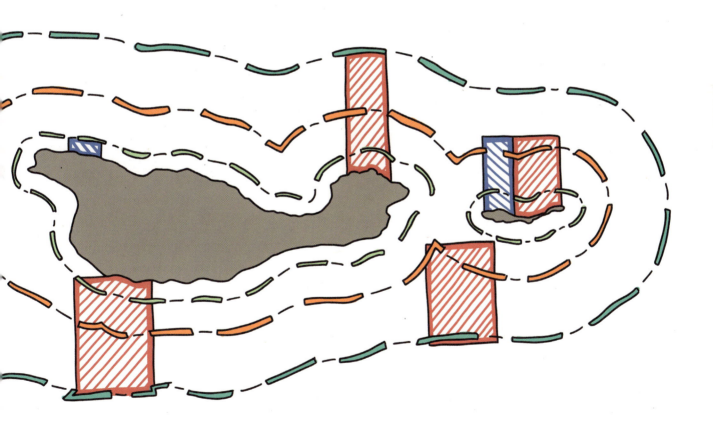

Photo by Pedal Born Pictures

WE ARE ANIMALS.

While we have delivery apps, microwaves, and frozen yogurt, we often forget that we are part of the same global food web as fish. Like fish, we live off the world around us. Unlike fish, we have distanced ourselves from our role in this planet-wide system.

For centuries, we have fed ourselves from the sea. Gradually, our relationship with this ocean harvest has changed. The products that we buy today look nothing like the things swimming around the Channel Islands. With this disconnect, we have consumed far too much. What we eat—and where it came from— does matter.

THIS IS FISH

Fish Oil

Canned Fish

Fish Tacos

FISH IS THIS

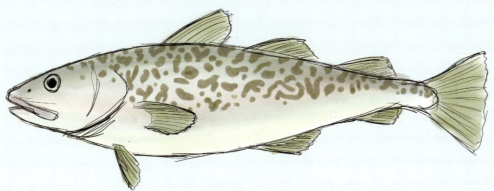

Pacific Cod

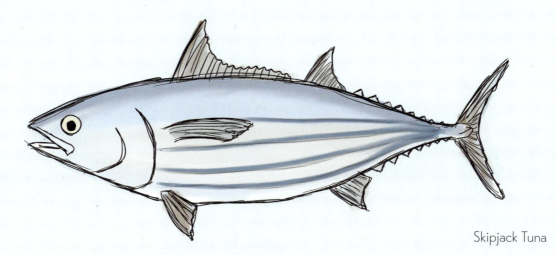

Skipjack Tuna

Vermillion Rockfish

ODE TO THE ROCKFISH

by Milton Love – *Professor of Fish, UCSB*

AGE 6 — Dad took him fishing on Malibu Pier. Declared he would be a fish biologist.

AGE 12 — Caught nine kinds of rockfishes. Decided to learn biology of rockfish.

AGE 32 — Earned PhD. Spent next 40 years studying biology of Pacific Coast fishes.

AGE 64 — Wrote rockfish book to teach everyone what he wanted to know at age 6.

I love rockfishes. I've got a tattoo of one on my arm, and I'll tell you why.

Rockfishes are America's Fishes. It's true. What America needs are fishes worthy of the task we have before us. We need fishes that are tough, fishes that are rough. We certainly don't need wimpy fishes like salmon. Salmon, and their cousins the trouts, are all flash and no substance. Why, the only way a salmon could hurt you is if you cut your finger opening the can. Rockfishes, on the other hand, would rather spine you a good one in the kneecap than talk to you. Even ones that have been sitting on deck for a few hours will stick you good if you try to pick them up.

So, why my sudden praise of rockfishes? Is it just the rambling of a marine biologist down on his luck? Or perhaps it's some madness brought about by an undigested bit of cheese from last night's supper?

No, I have loved these fishes since I was but a wee lad, dropping a line into the Pacific and catching so very many species of this remarkable group. Because the truth of the matter is that… rockfish rule. Yes, it's true. Just about every reef in California is just packed with these scaly beauties. Rockfishes tend to dominate many of the habitats off our coast. Unfortunately, overfishing by recreational and commercial fishermen led to the decline of a number of species. Fortunately, pretty tough restrictions on catches have led to a dramatic comeback of our spiny friends.

So let's honor these fishes of the 21st century, many of which make their home right around our beloved Channel Islands. Let's start by giving them their own anthem:

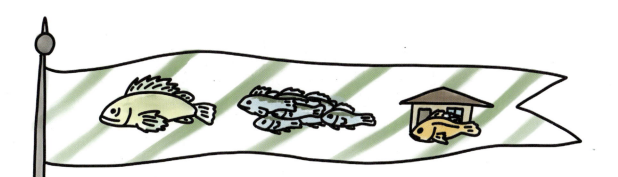

Oh here's to you who live alone,

And here's to you who school,

And here's to you who have a home,

Though that is not a rule.

Oh rockfishes, this is our wish,

We hold your banner high,

Though they might eat you

Raw or steamed or even in stir fry.

Assorted fishing lures for sale at
Hook, Line & Sinker in Santa Barbara.
Photo by Pedal Born Pictures

HOW FISHING CREATED CIVILIZATION

by Brian Fagan – *Professor of Anthropology, UCSB*

AGE 8	AGE 16	AGE 26	AGE 75
Taught to sail and understand fish by an English fisherman.	Went to sailing camp. Learned to catch and cook eels and herring.	Found hundreds of fish bones in 3,000-year-old camp in Africa.	Wrote a history of fishing, drawing on experiences fishing around the world.

Of the three ancient ways that humans used to get food—hunting, plant foraging, and fishing—only the last has remained important since we figured out how to farm and raise livestock some 12,000 years ago.

Yet ancient fisherfolk and their communities have rarely been studied. Why? Such communities held their knowledge close to their chests and seldom rose to power. And they passed knowledge from one generation to the next by word of mouth, not writing.

That knowledge remains highly relevant today. Fishers are people who draw their living from a hard, uncontrollable world that is largely indifferent to their fortunes or suffering. Many of them still fish with hooks, lines, nets, and spears that are virtually unchanged since the Ice Age. The world's first pre-industrial communities emerged in the Eastern Mediterranean around 3100 BC. Other states developed independently, somewhat later, in Asia and in the Americas.

Whether Sumerian, Egyptian, Roman, Cambodian, or Inca, these societies relied on the work of thousands of anonymous laborers who served on great estates, built temples, tombs, and public buildings, and produced the food that fed not only the ruler but also his armies of officials. Some of the most important laborers were the fishers, who along with farmers, were the most vital of all food providers. As city populations grew, fish became

a commodity, harvested by the thousands. Fishers transported their catches to small towns and then cities, bringing fish to markets and temples. For the first time, some communities became virtually full-time fishers, bartering or selling fish in town and village markets in exchange for other necessities. Their catches were recorded and taxed. The ruler and the state required hundreds, even thousands, of skilled and unskilled laborers. Their work might be a form of taxation, but the king had to support them in kind, often with fish.

The Land of the Pharaohs depended heavily on its fisher folk. Nile River catfish were easy to harvest, especially during the spring spawn, before they were gutted and dried in the tropical sun on large racks. The authorities assigned teams of fishers to catch specific quantities of fish within set periods of time, especially when the flood was receding. Large seine nets provided much of the catch, deployed and hauled in by teams of villagers.

The demand was enormous. Building the pyramids of Giza alone required thousands of people. The workers' settlement lay close to the royal tombs. In 1991 the Egyptologist Mark Lehner excavated two bakeries, including the vats for mixing dough and a cache of the large bell-shaped pots used for baking bread. A huge mud brick building next to bakeries contained troughs, benches, and tens of thousands of tiny fish fragments in the fine, ashy deposit covering the floor.

The fresh catches had to be dried and preserved immediately. Lehner believes that the fish were laid out on reed frames to dry on well-ventilated troughs and benches in a production line that provided protein for thousands of people. At its peak, the line must have employed hundreds of people and processed thousands of fish per

day—precise estimates are impossible. The fishers were thus only the first stage of an infrastructure of hundreds of people needed to process and store the dried catch for later consumption. The demands of this operation must have led to large, temporary fishing villages springing up at the same general locations every flood season.

The Ancient Egyptians were not alone. Mid-19th century travelers who crossed the Tonle Sap Lake in Cambodia after the monsoon as the water was falling reported catfish teeming so thickly under their canoes that one could almost walk across the water on their backs. The ancestors of these large fish fed thousands of Khmer laborers as they built the nearby stupendous temples of Angkor Wat and Angkor Thom in the 12th century. On the other side of the world, along the arid North Coast of Peru, the inshore anchovy fisheries, nourished by natural upwelling from the seabed, yielded enormous numbers of small fish that when dried and turned into meal, made a valuable protein supplement for farmers in fertile river valleys inland, such as the great settlement at Caral, about 193 kilometers (120 miles) north of present-day Lima. Caravans of llamas carried bags of fishmeal high into the Andes, where the fish became a major economic prop of the Inca empire. Tens of thousands of anchovies were netted, dried, and stored before being traded on a near-industrial scale.

Fish were major historical players in many places. Dried fish fed merchant seamen crossing the Indian Ocean from the Red Sea to India; dried cod from northern Norway was the beef jerky that sustained Norse crews as they sailed to Iceland, Greenland, and North America.

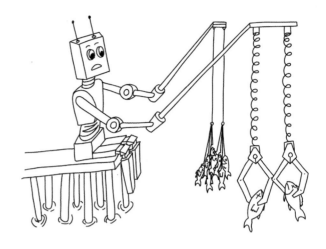

Those who caught the fish that fed pre-modern civilizations were anonymous folk who appeared with their catches in city markets, then vanished quietly back to their small villages in the countryside. Perhaps it was the smell of fish that clung to them, or the simple baskets, nets, and spears they used to harvest their catches that kept them isolated from the townsfolk. Perhaps they preferred to be taken for granted. But their efforts helped create, feed, and link great civilizations for thousands of years.

Centuries ago, urban populations numbered in the thousands, but the demand for fish was insatiable.

Today, the silent elephant in the fishing room is an exploding global population that considers ocean fish a staple. Deep-water trawls, diesel trawlers, electronic fish finders, and factory ships with deep freezers have turned the most ancient of our ways of obtaining food into an industrial behemoth. Even remote fisheries are being decimated.

Despite large-scale fish farming, humans face the specter of losing our most ancient practice of food-gathering—and thus leaving behind an ocean that is almost fishless.

This essay was originally published in *Zócalo Public Square*.

Black cod sits on ice at a fish market. For better or worse, we no longer have to go fishing to make a fish dinner.
Photo by Pedal Born Pictures

FISH WORLD

Of the roughly 8 billion people on our planet, **3 billion people** rely on fish as a key source of protein.

Annual fish consumption has more than **doubled globally**, from 9 kilograms (20 pounds) per person in 1961 to 20 kilograms (44 pounds) of fish per person in 2015.

As of 2018, there are estimated to be **4.6 million fishing boats** world-wide.

In many developing countries, the **exports of fish** account for more of the economy than the exports of most other agricultural products combined.

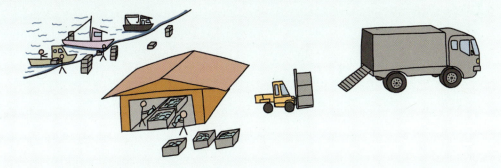

Over **800 million people** depend on fisheries and aquaculture for their livelihoods.

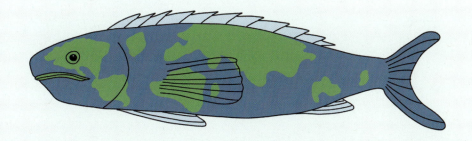

FISHING THE ISLANDS

The history of humans on the Channel Islands is a history of fishing. Many cultures have dropped a line or dived in these waters to make a living, or simply to find dinner. With different philosophies and tools, each group of fishermen had a unique impact on the island and channel fish populations.

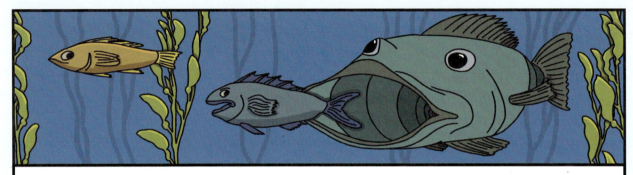

Forever: Fish ate fish. This was happening well before humans showed up. Giant sea bass gotta eat.

13,000 years ago through early 1800s: Chumash fished from their *tomols* all around the islands. They used hooked lines and harpoons to pursue everything from rockfish to swordfish.

Late 1800s: Chinese divers built large abalone camps on the islands, hauling up tons of this delicacy. In the early 1900s, Japanese and Americans replaced the Chinese. The abalone population eventually crashed.

Early 1900s: Island fishing boomed. Fishermen built shacks on the beaches of the islands, maximizing the time they could spend catching lobster, crab, and fish.

1980s: Squid fishing—now California's largest fishery—took off. Boats use giant lights, luring squid to the surface to catch.

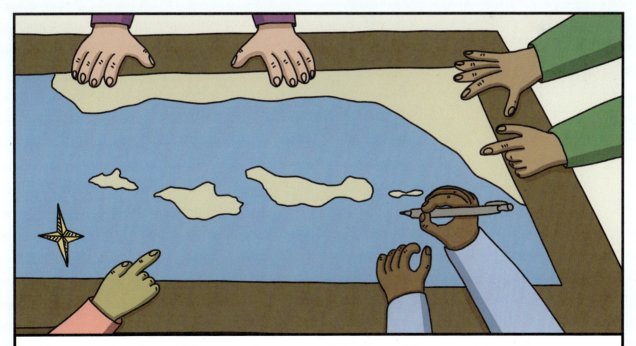

Early 2000s: A coalition of fishermen and scientists with the National Oceanic and Atmospheric Administration created marine protected areas (MPAs) to help fish populations recover.

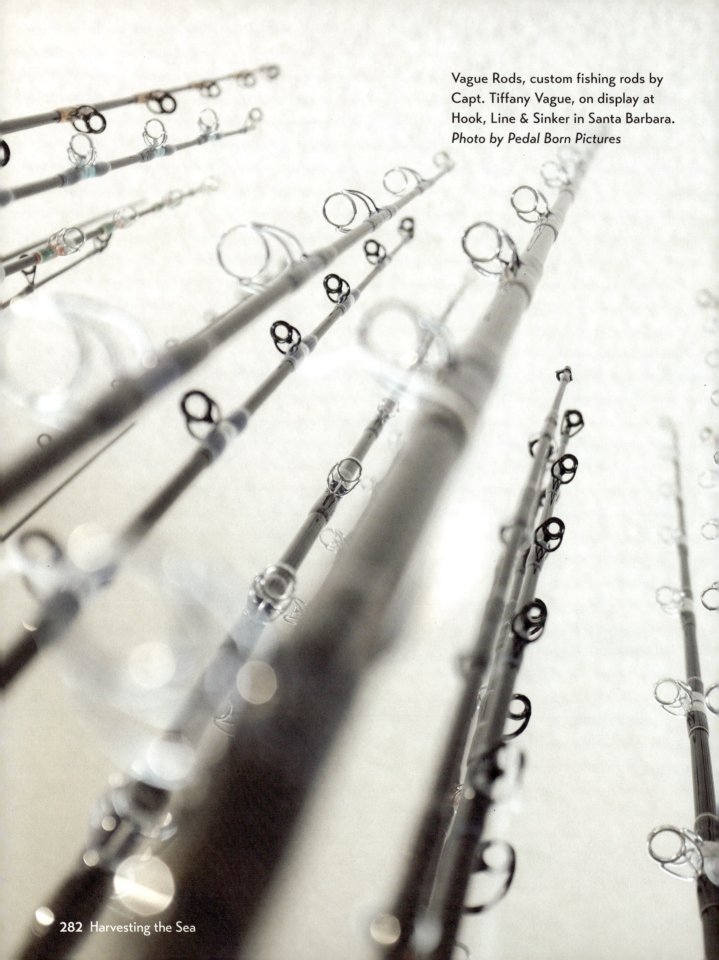

Vague Rods, custom fishing rods by Capt. Tiffany Vague, on display at Hook, Line & Sinker in Santa Barbara. *Photo by Pedal Born Pictures*

WHY WE FISH

with Captain David Bacon and Captain Tiffany Vague

Dad took him fishing before he could even hold a pole.

Stressed by computer center job, started charter fishing company.

Dad took her fishing. He held the rod while she operated the reel.

Got her captain's license. Now also builds rods and manages bait shop.

When did you start fishing as a career?

Captain David: I used to run computer centers. That line of work will kill a person. I earned my captain's license in my spare time, and I thought maybe I would put together a charter fishing business as a retirement career. Because of the result of stress, I decided that needed to happen earlier. Tiffany, my daughter, decided to join me, and now we have the tackle (fishing equipment) store too. I've been captaining the *WaveWalker* (my recreational fishing charter boat) full time since 1991.

Do you remember catching your first fish?

Captain David: Well that would be my daddy holding me on his arm, and he is holding the pole, and I am turning the handle at about six months old. I have been at this a while. Tiffany, same way, I was holding her, and she was holding the handle.

Do you remember your first fish in the channel?

Captain Tiffany: I was five, and my dad took me out on the *Hornet*. I remember to this day because

I was short, and I couldn't see over the railing. So they have pictures of me holding the fishing rod... staring at the wall. Dad says turn the handle, and I was wondering, "what are we doing?" The next thing I know, I brought in a little rockfish.

What is the hardest part about your job?

Captain Tiffany: Sometimes the biggest challenge is just getting the guests to accept what I know because I am a girl. Guys don't look at girls and think that they have the knowledge. But they haven't lived my life. Since I was born, it has been drilled into my head by my father and my grandfather. My schooling in fishing goes far beyond that of an average person.

How have you seen the fish in the channel change over the course of your career?

Captain David: You know, when I was a kid, we didn't really understand fisheries management. You would go out there and catch a bunch of fish, and say, "What a bonanza!" We didn't understand then that 80% of the fish are in 20% of the area.

So it was possible to not manage things carefully and do some damage. But we know that now and have adapted fisheries management to where it is an incredible science. We have generally so much better fish population management than we used to...and we have brought species after species after species back to abundance (lots of them around).

For example, one of our best fisheries now is white seabass. When I was a kid, you rarely caught one. Now there are days when we will go out and get the maximum allowable catch for everybody. That is because of good management. Fishermen putting in their time and money. We are the conservationists. We are not preservationists. That is an important distinction. There are many organizations that call themselves conservationists, but they want to lock everybody out. That's not conservation, that's preservation. Fishermen have been putting their time, money, and heart into this for a very long time. We believe in managing for sustainability. That includes us in the picture. That is the difference.

How do you define "sustainable fishing?"

Captain Tiffany: You catch what you eat. Obviously, with rules and regulations there are fish that you catch that are too small, so you have to let them go. But if you have a family of 6, then you catch however much they eat. But the ones who go, go, go, and then decide "I don't want this" and toss it in the trashcan–that's not sustainability.

What is your favorite dish to cook with the fish that you catch in the Channel?

Captain David: That changes around the season. You know, we do have seasons. Some years we have a great salmon run in the spring. Those are delicious fish. We've got white seabass, halibut, yellowtail, and lingcod. We've got a lot of good fish here. But, yeah, I'd hate to have to eat the same fish year round.

Why is it important for people to get out on the water and catch what they eat?

Captain David: I think we are at a place society-wise where that is kind of lost. People think, "Oh, you are hungry? You go to the store, you go to McDonalds." But nobody looks at that hamburger and thinks about a critter dying so that they could eat that. When you go fishing, you take a fish, you take it home. You are a little closer spiritually, thanking that critter for giving up its life so that your family can eat. That brings you to a totally different understanding as to what the food chain is. It's really important to get people out and give them that understanding.

Captain Tiffany: I see a lot of kids who are more into it because they are bringing home dinner. It's always been dad paying for the food, bringing home dinner, or mom goes to the grocery store. But now they are taking a part in it. Now they did the work, they caught it, they are bringing it home.

If you could give one piece of advice to a novice fisherman or fisherwoman, what would it be?

Captain David: I want them to understand that we are going out to immerse ourselves in the food chain. Stay aboard the boat, and you are probably at the top of the food chain. Nice place to be. We are taking home our dinner. It is going to taste a whole lot better than anything that you can buy in the store because it is fresh. But at the same time I want them to understand that we have a place in that food chain, and that our place includes managing it. Because we can, and we should.

Carolina Rig
LEADER

From: Hook, Line & Sinker
4010 Calle Real, Santa Barbara

$ 1.99

One of the many pieces of specialized fishing tackle on sale at Captain David and Captain Tiffany's shop.
Photo by Pedal Born Pictures

WAYS TO FISH

Thousands of years ago fishing meant standing over water with a sharp stick. While some folks like Captain Bacon and Captain Vague still catch fish one at a time, our planet-wide demand has led to new methods of fishing capable of pulling in thousands of fish at a time. You can see many of the techniques below in the waters around the Channel Islands.

TRAWL

What: Large, weighted net is dragged by a boat. Nets can be as big as five football fields and catch entire schools of fish.

Used to catch: Shrimp, halibut, sole, anchovies

Side-effects: High rate of bycatch (other species caught in the net accidentally), can scrape life off the ocean floor.

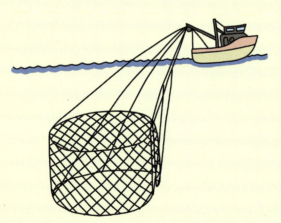

PURSE SEINE

What: A large wall of netting is used to encircle an entire school of fish. The bottom is then pulled closed like a purse.

Used to catch: Squid, anchovies, sardines

Side-effects: High rates of bycatch, especially young fish.

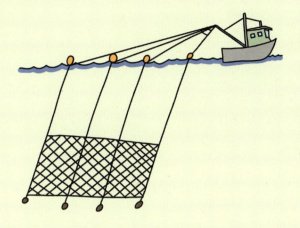

Gillnet

What: Weighted wall of net is dragged through the water. Fish swim through net which catches them by the gills.

Used to catch: Many types of fish including white seabass

Side-effects: High potential for bycatch; seals, turtles, dolphins, and sharks are frequently entangled.

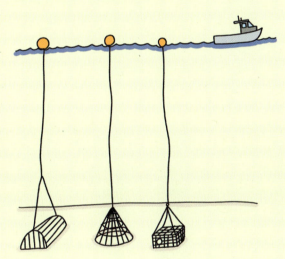

Traps and Pots

What: Small baited cages are set on the ocean floor and attached to a buoy on the surface. The fisherman periodically return and haul them up to check for catch.

Used to catch: Crab, lobster, shrimp, sablefish, cod

Side-effects: Can get cut from buoy by storms or rival fishermen, becoming "ghost traps" that keep catching.

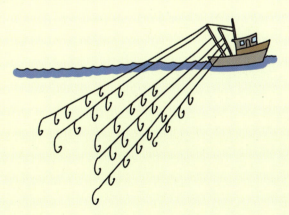

Troll

What: A series of individually-baited and hooked lines are pulled behind a moving boat.

Used to catch: Salmon, albacore tuna, mahi mahi

Side-effects: Relatively few. Fish are caught individually, and bycatch can be released easily.

COMMERCIAL CATCH

with Sam Shrout – Commercial Fisherman

AGE 15 — First abalone dive off of Isla Vista. Amazed by beauty of the sea.

AGE 17 — Hit rock while abalone diving. Now swims with an arm outstretched.

AGE 20 — Learned that fishermen have different opinions, but all support each other.

AGE 25 — On stormy days went for long hikes on the Channel Islands.

Do you remember your first catch?

Yes, it was my first day diving for abalone. I was diving in about 9 meters (30 feet) of water off Isla Vista. I got one dozen red and one dozen pink abalone in about one hour. I remember being absolutely blown away at how beautiful it was underwater. That was in 1974 or 1975.

Why do you do this for a living?

I have always done this for a living for the same reason: I enjoy the outdoors, I enjoy being independent, I enjoy our channel and the islands. I never got involved in fishing for the money. I always just worked hard and had a good time, and the money just came.

What made you decide to be a crab and lobster fisherman?

I decided to be a lobster fishermen about three years before the abalone fishery was closed. I could see that diving wasn't something that I wanted to have to do as I got older. In 1997,

when abalone went on moratorium due to withering foot syndrome [see page 301], I switched over to trap fishing.

Have you seen the lobster and crab fisheries change over the years?

That is the understatement of the century! When I started crab fishing virtually everyone used 5 centimeter x 10 centimeter (2 inch x 4 inch) wire mesh and only fished mildly. It was an amazing resource that seemed to be infinite for the 30 or 40 people who were fishing. That has changed in recent years. Now you can transfer crab permits, and there are many new participants in the fishery. People are fishing way, way harder with smaller and smaller wire mesh. The lobster fishery has also gone through major transformations. Permits are transferable, and many fishermen have paid over $100,000 just for the permit. There are many new lobster fisherman with nicer and nicer boats, better and better technology. Add to that the price of lobster going over $20 per pound, and you have a major growth in fishery effort.

We have just this season entered into a pot limit (limit on the number of traps–called pots–that one can place). I am optimistic that the pot limit will help reduce congestion.

What is your favorite dish to cook?

My favorite of all is sautéed bell peppers, mushrooms, onions, and garlic with lobster. Put that all on a warm flour tortilla with avocado, a little mayonnaise, and cheese. It is about the best flavor combination I've ever tasted. I also love rockfish grilled whole on the barbecue, and steamed crab claws chilled on ice, eaten in the hot sun with a few friends.

Where do you sell your catch?

Historically, the majority of the crab that I caught was delivered to markets in Los Angeles. I sold a small percentage to the public at the Saturday morning fisherman's market. Rockfish I sold exclusively to the public at the Saturday market. Lobster—the vast majority of it is shipped to Los Angeles and exported to Chinese markets.

Why is it important to buy local seafood?

Santa Barbara is such a productive harbor that it would actually be virtually impossible to sell all of the seafood that comes into this harbor to the Santa Barbara area. I do hope that many locals venture down to the seafood markets and buy

and consume local fish. Let's face it, the closer you get your food to the source, the fresher and healthier it will be.

You have participated in several conservation projects led by groups like NOAA. Why?

My love of the sea encourages me to be involved with anything that will help the environment—any projects that help ensure the resource is always getting stronger and healthier. I have been involved in many projects that I abandoned because I couldn't see a clear benefit to the environment, resource, or fishery itself.

If you could give one piece of advice to someone who is just becoming a lobster fisherman, what would it be?

Please don't get involved in the fishery because you think you are going to make a fortune. Be a fisherman because you want to be a steward of the sea and enjoy a life of beauty and outdoors. There are no new islands or reefs or fishing grounds that you are going to go off and find on your own and be able to stay out of other peoples' way. Eventually you will be in the fray, another person fishing on a reef that historically had one or two lobster traps on it that now has 15 or 20 on it.

LOCAL FISHERIES

The Channel Islands are home to a variety of commercial fisheries. In 2012 NOAA broke down the catch from within Channel Islands National Marine Sanctuary as follows:

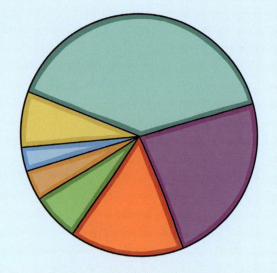

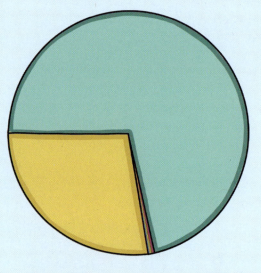

By percentage of profit made:

40% - Market Squid

23% - Urchin

16% - Spiny Lobster

6.5% - Crab

4% - Prawn and Shrimp

3% - Sea Cucumber

7.5% - Other Fish and Shellfish

By percentage of weight caught:

72% - Market Squid

0.2% - Urchin

0.005% - Spiny Lobster

0.02% - Crab

0.001% - Prawn and Shrimp

0.003% - Sea Cucumber

27.8% Other Fish and Shellfish

What is a fishery? The United Nations Food and Agriculture Organization defines one as:

"A unit determined by an authority or other entity that is engaged in raising and/or harvesting fish. Typically, the unit is defined in terms of some or all of the following: people involved, species or type of fish, area of water or seabed, method of fishing, class of boats and purpose of the activities."

 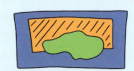 

In short, a **fishery** is the fish, the region in which the fish are caught, and the people who do the catching.

Here is a look at three of the largest commercial fisheries around the Channel Islands (based on 2012 data):

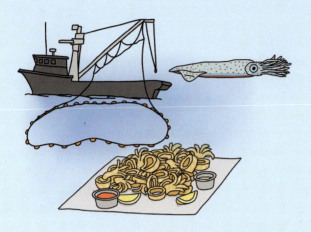

MARKET SQUID FISHERY

Season: October-March

Method: Purse seine with lights to attract squid

Total catch: 11,542,840 kilograms (25,447,606 pounds)

Total catch value: $7.46 million

Most of the squid caught in California comes from the channel and is brought ashore in Ventura, Port Hueneme, and San Pedro. Eighty percent is sent to Asia for cheaper processing. Some of this squid ends up back in the U.S.

SEA URCHIN FISHERY

Season: All Year

Method: Divers harvesting by hand

Total catch: 2,855,057 kilograms (6,294,324 pounds)

Total catch value: $4.24 million

Santa Barbara sea urchins are prized as some of the highest quality on the planet. They are sold as uni in sushi bars and fish markets from New York to Japan. [To learn more, jump in with a diver on page 236.]

SPINY LOBSTER FISHERY

Season: October-March

Method: Pots attached to buoys on the surface

Total catch: 81,056 kilograms (178,699 pounds)

Total catch value: $2.98 million

Santa Barbara harbor often brings in more lobster than anywhere else in California. Seventy-five percent of this lobster is sold to Asia. There is also a large recreational fishery where divers catch the lobster by hand.

OVERFISHED

Looking at the fish counter in your local grocery store, it might look like there is plenty of fish to go around. There are always fresh fillets ready for cooking and shrimp sitting on ice. The market shelves never seem to run out. Unfortunately, the ocean tells a different story.

A 2016 United Nations study found that of all the commercially-fished species they monitor:

58.1% are fully fished (can't sustainably catch any more)

31.4% are overfished (population can't sustain itself)

Since the 1970s, annual global catch has doubled to approximately

80 million metric tons.

This means that if global growth in fishing continues,

90% of the fish we catch are in danger of disappearing.

LOCAL EXAMPLE: GIANT SEA BASS

The giant sea bass serves as a cautionary tale of how overfishing can impact fish populations around the Channel Islands. These huge fish can weigh in at up to 227 kilograms (500 pounds), making them a great trophy fish and commercial catch alike. Unfortunately, our appetite for these gentle giants nearly drove them to extinction. Here is a brief timeline of the giant sea bass's sharp decline in California:

1800s: Commercial fishing of giant sea bass began.

1930s: Commercial catch peaked. Recreational fishing for giant sea bass began to increase.

1963: Recreational catch peaked. Targeting of fish that gathered to reproduce caused population collapse.

1981: California banned intentional commercial and recreational fishing for giant sea bass.

1996: The International Union for Conservation of Nature listed giant sea bass as "critically endangered."

Today, divers such as Kathy deWett-Oleson have been seeing more and more giant sea bass around the islands [see page 228 for her story], suggesting that this magnificent fish is on the road to recovery.

Photos courtesy of Santa Cruz Island Foundation Archives

The California sheepheads at Anacapa Island's Cathedral Cove were very aggressive this summer. This huge male took interest in his own reflection from my camera housing.
Photo by Douglas Klug

This brilliantly colored
juvenile garibaldi has
bright blue spots that will
disappear as it grows older.
Photo by Douglas Klug

RECOGNIZE WATER

by Laura Francis – *Marine Biologist, Educator, NOAA*

AGE 5 — Began collecting shells and sea glass on the beach near Santa Barbara.

AGE 11 — First visit to Channel Islands. Ignited a passion for the ocean.

AGE 18 — Studied at UC Berkeley and got scuba diving certification.

AGE 27 — Landed dream job: NOAA Channel Islands education coordinator.

I have a vividly clear memory of my first Channel Islands experience. After a hearty egg and muffin breakfast with my dad, 11-year-old me headed out to Anacapa Island with my sixth grade classmates. During the crossing we spotted countless seabirds, dolphins, seals, and sea lions—and a couple of humpback whales! When we anchored off Anacapa Island, some of the naturalists went diving and brought up colorful sea slugs called nudibranchs, sea stars, sea cucumbers, abalone, and sea urchins. The most memorable ocean inhabitant that I encountered that day was a mermaid's purse: a pouch with a tiny wriggling baby horn shark inside! That day I decided I wanted to be a marine biologist when I grew up.

Back then in 1978, the islands were considered wild and remote. Not many people had the opportunity to experience them. It was not until 1980 that the northern Channel Islands—Anacapa, Santa Cruz, Santa Rosa, and San Miguel, as well as Santa Barbara to the south—were designated as a National Park (the land and waters out to 1 nautical mile) and a National Marine Sanctuary (from high tide out to 6 nautical miles).

Most people are familiar with our national parks system on land. Fewer are aware that we also have a national system of underwater parks managed by the National Oceanic and Atmospheric Administration (NOAA) Office of National Marine Sanctuaries. These underwater treasures span over 1.6 million square kilometers (600,000 square miles) of ocean and Great Lakes waters. As of 2020, they include 14 marine protected areas and two marine national monuments. The system works with diverse partners and stakeholders to protect, research, educate, and promote responsible, sustainable use.

Despite this protection, by 1998 some fish populations around the Channel Islands were suffering due to past overfishing and other natural and human-caused stresses. A group of concerned citizens, including recreational fishers, scientists, and the public, requested that the California

Fish and Game Commission establish a network of Marine Reserves—areas protected from all fishing—around the islands. A Marine Reserves Working Group was created. It represented a full range of community perspectives including the general public, commercial fishers, recreational fishers and divers, scientists, and policymakers. The goal of the group was to consider which areas to set aside to protect marine habitats, ecological processes, and specific animal and plant populations. All of this while also maintaining long-term economic viability and sustainability of fisheries. No small task.

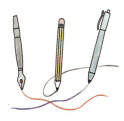 After almost two years of working together on these challenging and seemingly competitive goals, the group almost achieved complete consensus. There were disagreements, but ultimately they presented a couple of different proposed maps of new marine reserves to the Marine Sanctuary, which in turn brought a proposal to the California Fish and Game Commission. In 2003, the State of California implemented a network of 11 marine reserves and two marine conservation areas allowing limited take of lobster and pelagic (open ocean) fish. This was expanded by NOAA in 2007 to include federal waters. It was the first network of its kind in California, and at the time the largest network of marine reserves in the country, encompassing about 20 percent of the Channel Islands National Marine Sanctuary [see map on page 264].

Since their designation almost 17 years ago, scientists have found that, overall, sea life inside these reserves is bigger and more abundant than outside the reserves. This is an incredible success story of diverse stakeholders coming together to protect an ocean space that they care about.

Olympic Coast NMS

These shaded spaces represent the National Marine Sanctuaries (NMS) that NOAA manages on the western coast of the United States.

Each sanctuary is a balancing act between the needs of local communities, industries, and crucial ecosystems that call them home.

Greater Farrallones NMS

Cordell Bank NMS

Monterey Bay NMS

Channel Islands NMS

As human pressure on our ocean increases, it becomes ever more critical to create protected areas that replenish biodiversity, sustain important ecosystems, provide educational and recreational opportunities, and nourish the growing human population.

For me as an educator and scientist, it has been fantastic to be able to use the Channel Islands as a living laboratory and classroom. These protected areas below the sea are the perfect place to inspire teachers and students about the importance of a healthy ocean environment. Hopefully, more kids will get a chance to look off the bow, take in the sea spray, and have their sense of wonder and stewardship ignited by the creatures living below the surface—just like I did over 40 years ago.

FARMING THE SEA

Despite increased regulation and management of marine protected areas, wild fish stocks are still on a steep decline. One possible solution is aquaculture: farming our seafood. Humans have been doing this for centuries, with mixed results. At its worst, aquaculture can pose a toxic threat to wild ecosystems. At its best, it could be a dynamic and sustainable way to help feed the growing population of this little blue marble we call Earth.

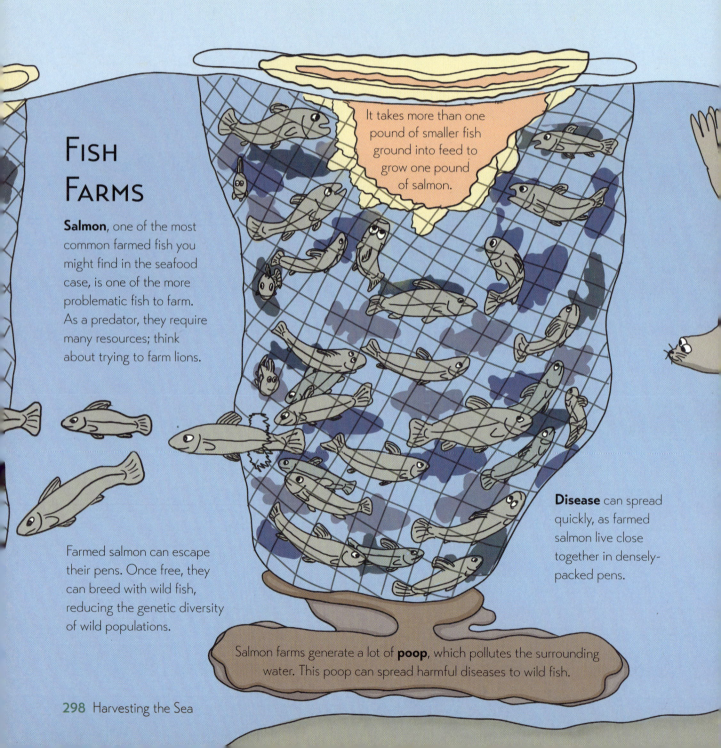

FISH FARMS

Salmon, one of the most common farmed fish you might find in the seafood case, is one of the more problematic fish to farm. As a predator, they require many resources; think about trying to farm lions.

It takes more than one pound of smaller fish ground into feed to grow one pound of salmon.

Farmed salmon can escape their pens. Once free, they can breed with wild fish, reducing the genetic diversity of wild populations.

Disease can spread quickly, as farmed salmon live close together in densely-packed pens.

Salmon farms generate a lot of **poop**, which pollutes the surrounding water. This poop can spread harmful diseases to wild fish.

OCEAN GARDENS

Instead of focusing on a single species, new sea farmers, such as Bren Smith of GreenWave, grow several species next to each other—healing the ocean while feeding us. Think of these new aquacultures as complete ecosystems rather than single-species assembly lines.

Farms like this protect us from storm surges and serve as a home for countless species of fish.

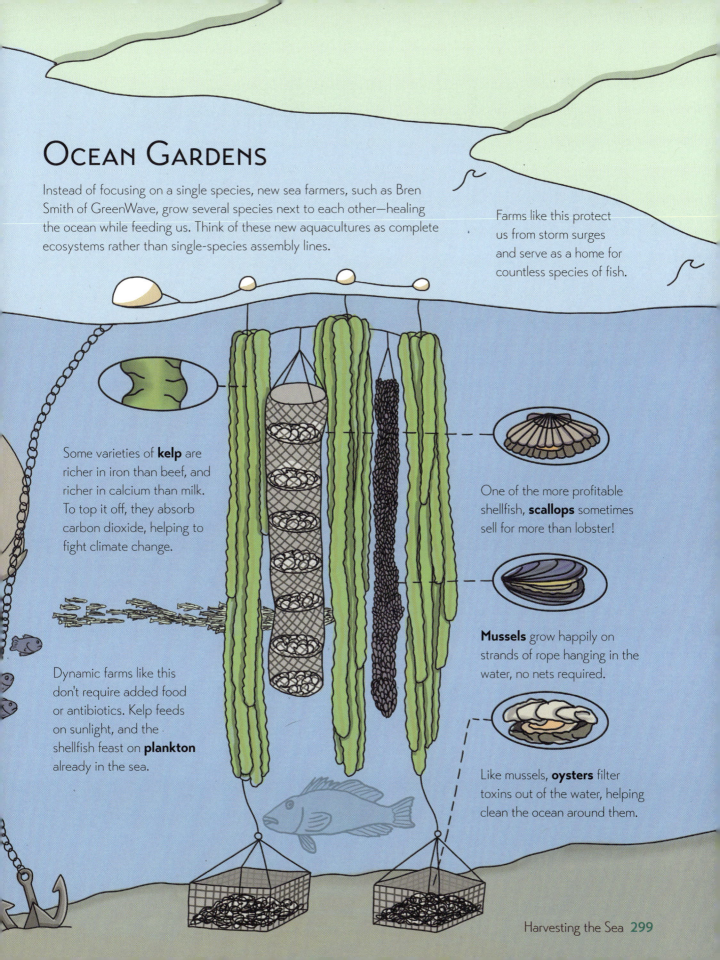

Some varieties of **kelp** are richer in iron than beef, and richer in calcium than milk. To top it off, they absorb carbon dioxide, helping to fight climate change.

Dynamic farms like this don't require added food or antibiotics. Kelp feeds on sunlight, and the shellfish feast on **plankton** already in the sea.

One of the more profitable shellfish, **scallops** sometimes sell for more than lobster!

Mussels grow happily on strands of rope hanging in the water, no nets required.

Like mussels, **oysters** filter toxins out of the water, helping clean the ocean around them.

Culturing Abalone

by Doug Bush – Owner, Cultured Abalone

AGE 11 — Visited Maine and ate mussels collected right from the rocks.

AGE 19 — Moved to Southern California and swam in Pacific for the first time.

AGE 25 — Visited a fish farm in Malawi while teaching biology in the Peace Corps.

AGE 33 — Moved to Santa Barbara, started working on an abalone farm.

A lot of people ask me how I ended up farming abalone. All my life I have really liked little creatures: the little animals that are shy and hide under rocks and look like aliens from another planet. When I was young, I liked to crawl around in a creek looking for crayfish, frogs, and salamanders. I also loved to crawl around in tidepools, catching crabs and feeding crushed mussels to anemones. My passion for swimming turned into a love for surfing, and I really enjoy cooking and eating delicious seafood. So I think I'm pretty lucky because I get to do something that blends all of these things together.

Abalone are incredible little sea creatures. They are snails, just like the snails you might find in your garden. However, instead of feasting on your basil and lettuce, they eat the leafy blades of seaweeds that grow on our California reefs. During the day they hide deep in the cracks of the rock reef, and emerge in the evening to cruise around and munch on the green, red, and brown species of algae that grow in our waters. They carry a shell on their back to protect them from being eaten, but it doesn't always work.

Abalone are a favorite food of the sea otters that swim in the kelp forests and, for several thousand years, of the humans that lived on the beaches of California.

Each abalone shell tells a story. The color of the shell is a result of the seaweeds that the abalone eats. The red abalone has a red shell because it lives at the depth predominantly inhabited by red algae. The red pigments in the algae accumulate in the shell as the abalone grows. The inside of the abalone shell is a wonderful swirl of iridescent colors called "nacre." The colors in nacre come from patterns in the thin layers of crystallized calcium carbonate, and from the way that these layers reflect light. Pieces of abalone shell nacre are prized for use in jewelry.

While you can no longer collect abalone in the Santa Barbara Channel, or anywhere else in California, our farm grows red abalone that you can still eat for dinner. We raise abalone from eggs right up to the market size, which is about 9 centimeters (3.5 inches) long. The eggs are just barely visible to the naked eye; about as small as the smallest dot you could make with your sharpest pencil. A single female abalone can produce about one million eggs for a single spawning. This is what we do in our hatchery when we want to produce baby abalone for our farm: We fertilize the eggs and hatch the embryos, then care for the tiny abalone larvae in special incubators with clean, cold ocean water for about one week. The water in these tanks is pumped directly to our farm from a series of pipes 12 meters (40 feet) deep in the Santa Barbara Channel. After that, they are ready to get transferred to trays where they grow into tiny versions of their adult form and start eating a thin film of algae. These trays are designed to act like the multidimensional rock bottom of their natural environment. About three years later, after eating lots and lots and lots of seaweed, the abalone are ready for market.

In farming abalone, we also farm and harvest seaweed. We feed our abalone both giant kelp that we sustainably harvest from the dynamic local coastal kelp beds, and various species of native algae that we cultivate in tanks on site. This provides a diverse natural basis for their nutritional needs and a final product with exemplary taste and quality. We don't use composite feeds with terrestrial proteins or antibiotics.

Running a farm means you have to be ready and willing to do just about anything; whatever needs to get done to keep the business moving forward. I work with chefs and people who love to cook and eat abalone. I work with researchers, ocean stewards, and with people from the state of California to make sure that the ocean resources are being managed well for the future. My business depends on a clean and healthy ocean environment. I need to fix motors for pumps and figure out the best kinds of seaweed to feed to the abalone. I get to work outside, but sometimes I need to work at a desk. Aquaculture, and shellfish aquaculture in particular, is a chapter in the history of California seafood that we are just beginning to write.

ABALONE IN THE CHANNEL

For centuries, abalone were a food source for Chumash and sea otter alike. In the late 1800s, the Chinese began harvesting this shellfish, followed by the Americans and Japanese. By 1900, abalone were in a steep decline. In the 1980s, a disease called "withering foot syndrome" wiped out much of the population. Abalone-harvesting around the Channel Islands—and on the California coast as a whole—is now illegal. However, there is evidence that some species, including the red abalone and black abalone, are starting to recover around the islands.

Choose

It's easy to see fishermen as the ones responsible for overfishing. But why do they fish in the first place? They do it to provide for you, the consumer. Each time you buy or order fish, you vote with your dollars. That said, making the right choice at the market or restaurant takes some thought. The Monterey Bay Aquarium Seafood Watch app or website is a good place to start. With one of those in hand, here are some things to look for:

1. What Species is it?

Tuna isn't just tuna. Salmon isn't just salmon. Both have many different species: from coho to king salmon, skipjack to albacore tuna. Some are more sustainable to eat than others. Figure out what species that fillet or steak is.

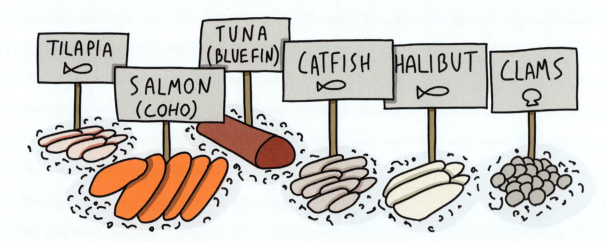

2. WHERE WAS IT CAUGHT?

Within fish species, there are distinct populations in different parts of the world. The skipjack tuna in the South Pacific Ocean might be doing better or worse than those in the Indian Ocean.

3. HOW WAS IT CAUGHT?

Not all forms of fishing are created equal. Giant nets can scoop up dolphins, sharks, and turtles, in addition to your tasty fish dinner. A single hook in the water, on the other hand, catches just a single fish.

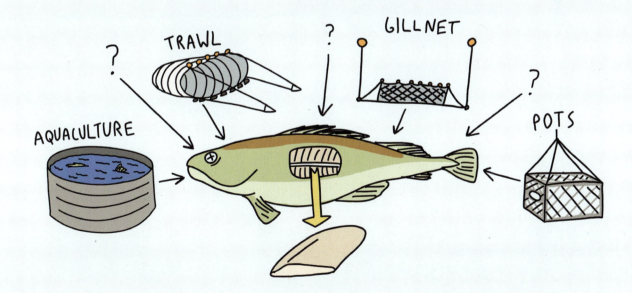

If you don't see a sustainable choice, tell the market or restaurant. The more people that ask for a product, the more likely restaurants and markets are to serve or stock it. Lastly, it is worth asking a more difficult question: given the state of global fisheries, should you buy fish at all?

SUSTAINABLE?

by Carl Safina – Conservationist

AGE 3 — Caught first fish, a hand-sized porgy. Decided he loved water.

AGE 5 — Played tug-of-war with eagle at zoo. Saw animals relate to others.

AGE 14 — Given great horned owl by music teacher. Started training hawks.

AGE 22 — Volunteered to help study terns. Saw a future in wildlife research.

TRAWLING THE BOTTOM

Coastal living, fishing, and seafood have been with us since, roughly, day one. The question on our plate today is: How much longer will the fish be joining us for dinner? One hint of the future had come centuries ago to King Charles I, who in 1631 stated:

And the former abundance of fish is turned into such scarcitie and deareness, that...especially our citie of London, and even our owne Court, are many times unprovided for their necessary dyet... therefore...the nets heretofore called traules...which is notoriously known to destroy the said frie & spawne...is...forbidden by the law.

In 1884 scientist and "Darwin's Bulldog" Thomas Huxley, who was then president of the Marine Biology Association, declared his belief that sea fisheries were "inexhaustible." He was careful to note that he was speaking in reference to the fishing pressure of his time, and he noted the exceptions of salmon and oysters which even then

showed signs of fatigue. But the audience heard what it wanted. His quote has often been used to illustrate a notion of oceanic inexhaustibility that lasted a century in the popular mind.

By the 1930s we found out that amber waves of grain could become dust-bowls, but we believed the sea would somehow remain invincible to all conceivable assault. As recently as the 1960s, whenever the question arose of how to feed the baby-boomed, population-bombed future, thoughts turned seaward. By then, frontiers on land were largely a thing of the past; the ocean

presented a final earthly frontier. The mentality of exploitation combined a sense of lawless freedom and a gold rush-race for riches.

Fishes used to have two great reserves in the sea, known to fishermen as "too far" and "too deep." But after fishing experienced its electronic coming-of-age, fish could only run; they could no longer hide. After World War II, detection technologies developed for fighting enemies at sea quickly found adaptation for what amounted to a veritable war on fishes. Sonar technology allowed boats to see fish schooling hundreds of feet below the surface. LORAN (a type of long range radar navigation) allowed boats to instantly pinpoint and return to any rockpile or drop-off where fish congregated in the seemingly trackless distances of the ocean. Radar allowed boats to fish safely and unrelentingly through fog that might previously have suspended operations. And while we could see the fish anywhere, we spun nylon monofilament into nets and lines virtually invisible to fish.

TURN THE TIDE

Ironically, it was communist countries' intensive fishing just off the beaches of New England during the Cold War that brought the first widespread cries of overfishing. By the time the U.S. enacted a law claiming sovereignty over all waters within 200 miles of its coast, in 1976—specifically to protect its own fishermen and the fishes from the fishing power of foreigners—the notion that an ocean could be depleted by boats towing nets had gained international traction.

In the 1990s and early 2000s, successive new scientific reports removed most remaining denial that fishing had largely depleted the prey on which

it depends. Among the more shocking reports were the following findings:

• Because of depletion of large edible fishes, fisheries are forced to target animals lower on the food web. In the most startling example, new fisheries are targeting jellyfish for human consumption.

• One-quarter of all sea life caught is unwanted and discarded dead. This "bycatch" is driving serious declines, endangering sea turtles, albatrosses, other seabirds, and certain fishes. In shrimp fishing, 10 kilograms (22 pounds) of unwanted juvenile fishes and other sea creatures are commonly discarded for each kilogram of shrimp caught.

• Data on fish catches shows that, compared to 50 years ago, when modern data sets began to be compiled, the abundance of large fishes such as tunas, sharks, cod, and groupers has declined roughly 90 percent.

TOWARD IMPROVEMENTS

Increasing recognition of these problems has led to changes in some fishing practices, legislation, and international cooperation. But no country can claim that their fishing problems have been solved, or that their new practices are running smoothly with high probability of long-term recovery and sustainability.

Whether ocean fishing remains viable depends on whether we rebuild fish populations and then limit catches. In a world facing still-increasing human population, this will be challenging. Fishing power must be reduced by about half. One way of doing it is a system of transferable fishing quotas (a maximum amount of a particular fish that may be caught). In some fisheries in Alaska, for example, fishing power has been reduced by allowing boats to buy and sell shares of the allowed quota. This has allowed some smaller-scale fishermen who are having a hard time paying for their boats to sell out, and other smaller-scale fishermen to, in turn, increase their profitability. For this to work economically, catches have to be well-capped and enforced. For it to work socially, safeguards limiting share ownership must be in place to prevent large corporations from swooping in and taking control of all shares of a quota. Alaska's system provides good examples of both.

Many ask whether it would be best to stop hunting wild fish and focus on fish farming. While fish farming is the fastest-growing sector in agriculture, it is not necessarily an answer to ocean woes. Fish farms are often made by destroying natural habitats that support diverse wild populations and human fishing communities. Many fish and shrimp must be fed fish caught from the ocean—meaning that it actually takes more protein to raise these fish than you get by consuming them. Yet some fish and shellfish are raised in environmentally-safe ways. The way forward lies in developing progressively less-harmful farming methods and supporting best practices.

Marine reserves that are closed to fishing have become a focus of debate in recent years. The United States, New Zealand, Australia, the Philippines, and several other countries have established such reserves. What is evident is that the size and abundance of fishes, and their ability to reproduce, increases in reserves. It is less evident that this leads to improved fishing outside the reserve boundaries. Whether it does probably depends on the size of the reserve.

Consumers of seafood can play a large role in improving ocean fishing and farming practices. Several organizations, such as the Safina Center, Environmental Defense, and Monterey Bay Aquarium, analyze various seafoods' environmental considerations, and publish consumer advice recommending menu choices that seafood enthusiasts can enjoy with a clear conscience. Increasing awareness, celebrity-chef involvement, and news media coverage have made the seafood experience more meaningful for choosy seafood lovers.

The answers to ocean recovery lie in fishing slower than the fish can breed, farming seafood in ecologically less destructive ways, and giving consumers the information they need to vote with their conscience and their wallet. There is time. And, yes, there is hope.

When clear water, calm seas, sunlight, and a healthy kelp forest combine, and I'm lucky enough to be in the ocean with the right lens, I kind of go crazy with the camera, intent on capturing all that magic.
Photo by Douglas Klug

I cast my line out
Drawing my line out farther and farther
As it disappears into the sea below

I cast my line out
Clicking back the reel
Looking for some sign of a sea-dwelling creature
Or a yield in the wind

I cast my line out
I now feel a hunger
A hope

I cast my line out
The sea calms
The crew catch fish after fish after fish
I sit there for hours

I cast my line out
Hoping to be granted at least one fish
Glaring down at them passing under the boat
Taunting me

I cast my line out
My bait is taken off
I figure it is too late to catch one of these mighty creatures
I almost stop

I cast my line out
I am too afraid to stop

I cast my line out
I feel this is going to be my last chance
I have to catch a fish

The moon lights the water
I cast my line out
And I reel in a crab

"I Cast My Line Out"
by Sydney Long, Student

Photo by Douglas Klug

CHAPTER 8

OILY
FOOTPRINTS

2015 Spill

 = Active Oil Rig

= Decommissioned Oil Rig

= Oil Processing Plant

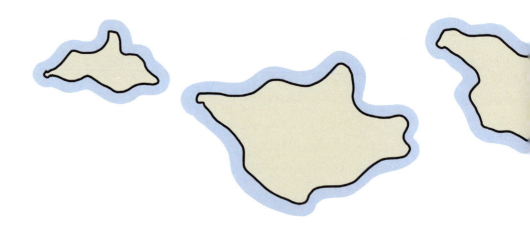

Oil Drilling in the Channel - 2019

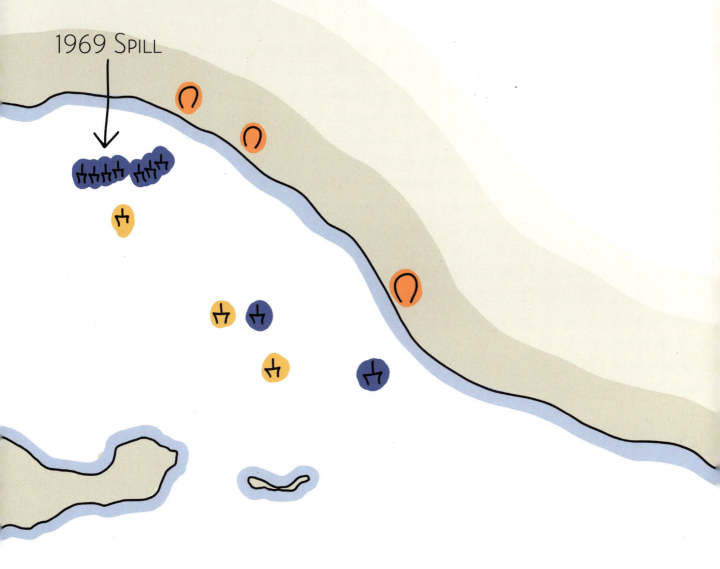

1969 Spill

Photo by Douglas Klug

THERE IS NO SUCH THING AS AWAY.

Even the most remote islands are not truly isolated. The sky above us is the same as the sky above them. Our ocean is the same ocean that surrounds them. No place—land or sea—is safe from our footprints.

The Channel Islands are ground zero for these footprints. Giant oil platforms stand as reminders of a spill that sparked world-wide awareness. Everything from plastic straws to car tires can be found on the once-clean island beaches. But it doesn't have to be this way. Together we can slowly wipe away our prints on these not-so-distant shores.

OIL IN THE CHANNEL

7,000 Years Ago

What: Small semi-solid pieces of oil seeped from cracks in the sea floor and washed ashore. This tar was used to waterproof *tomols* and baskets. Since it was never burned, no carbon dioxide was released.

Who: Chumash and other coastal peoples

How: Collected by hand from the beach.

Quantity: Only what seeped up naturally from the seafloor and washed ashore.

The Year 2013

What: Crude oil extracted from the seafloor, then processed into products such as gasoline (burned in cars, releasing carbon dioxide) and plastic (often ending up back in the ocean).

Who: Oil companies including Venoco and ExxonMobil

How: Drilled into channel seafloor, built oil platforms, pumped oil up from the deep.

Quantity: 2.5 million barrels (1 barrel = 160 liters = 42 gallons), sold for approximately $241 million.

WHAT A TIME TO BE

Oil, climate change, plastic in the ocean—pretty bleak stuff. However, as you read this chapter remember that this isn't one big inevitable disaster. We humans have been on Earth for a long time.

Over the centuries, we have had many different relationships with the planet and its furred, finned, and leafy residents. While the current situation might not look so pretty, if you look back 100 years, 1,000 years, 10,000 years, you can see that it doesn't have to be like it is today.

If we listen to the world around us—and use our creativity and inventiveness—we just might be able to turn this ship around. If we succeed, imagine what the planet could look like in 100 years, 1,000 years, or 10,000 years.

TIMELINE

A LONG, LONG TIME AGO

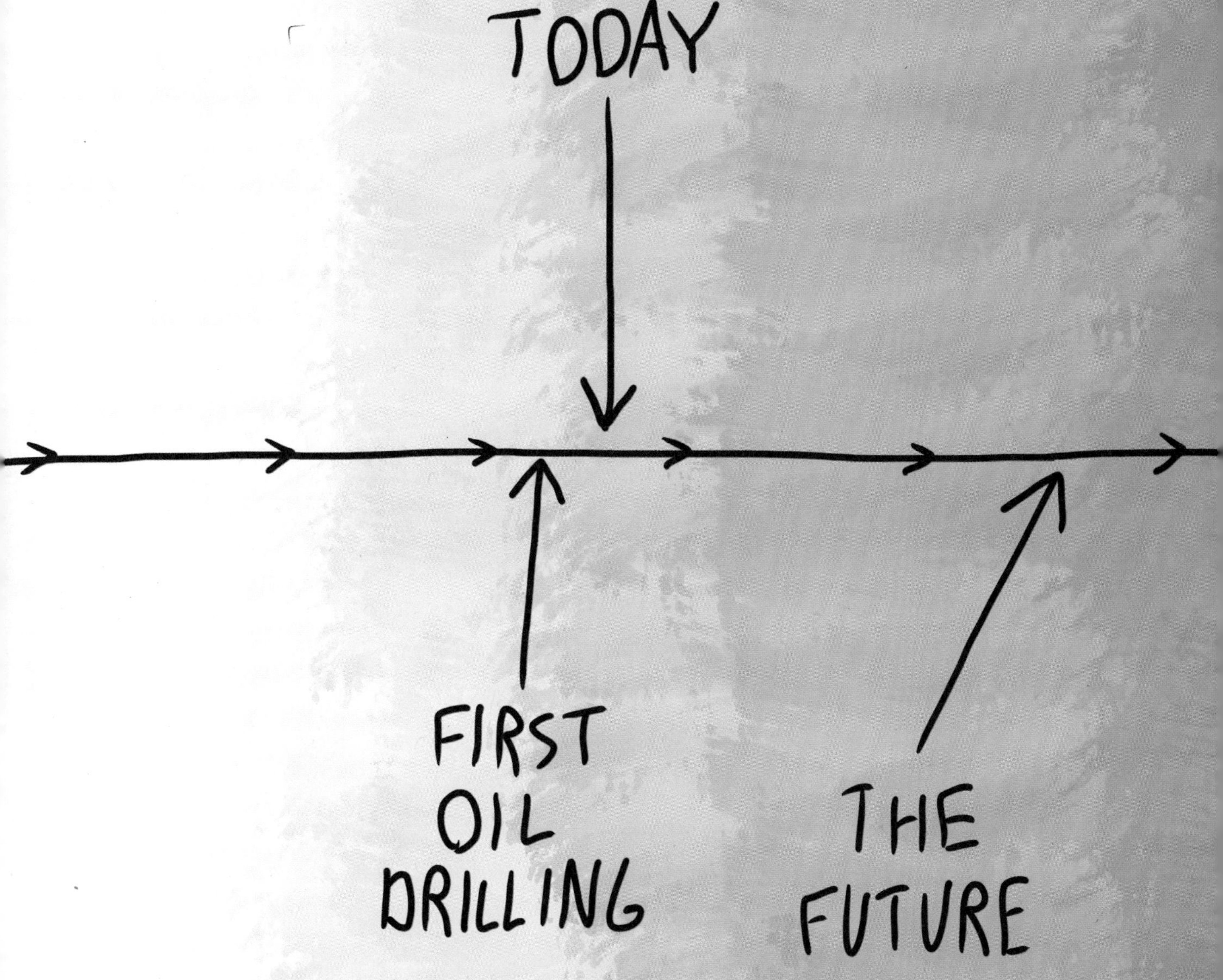

TODAY

FIRST
OIL
DRILLING

THE
FUTURE

SPREADING OIL

As soon as we started to pump the crude oil buried deep within our planet up to the surface, everything changed. The products that we create from this sticky black goo now pollute much of our air and water. Every part of the planet—every island—had evolved to survive without this oily presence. We use it every day, yet rarely think about where it comes from, where it is going, and how this impacts our big blue home.

WHAT IS IT?

The crude oil—the stuff that we pump up from the ground— is made of long-dead plants, animals, and algae.

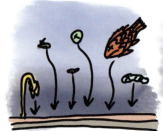   

These living things died millions of years ago and sank to the bottom of the sea.

Over time, they were covered by soil and sand, sinking deeper beneath the surface.

Pressure and heat slowly broke down these organisms into a dark black goo.

This goo—now formed into highly pressurized pockets that we call deposits—is crude oil.

BELOW

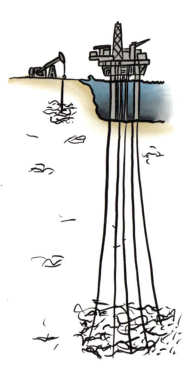

Today, we drill deep into the earth both on land and below the sea, all in search of deposits of this ancient material. Because it is under so much pressure, the pipes and pumps that we use to bring it to the surface sometimes burst, leading to oil spills.

From Oil to Infinity

For all of its downsides, crude oil is a pretty incredible substance. We can use a variety of chemical processes to turn it into everything from a fuel that helps us travel the planet to medical devices that save lives. Crude oil has changed nearly every aspect of the way we live. However, these benefits come with many unintended consequences.

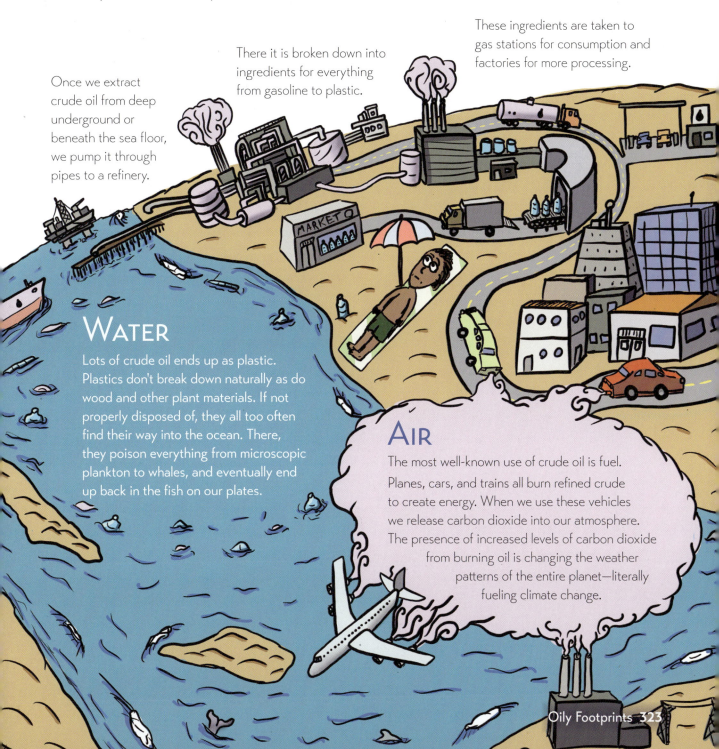

There it is broken down into ingredients for everything from gasoline to plastic.

These ingredients are taken to gas stations for consumption and factories for more processing.

Once we extract crude oil from deep underground or beneath the sea floor, we pump it through pipes to a refinery.

Water

Lots of crude oil ends up as plastic. Plastics don't break down naturally as do wood and other plant materials. If not properly disposed of, they all too often find their way into the ocean. There, they poison everything from microscopic plankton to whales, and eventually end up back in the fish on our plates.

Air

The most well-known use of crude oil is fuel. Planes, cars, and trains all burn refined crude to create energy. When we use these vehicles we release carbon dioxide into our atmosphere. The presence of increased levels of carbon dioxide from burning oil is changing the weather patterns of the entire planet—literally fueling climate change.

A fog bank lifts at sunrise off Santa Cruz Island.
Photo by Pedal Born Pictures

EXPLORING FOR WHAT?

by Liz Taylor – *President, DOER Marine*

AGE 3	AGE 5	AGE 9	AGE 32
Dad took her to collect clam and oyster specimens in Tampa Bay.	Mom taught her how to preserve algae that she collected.	Took first scuba dive in Hawaii, wanted to go deeper.	Co-founded DOER Marine to develop new ocean exploration tech.

It was inevitable that I would wind up exploring the deep for a living. My dad was an invertebrate zoologist who took me out to help collect sea worms, clams, and oysters in Tampa Bay. My mother, marine botanist and explorer Sylvia Earle, taught me how to collect algae specimens that we mounted and dried in a home herbarium set-up. On trips to the beach, hours were spent eye-to-eye with fierce fiddler crabs watching rainbows of coquina clams upend themselves and dig back down into the sand.

I got my first informal scuba diving lessons during a trip to Hawaii. It was wonderful to be able to follow a fish down into deeper water without a one-breath constraint. However, time and depth are still very limiting factors in scuba diving. I watched how this frustrated ocean explorers, and saw a great push towards subsea habitats and submersible development as I grew up. Eventually, I became president of Deep Ocean Exploration and Research, a company dedicated to developing new submersible and remotely-operated vehicle technology to explore the ocean.

Even as we proved the usefulness of compact submersibles for science, there was pressure to use them—and the technology used to develop

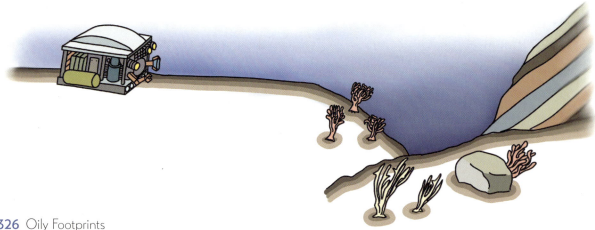

them—in the oil, gas, and mining industries. In 2015, I was participating in Mission Blue II (a TED-Talks-at-sea) aboard a vessel in the Solomon Islands. The subject of deep sea mining came up. I brought up the uncomfortable topic of scientific technologies being used not only to explore the ocean but also to scope out areas for mining exploitation. We had all seen it. Even the venerable Woods Hole Oceanographic Institution succumbed.

The submersible *Alvin*, a workhorse of deep sea research, was hired by Nautilus Minerals to investigate areas in the South Pacific for mining. One of the scientists who participated in the mining survey was on the ship with us. She explained that she signed up for the project because it was likely her only opportunity to study deep sea ecology. She hoped that a case could be made to protect some of the areas from what seemed inevitable destruction. For a non-profit scientific institute to undertake a commercial survey was questionable, but for a deep sea ecologist to be placed in the position of documenting the deep—knowing that the findings would be used to justify mining—was simply depressing. It also pointed to the real problem of money. Industry is well-funded. Science is not.

In 2010, we saw firsthand how far extractive industry could go: the Deep Water Horizon oil rig burst, spewing 795 million liters (210 million gallons) of crude oil into the Gulf of Mexico. It was the worst oil spill in the history of oil extraction. In response, we founded Deep Hope. The objectives are pretty simple. Build two submersibles combining all that we've learned over the past 25 years. Get out and dive the submersibles, not only with scientists but with artists, musicians, teachers, students, and even politicians. Let people see for themselves what is at risk of being lost for good if we let our extraction run unchecked.

Our own Channel Islands are where we plan to test the Deep Hope submersibles. There are still extractive activities taking place right along the coast: oil rigs in plain view from beaches that have tar balls both from natural seeps and past spills. When we are lured by the promise of quick wealth, it is tempting to cast exploration aside and embrace exploitation. In the sea, it is especially tempting in an "out of sight, out of mind" way. Deep Hope will show people that nothing is truly out of mind. Only through this direct exploration and sharing of knowledge can we hope to counter the siren song of exploitation.

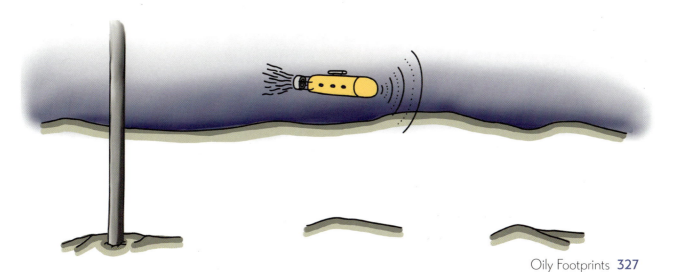

THE OCEAN IS BOILING

by Kate Wheeling & Max Ufberg - *Pacific Standard*

KATE AGE 11	**MAX AGE 11**	**KATE AGE 27, MAX AGE 27**
Discovered journalism by thumbing through her dad's old *National Geographics*.	Discovered a knack for writing thanks to an essay contest in 7th grade.	Worked together as journalists at *Pacific Standard* magazine, where they covered the environment and climate change.

On the morning of January 29, 1969 *Santa Barbara News-Press* reporter Bob Sollen received a call from an anonymous source. The voice at the other end of the line rang out clear and urgent.

Bob Sollen (former Santa Barbara News-Press reporter): *They said, "The ocean is boiling!" I don't know who it was, or what position they were in, but they were alarmed by it. For some reason I figured it was one of the workers out at the platform.*

For nearly 24 hours, gas and thick black oil had been bubbling to the water's surface, and, with each lapping wave, the sludge inched closer to the California coastline. The day before, the workers on an offshore oil rig called Platform A were removing the drill pipe from a freshly-bored well when gas and drilling mud erupted onto the platform. Though the crew managed to plug the top of the well, the highly pressurized gas and oil continued leaking into the water through cracks in the upper layer of the ocean floor.

Paul Relis (first executive director of the Community Environmental Council): *We hadn't had big oil spills and it seemed so foreign to this place, this beautiful coastline—all of a sudden you go down to the water's edge and it's just like heavy, black soup.*

Somehow I got my way into a single-engine small plane that flew over the actual source of the oil spill. I remember looking straight down into this huge upwelling of black out of the ocean. And I just instantly thought, this is going to change the world.

Bud Bottoms (co-founder of Get Oil Out!): *You went to Hendry's Beach, there was no noise of the waves breaking, just…slop, slop, slop, slop. And people just stood there and cried. All our beaches were black. You'd see surfers standing there with their boards, and their boards were covered in black.*

As the birds would come out of the water, they would try to clean their feathers and they'd ingest the oil. People picked them up and put them in boxes, took them down to a cleaning station. There were thousands of birds; I don't think they saved one of them.

Sea lions took a real beating too, over on San Miguel Island. The babies couldn't suckle their mothers because she'd have tar on her tummy, so that would kill them. It was a mess.

Platform A was owned and operated by Union Oil, a company headquartered in nearby El Segundo, California. With no contingency (backup) plan and no federal regulations in place, it took Union Oil months to contain the blowout. Eleven-million liters (3 million gallons) of crude oil spilled into the Pacific, spreading across more than 2,071 square kilometers (800 square miles) of ocean, coating 56 kilometers (35 miles) of beach and killing more than 3,600 seabirds and countless marine mammals and fish.

Relis: *I thought these oil companies and the federal government had some sort of a game plan, but this was a joke. They were throwing straw down on the beach to lap up the oil with pitchforks and hiring people off the street! I mean, this was funky. That was kind of eye-opening—that big companies and big government could be so incompetent.*

Santa Barbarans of all ages mobilized against the profound degradation of their otherwise-pristine seaside city, long known as "The American Riviera." Demonstrations took many forms: There were dozens of local protests against Union Oil, which saw residents lashing out at ecological injustice; there were grassroots factions such as Get Oil Out! which distributed pamphlets and bumper stickers, and there was the lawsuit against Union Oil, filed jointly by the city, county, and state.

Bottoms: *We were invaded by the oil companies. We didn't want that out in our oceans, you know? I mean, I spearfished, took lobster. I fed my kids out of the ocean for years.*

I was so disturbed, I yelled out, "We've got to get the oil out!" And my boss goes, "Yeah, that's good, get it all out, goo. G-O-O."

Denis Hayes (*coordinator of the first Earth Day*): *GOO! was reducing things to that kind of bumper-sticker level, which you really needed if you were going to be communicating with large crowds.*

Bottoms: *So I said, "Let's run up a petition to get it out, to get the people of Santa Barbara to get it all out of the channel." So we wrote up this petition, and we didn't know anything; we were just conservation-type people. But we wrote the petition, and in no time flat we had over 200,000 signatures from around the world to get oil out of the Santa Barbara Channel. [At the time, the city of Santa Barbara had a population of 75,000.] One time we invited everybody to come to the beach with their mirrors and build a wall along the sand and shine their mirrors on Platform A. We had kids that would go to the beach and get little bottles and fill them with oil. There'd be 200 oil flasks, and we sent them to every legislator, from city officials to the feds. Just continuous guerrilla warfare for the cause.*

There was a guy who met with the Union Oil top dog and dumped oil all over his desk. There was a guy who was a bomber pilot during World War II, and he said, "I've got a crew that wants to take out that platform." And I was like: "I don't know about that, just do what you want to do but gently. But I don't want to know." [The plan ultimately did not go through.]

The blowout—then the largest in United States history—drew global attention, as images of oil-coated marine life circulated in news reports around the world. That reporting got people thinking about how to balance their desires for

Union Oil Platform A, which infamously blew in 1969.
Photo by David "Doc" Searls

economic progress—and cheap energy—with the emerging idea that humans have a moral obligation to protect the environment.

The spill was followed by decades of bipartisan environmental action: Members of Congress worked across the aisle to create the first Earth Day in April of 1970, as well as several key acts of environmental legislation. For Union Oil the spill represented a colossal failure, one made worse by its own executives' apparent lack of heart. "I am amazed at the publicity for the loss of a few birds," Union Oil president Fred Hartley infamously said after the spill.

Hayes: *Senator Gaylord Nelson was flying from Los Angeles up to Seattle for a meeting while the spill was going on. He was horrified by the extent of it [seen] from the plane window. So Santa Barbara played a key role in prompting him to develop the idea for Earth Day. In the run-up to the protests of the war in Vietnam and the early days of the civil rights movement, there had been teach-ins on college campuses. He thought that would be a useful thing to do for conservation issues broadly.*

Relis: *I talked to Hayes about Earth Day and basically thought, well, that sounds like a cool idea. So we closed the streets and held the first Earth Day.*

Bottoms: *We had lectures on all kinds of things: how to plant a seed, beehives, how to live off the land, all kinds of things like that.*

It would be a stretch to say the oil spill precipitated the modern environmental movement. But the disaster certainly called forth a more tactical and clear national effort, and imbued environmentalism with the kind of energy that had already mobilized the push for women's equality, civil rights, and peace in Southeast Asia.

Relis: *I'd seen the ecology center up at UC Berkeley. It was sort of an active center for new ideas, new thinking. The first thing we did, we secured a storefront downtown and we replicated what the Berkeley ecology center was: bookstore, meeting place, paintings on the walls. It was a real trippy kind of place. Then we decided to build a quarter-acre organic garden.*

Early on it struck me that maybe Santa Barbara itself could be a laboratory for raising environmental consciousness and implementing ideas that could start here and move elsewhere.

Bottoms: *We just had a bunch of crazy, wild things to stop fossil fuel. Because we knew that was a killer.*

Relis: *We weren't going to purely regulate our way out of this. We were going to have to build a whole new infrastructure, and that oil infrastructure took about 50 to 75 years to build. Why would we think an alternative infrastructure was going to happen overnight?*

There would be many more spills in the U.S. in future years, but never again would industry and government officials be so ill-prepared. All that protest, and all those new laws, thanks in large part to the fuss over "the loss of a few birds."

Adapted from " 'The Ocean is Boiling': The Complete Oral History of the 1969 Santa Barbara Oil Spill," published in *Pacific Standard*.

SANTA BARBARA CHANNEL
OIL HISTORY

1897 First offshore drilling in the world took place off of Summerland.

1920s Oil fields discovered and drilled throughout the county, from Santa Maria to Ellwood.

1958 Onshore oil fields dried up. Platform Hazel, the first offshore platform, was built.

1967 Against strong protests, the first platform was built in federal waters: Platform Hogan.

1969 Union Oil's Platform A blew, spilling 80,000 to 100,000 barrels of oil into the ocean.

1970s Offshore oil production exceeded onshore oil production in Santa Barbara county.

1995 Santa Barbara County oil production hit an all-time high: 68,798,091 barrels.

2015 Refugio Spill, platforms in the channel temporarily shut down.

2017 Venoco filed for bankruptcy, decommissioning Platform Holly. Ended all active drilling in state waters of the channel.

A worker lays straw down on the oil-covered waters of the
Channel in an attempt to absorb the crude from the 1969 spill.
Photo by James Chen

PLASTIC

Two-hundred years ago things weren't cheap. Most everyday items were made of wood, stone, fabric, or metal. They might cost you more than a day's wages to buy. When we discovered how to make things out of plastics, that all changed. We were now able to create this wonder material from what seemed like an endless supply of crude oil buried beneath our planet's surface and deep below the seafloor. It could be molded into almost any shape and was much easier to work with than stone or metal. For the average person, plastic became so normal that we stopped paying attention to where it came from, and where it ended up.

MORE THAN BEFORE

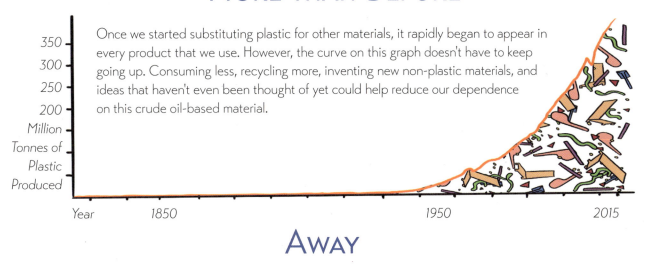

Once we started substituting plastic for other materials, it rapidly began to appear in every product that we use. However, the curve on this graph doesn't have to keep going up. Consuming less, recycling more, inventing new non-plastic materials, and ideas that haven't even been thought of yet could help reduce our dependence on this crude oil-based material.

350
300
250
200
Million
Tonnes of
Plastic
Produced

Year   1850   1950   2015

AWAY

Plastics are incredibly durable. If left alone, most won't **biodegrade** (be broken down by living organisms in the soil). This is great for a product that is meant to be used forever. For products that are used only once, or for just a few years, it's not so awesome.

After a piece of plastic has served its intended purpose, it begins a journey that won't end for a long time and often ends in the sea. Throwing plastic "away" can frequently mean throwing it into the ocean, where it just might find its way onto the shores of the Channel Islands.

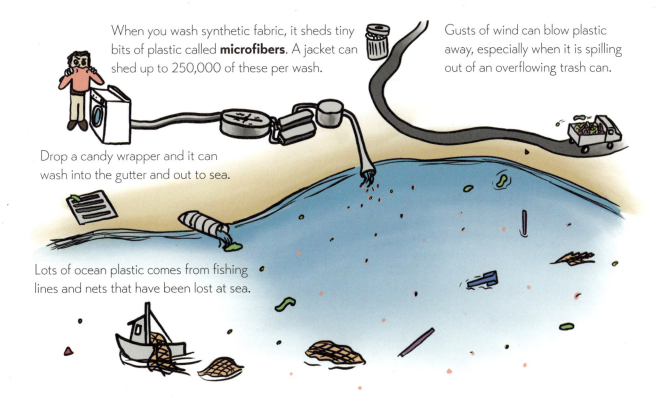

When you wash synthetic fabric, it sheds tiny bits of plastic called **microfibers**. A jacket can shed up to 250,000 of these per wash.

Gusts of wind can blow plastic away, especially when it is spilling out of an overflowing trash can.

Drop a candy wrapper and it can wash into the gutter and out to sea.

Lots of ocean plastic comes from fishing lines and nets that have been lost at sea.

Swirls with Plastic on Top

Once in the ocean, plastic gets around. Some of it will eventually sink to the ocean floor. Other pieces float near the surface where they are transported across the globe by wind-driven currents called gyres. Sometimes this plastic can get concentrated into patches in the middle of the ocean.

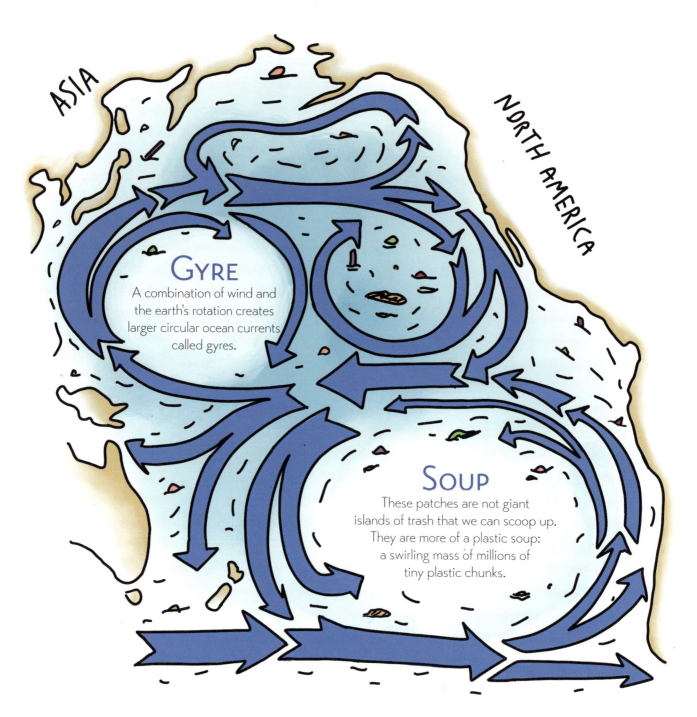

ASIA

NORTH AMERICA

Gyre

A combination of wind and the earth's rotation creates larger circular ocean currents called gyres.

Soup

These patches are not giant islands of trash that we can scoop up. They are more of a plastic soup: a swirling mass of millions of tiny plastic chunks.

Tiny

Once in the ocean, plastic gets slowly broken down by churning ocean currents and sunlight in a process called photodegradation. This leaves the ocean full of tiny pieces of plastic less than five millimeters (0.2 inches) long called **microplastics**. A 2017 study estimated that there are 51 trillion microplastic particles in the ocean.

Eat it

Once it is "away" in the ocean, plastic starts to affect everything. Tiny plankton and fish often mistake microplastics and microfibers for food. Once they consume these toxic meals, they keep both those plastics and the harmful chemicals those plastics contain in their bodies. We call this **bioaccumulation**.

Larger fish then eat these smaller animals, absorbing all of the plastic and chemicals present in their daily meals. When we eat these fish, we in turn get even more of these nasty side dishes in our systems. Thanks to this process—called **biomagnification**—even a pristine-looking fillet of fish often has plastic and toxic chemicals in it.

PARADISE TOSSED

by Emma Wagner – *Student*

AGE 5	AGE 11	AGE 14	AGE 18
Investigated tide pools and boogie-boarded in the waves for hours on end.	Went on their first bike trip. Experienced the beauty of the land.	Visited Channel Islands with Santa Barbara Middle School.	Pursued a degree in Sociology & Anthropology at Lewis & Clark College.

I spring into motion and pounce on the small white ribbon blowing in the wind. I snatch it up and stuff it into the big trash bag clutched in my sandy hands. Over the past few hours, I have proudly become an expert on differentiating between small white ribbons and small white pieces of seaweed. This may not sound like something to get excited about, but I am thrilled to have mastered the art. For the first time in an hour, I pause in my search and look around. I am on Santa Rosa Island combing the beautiful, white sand beach for human debris.

Every year, my school's ninth grade class comes to Santa Rosa in order to eliminate and analyze the manmade litter that has washed up on the shore. Each time, we clear all the trash from the beach. A year later when the new class returns, more debris has made its way to this paradise.

Out of the 50 billion plastic bottles consumed each year in the U.S., 156 of those bottle caps and plastic pieces end up on Santa Rosa Island. Considering the United States is 10 million square kilometers (3.7 million square miles) and Santa Rosa Island is only 215 square kilometers (83 square miles) total, it is shocking that any trash at all would end up on this small fragment of Earth.

Walking along the sandy, plant-strewn bluffs, I notice small tracks dotted here and there; the only indication that others have been on this island before us. I come across paw prints several times before the obvious sinks in: Animals live here and we are uninvited guests in their home.

While our school is here to help these animals and their environment, the rest of the world is unknowingly and simultaneously damaging their habitat. The fact that humans ignorantly yet significantly intrude upon the island home and vandalize its perfection with their carelessness saddens me.

I continue to walk down the beach, stopping when I see a group of my classmates clustered around something rolling in the waves. At first glance, I think it is a log, maybe fallen off an old boat. Then I get closer and realize that what I previously thought was a log is actually a sea lion, all the life gone from its eyes. As the tide gently rocks the sea lion back and forth, I can see my own hopelessness mirrored in its limp body. The cause of the sea lion's death is evident: a dilapidated car tire cut into the skin of its neck, quelling any hope of breath the creature once had.

I am told that some sort of animal in this condition is found each and every year. Whether it is a strangled sea lion or a bird with a stomach full of plastic, they are all similar, and all killed by the same thing: us.

As I stuff another piece of plastic into my bag, I realize the impact that we humans have on this stunning place and others like it, and I am left with the helpless feeling that my heroic efforts to turn the tide of damage may be futile.

A group of sea lions play beneath the waves off Santa Barbara Island. *Photo by Katie Davis*

ALBATROSS

by Chris Jordan – *Photographer*

AGE 10 — Grew up in an artist household: mom painted, dad took photos.

AGE 23 — Worked as a lawyer for 10 years, then quit to pursue passion for photography.

AGE 38 — Photographed giant piles of garbage, documenting our mass consumption.

AGE 45 — Found majestic albatross, focused on capturing beauty ever since.

Artist, activist, and photographer Chris Jordan has spent several years documenting the plight of the albatross on Midway Island, located in the middle of the Pacific Ocean.

Biologists have put tracking devices on albatrosses, and are astonished to learn that the birds regularly fly 16,000 kilometers (10,000 miles) in a single feeding trip. They catch their food on the ocean surface, in a quick zooming grab. An albatross might scoop up only one bite of food in 800 kilometers (500 miles) of flying. But in a week she will have a whole belly full to bring home to her chick.

Albatrosses can't know what plastic is. Their instinct is to trust what the ocean provides, as they and their ancestors have done for millions of years. The parents serve as a living umbilical cord: directly from the sea, to the stomachs of their chicks. Every bite of food they have ever eaten, every molecule they are made of, came from the sea. In this way, there is no boundary between the albatross and the ocean.

When her belly is full, no matter where she is in the Pacific, she turns and flies thousands of miles to her island home and nest. What she doesn't know, because she can't know it, is that along with the nutrients in her belly she is carrying something toxic and sharp, and it's headed for the soft membrane within the stomach of her baby.

Kneeling over these scenes is like looking into a mirror. Here we face one surreal consequence of our collective choice. This is our culture, turned inside out.

To see more of Chris's work, visit www.albatrossthefilm.com and www.chrisjordan.com.

HISTORY OF THE STRAW

In 2018 Americans used almost 500 million disposable straws, most of them plastic, every day. That is a ton of plastic waste. Humans have used straws for thousands of years. But they haven't always been plastic.

3,000 BC - Ancient Sumerians use hollow sticks to drink beer.

300 CE - Chinese use hollow reeds to drink wine.

1500s - The *bombilla*, a metal straw used for drinking mate, is invented in South America.

1800s - Straws made of rye stalks used in the United States.

1901 - United States produces 165 million paper straws.

1928 - United States produces 4 billion paper straws.

1907 - Leo Baekeland invents Bakelite, the first synthetic (non-naturally occurring) plastic. This sparks a revolution in the materials that we use to make everyday objects.

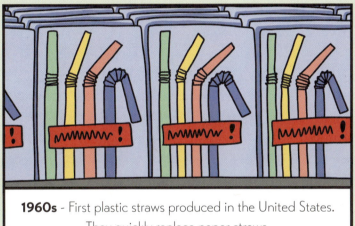

1960s - First plastic straws produced in the United States. They quickly replace paper straws.

1980s - Plastic straws get weird with the "jumbo straw" and "crazy straw."

2015 - A study estimates that there are 7.5 billion discarded straws on beaches across the U.S.

2018 - City of Santa Barbara joins communities across the country in banning plastic straws.

PLASTIC DIARY

by Julia Keane – *Educator, Explore Ecology*

AGE 10	AGE 13	AGE 19	AGE 22
Visited the aquarium. Dreamed for months of swimming with sharks.	Presented a slideshow about fiddler crabs during family talent night.	Sank up to her waist in mud while helping kids restore wetland plants.	Drove across U.S. to join AmeriCorps. Became an environmental educator.

For Christmas last year, I asked my family for all the reusable products I could think of to add to my growing stash. Of what was on my list, I received Bees Wrap, three types of reusable bags, and a pack of cleaning brushes for my reusable straws. You would think that after getting this haul I'd have no problem reducing my plastic waste to zero. These gifts have become a huge plastic-saver in my life when it comes to food. However, since life does not revolve around the three meals you eat a day— no matter how badly we want it to—there are other places where single-use plastic entered my waste stream. I decided to record all of the plastic that I use in a single week, and the results were quite surprising.

Since I go from the beach to classrooms to the office every day, I bring my own lunch. Usually, I prepare a big meal to eat throughout the week, portioning it out into glass containers. But snacks are what keep my energy up during the day, and I had just run out. So I bought a box of granola bars, each one wrapped in single-use plastic. My whole lunch, except for this one thing, is zero waste. Not bad. But then I got back to the office after a day of teaching and saw my coworker had refilled the candy jar. I couldn't turn down chocolate, so I unwrapped yet another piece of plastic.

The next day, my friends and I went out to lunch at a cafe within walking distance. As soon as I got there, I realized I forgot my metal water bottle. I challenged myself to stick it out until we got back to work. But my lunch ended up being spicy, so I caved and used one of their plastic cups.

As the week went on, I started to notice the food I bought in bulk, like tubs of hummus or yogurt, was running low. After cleaning out my fridge, I realized the majority of the items in there were actually packaged in plastic. I just learned in a meeting with the city's recycling department that a lot of those items aren't valuable at recycling centers anyway. As I went through my usual routine, the pile started getting bigger. Flossing or even using makeup became hard to do without noticing the big plastic elephant in the room. Treating myself to a shopping trip at a local thrift store left me with not only a new wardrobe but a handful of plastic tags.

The end of the week was finally here. It was date night, so we chose a local taco stand that got great reviews. Even though we were dining in, everything was served on plastic. Plastic plates, forks, and salsa cups were strewn about our table. Ironically, the napkins were made from recycled paper. I went home after the meal feeling stuffed, but a little discouraged. I thought I was practicing what I preach. So it surprised me that single-use plastics are still very much a part of my life. I empower students to find areas in their lives where they can creatively reduce and reuse. Some of those strategies that I use in my own life. Buying in bulk, walking to lunch, or shopping at thrift stores are a great way to shrink your carbon footprint. But it's important to go one step further.

Looking at the list of single-use plastics that I used this week, it's easy to say, "This wasn't a normal week." As in, "This wasn't how I typically live my life and so I shouldn't be judged." But the fact is that there are no "normal" weeks, so why wait? I needed to find room for growth within my lifestyle and make some changes. I noticed that I use the most plastic when I'm unprepared. Whether that means I forgot my reusable straw

at my house (which happens more often than not) or that I didn't have time to cook homemade snacks. Taking a couple of minutes from binge-watching a show on Netflix to make some granola, or putting together a "reusable kit" for my car, can make a difference. Another area for growth was my grocery store habits. Making a switch to paper, metal, or glass packaging is a simple way to cut down on a majority of my plastic use.

Facing the plastic in my life was overwhelming, but it gave me the chance to reflect on a few choices that I didn't know I had. Managing our use of plastic can cause a ripple effect of healthier actions, benefitting not only ourselves but all living creatures on this planet.

Single-use plastics I used this week:
3 granola bar wrappers
3 chocolate wrappers
1 plastic cup
1 take out container lid
tags from new clothes
1 large yogurt container
1 sliced cheese package wrapper
1 plastic bag from the deli for turkey meat
1 plastic fork
1 plastic plate from restaurant
2 salsa bar cups
5 pieces of plastic floss
1 plastic liquid eyeliner bottle
1 plastic packaging for new liquid eyeliner
1 plastic packaging for new medicine from pharmacy
2 dryer sheets (made of plastic)
2 band-aids with packaging
1 plastic empty coffee bag
1 plastic hummus container
1 plastic carrot bag
1 plastic wrapper from frozen pizza

A container ship carries millions of pounds
of goods past Anacapa Island.
Photo by Robert Schwemmer

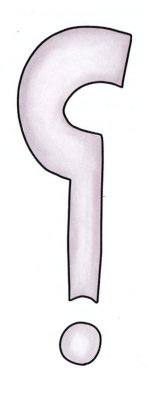

PEOPLE MAKING A DIFFERENCE

Sometimes, all it takes is an idea. A new way of making things. A new way of doing business. Bright minds from across the planet are finding innovative ways to address our addiction to crude oil products such as plastics and gasoline. Here are just a few:

ROBERT ANDERSON

In the 1830s, long before gas-powered automobiles clogged our highways, Scottish inventor Robert Anderson attached a non-rechargeable battery to a carriage. This was the first electric car. It would be another 100 years before electric car technology could be mass produced. Today, major car companies, including General Motors and upstarts such as Tesla, are pushing the electric vehicle as a serious alternative. All because a Scotsman decided that electricity might be the best replacement for the horse.

Ben, David, and Kevin

While working with fishermen in Chile, Ben Kneppers realized that discarded old fishing nets were one of the planet's largest sources of marine plastics. Seeing these nets as a resource rather than trash, he and his friends David Stover and Kevin Ahearn started working with Chilean fishermen to collect old nets and chop them up into plastic pellets. Bureo was born. Their goal: to show people that this "trash" is in fact a valuable material that can be made into a variety of new goods. Their first product: a skateboard deck made from 100 percent recycled fishing nets.

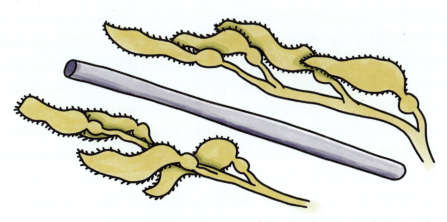

Chelsea Briganti

Growing up in Hawaii, Chelsea fell in love with the ocean. While studying industrial design, she began to think about ways that we could make products out of materials other than plastic. Chelsea founded Loliware to develop an alternative to the one-use plastic beverage sipper: a 100 percent kelp-based straw that lasts 18 times longer than a paper straw when submerged in liquid, and doesn't require the chopping down of new trees to manufacture. People have taken notice, and Marriott Hotels has even placed an order.

HOW TO PROTECT ISLANDS

Even though the Channel Islands are protected as part of a National Park and Marine Sanctuary, they are still not immune to our changing world. Lines on a map don't stop oil spills, climate change, or the flow of microplastics. Just as we discovered and innovated around fossil fuels, we have also developed some pretty cool alternatives. To protect these islands, and save the larger island planet we live on, we need to embrace these new ways of thinking.

REDUCE

The amount of things we buy and throw away is at a high. We don't need to invent new technologies to fix this. Consume art, education, and entertainment, not stuff.

RECYCLE

After an object has served its purpose, it can be turned into something else. No new resources need to be mined. Just be careful: Not everything is so easy to recycle, and this whole process takes energy.

MOVE

Ditch the car. Bicycles are super efficient and run on you. Trains and busses can move lots of people together over longer distances and can run on electricity.

Fix Carbon

We have disrupted the once-natural carbon cycle in our atmosphere. It might not be as visible as trash on the beach, but this part of our footprint is much more serious. Healing the planet and protecting our islands starts here.

By pumping more carbon dioxide into the atmosphere, we are causing more heatwaves, droughts, and hurricanes.

Algae and plants "clean" air when they breathe, pulling carbon from the atmosphere. If we grow more of both, we can clean the air.

This is one way to heal our planet. It won't solve everything though. We need more outside-the-box thoughts like this to turn things around.

Conserve

Natural spaces need to be protected. Plants, algae, mushrooms, and animals are all a part of the balance that keeps us, and our planet, healthy. Everything needs a home.

Renew

We can get our electricity from renewable sources that don't create more carbon. Solar panels harness energy from the sun. Turbines do so with wind.

Eat Local

Over the last 100 years, we have moved away from local food sources. If we can start creating food closer to the mouths that need it, less energy will be needed to move it around the world.

WE HAVE A CHOICE

by Paul Relis – Community Environmental Council

AGE 10
Discovered a magical pond full of frogs in the middle of an oil field.

AGE 22
Experienced the '69 oil spill. Dedicated life to protecting the environment.

AGE 23
Founded Community Environmental Council, a "think-and-do" tank.

AGE 58
CEC committed to a "fossil free" future for the Santa Barbara region.

The fossil fuel age has been with us now for a little more than 100 years, or about four generations. There's hardly a soul alive who has not been touched in almost every aspect of his or her life by the power of oil. But as we know, there is a shadow side to all things that blaze with light and power.

Today, ask the families residing along the freeway corridor to the Ports of Long Beach and Los Angeles about how they've been harmed by oil, and they'll reveal a sad litany of statistics concerning the high incidence of air pollution-caused cancers. Ask a U.S. general what it means to the military, and he or she will reveal the strain our oil dependence places on the entire armed forces; how it puts troops needlessly in harm's way around the world. Ask the scientists, the 97 percent who have validated human-induced climate change, not the flabby-headed noisemakers on television who go on and on, denying the human impact on the natural world and climate. Let these scientists explain what understanding they have gained when they measure the snowpacks in the Sierra for water content, the ice sheets in the Arctic, the

temperatures of the world's marine currents, the rising acidity in the oceans, and what this means for the coming decades as climate change seizes the world stage and the migrations to cope with its effects begin.

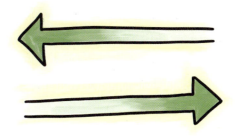

TWO PATHS

When faced with these problems, there are two basic courses of action. For those so inclined, there is the action of inaction, denial, resistance to change, and statements that there are forces at work that are beyond our insight and beyond our control. Under the guise of caution—of "not knowing enough," not being "certain"—the case is made to wait and see. Such inaction in the face of overwhelming scientific evidence is similar to a family, its finances going underwater, wishing against all evidence to the contrary, that its members will be rescued, that a check will arrive in the mail, or an aunt will die just in time with a bequest to relieve them of the heavy burden of having to change their lives. In doing so, we would retreat in fear before the task, deciding that it's just too big and too difficult to address.

The second choice—the one that I'm most comfortable proposing, one that is a product of my experience—is to consider this immense and still-abstract problem and break it down into understandable and manageable pieces. Unlike 40 years ago when I began to experiment in finding ways out of our fossil fuel dependency, we are equipped with a powerful array of technical and policy tools to build this new world.

We have decades of home-appliance development delivering water heaters, refrigerators, dishwashers, and heating and cooling systems that use much less energy than their predecessors; we have transport vehicles today that can run reliably on alternative fuels such as renewable natural gas or electricity produced from the sunlight; we are designing buildings that are mimicking natural systems, buildings that are pointing the way to the creation of living environments that can photosynthesize and purify air and water in ways that we could barely dream of 40 years ago.

More importantly, we have countries, including Sweden and Germany, and U.S. states, including California, that are well along in building a renewable energy infrastructure that is undeniably changing how we meet our energy needs.

BACK TO THE ISLANDS

In 1969, when I gazed out the window of that small airplane and looked into the maw of that artesian-like well of blackness spewing into the Santa Barbara Channel, I saw no hope, only darkness and death. And, considering how many experts forecast our running out of natural resources, the depletion of the fish in the ocean, the poisoning of our land and water, the befoulment of our air, the frightful loss of species, and horror after horror, it all seemed reasonable enough to me: the mounting evidence was there, demonstrating man's tendency to be blind and bury nature's presence in the modern world.

But all this didn't deflate my spirits or unravel me psychologically. Strangely, it had the opposite effect. It awakened a creative spirit and a resolve to bring forth what I thought might be healing influences, such as gardens, such as recycling and green buildings, and, more recently, renewable energy facilities. The very making of these artifacts had a therapeutic impact on my state of mind.

Yes, I may prove to be a fool to think that we can still make a difference, to work as if our tomorrows can be influenced by what we do today, when a century of burning fossil fuels is up there in the atmosphere and will be there long after the burning of fossil fuels is no more—long after you and I are no more. But one thing I do know, and I'm absolutely certain of this: No person, group, or institution knows fully what the future holds.

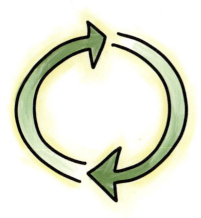

IMAGINING A FUTURE

I have heard many people say to me:

"You can't get people to recycle or compost; that's for Boy and Girl Scouts. Besides, people just won't invest the time and effort to separate their waste materials."

"You can't build a functioning hybrid or electric vehicle that people will buy. People won't ride bicycles or walk to work, let alone prefer living in towns and cities where they are readily available."

"They won't give up their plastic shopping bags or pay more for organic food. You can't make renewable energy from organic waste, your grass clippings, and discarded food; it's too expensive compared with landfilling the waste."

I have experienced all these "can't-be-done's," and I remember well all those who told me with their finger-wagging certainty that these were irrelevant ideas that would never go mainstream. Their views, once so dominant and seemingly unchallengeable not so many years ago, have receded as more sensible and sustainable ones replace them.

There are green shoots appearing all over the planet, even as our dependence on fossil fuels remains so seemingly impossible to solve. They are the creations of people propelled by an inner need to do something: to build alternative constructs, new products and services, new technologies that can perform work, make goods, and meet human needs while relying on fossil fuels more sparingly or not at all. The green shoots are beginning to weave a tapestry. It's faint now but it is growing. The will and the means to do more will only build as the urgency of our condition becomes undeniable.

Adapted from excerpts of *Out Of The Wasteland: Stories From The Environmental Frontier* by Paul Relis.

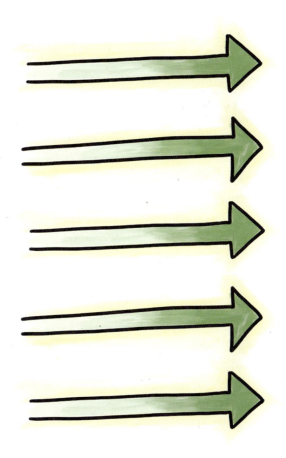

Chumash paddlers pass an
oil platform as they cross the
channel in the *tomol 'Elye'wun.*
Photo by Robert Schwemmer

Giant kelp sways in the current, absorbing carbon dioxide and helping produce oxygen that we breathe. *Photo by Robert Schwemmer*

No Islands

Don't panic. Seriously, don't. Yes, our reliance on crude oil is huge. And yes, the amount of plastic in our oceans seems really scary. But you can make a difference. It is going to take a lot of small local actions by individuals like you to turn things around. Small actions add up and fuel the movements that we desperately need. Here are a few ways that small can get big:

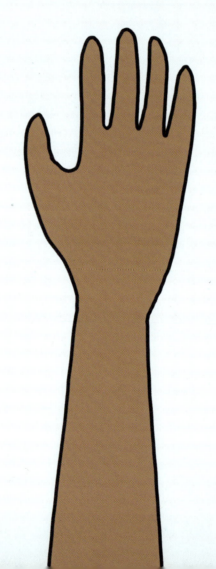

NATURE FRIEND

We protect only what we know. Take a friend down to the beach or into the woods. Show them why these places matter.

CITIZEN SCIENCE

Even PhDs need assistance. Help local scientists monitor water quality in your creeks or count migrating species.

VOTE CHANGE

Vote for politicians with records of supporting the environment and ballot measures that put the planet first.

BOYCOTT

Don't buy from companies that use disposable plastic packaging. This puts pressure on them to change.

BE LOCAL

The more people who demand locally made products, the more likely a store is to carry them.

We lean over the edge of the boat
And watch the dolphins play in the water
And we think:
They are not so different from us

We watch them have complex relationships
Conversations
And games
And we think:
They are not so different from us

We read the headlines about how injured our world is
And we think about the people who are so
Wasteful and ignorant
And we think:
We are so different from them

But then we realize:
We still burn fossil fuels
We still throw away plastic instead of recycling
We still rely on so many things that injure the world
And we think:
They are not so different from us

"Earth Island"
by Eric Permé, Student

Photo by Robert Schwemmer

ONWARD

Looking out to sea, the Channel Islands no longer seem so small and distant. From the brown pelican to the giant sea bass, all island residents are our neighbors. These Channel Islands serve as a constant reminder of the beauty of our little blue marble—and our footprints upon it.

Despite the patches of plastic on the beach and the oil platforms in the Channel, the islands also show us how we can begin to right our wrongs. Just look at the island fox, which we brought back from near extinction faster than any species in history. Dive into the kelp forests and you will see an abundance of fish species on the rebound. Communities across the globe now look to these isles as a model for how to sustainably protect their own islands.

It all starts with listening. Pay attention to what the elders of these islands tell you—both those with feet and those with flippers. Remember their stories, and notice their differences. By seeking to better understand our island neighbors, we can better understand ourselves and our role on this planet—which is really just one big island.

TAKE ACTION

To learn more about the issues discussed in this book—and take action—check out the following organizations who work on and around the Channel Islands:

Channel Islands National Park
Check current conditions on the islands, download a hiking map, and book a campsite.
nps.gov/chis

Channel Islands National Marine Sanctuary
Dive into the undersea park that surrounds the islands.
channelislands.noaa.gov

The Nature Conservancy
Learn about the conservation organization that manages the western portion of Santa Cruz Island.
nature.org/santacruzisland

Wishtoyo Chumash Foundation
Visit a traditional village and learn about Chumash culture past and present.
wishtoyo.org

Santa Barbara Museum of Natural History
Check out pygmy mammoth bones, a Chumash *tomol*, and more.
sbnature.org

Santa Barbara Botanic Garden
See and smell endemic island plants and learn what we can do to protect them.
sbbg.org

The Western Foundation of Vertebrate Zoology
See thousands of bird specimens, and learn about island bird populations and pesticide impacts.
wfvz.org

Santa Barbara Maritime Museum
Learn more about the ships that have sailed—and sunk—around the islands.
sbmm.org

Santa Barbara Zoo
See a real live island fox and learn what you can do to help protect similar creatures.
sbzoo.org

Explore Ecology
Join a beach cleanup and learn what you can do to reduce your impact on the planet.
exploreecology.org

Heal the Ocean
Take action to prevent sewage and waste from being dumped into the ocean.
healtheocean.org

Santa Barbara Channelkeeper
Help monitor water quality in your local creek,
which flows into the ocean.
sbck.org

Island Packers
Hop on a boat, meet a naturalist,
and set foot on the islands themselves.
islandpackers.com

Channel Islands Restoration
Restore native habitats on the islands
and the mainland.
cirweb.org

Santa Rosa Island Research Station
Learn how school groups can spend time
at this university-run field station.
csuci.edu/sri/

Friends of the Island Fox
Learn everything you ever wanted to know about
this keystone species.
islandfox.org

Santa Cruz Island Reserve
Apply to do research at or schedule a class visit to
this UCSB-run reserve.
santacruz.nrs.ucsb.edu

The REEF at UCSB
Get up close and personal with the creatures
that live in a kelp forest.
msi.ucsb.edu/reef

Nautilus Live
See new deep sea creatures on live, remotely
operated vehicle (ROV) dives across the globe.
nautiluslive.org

MERITO Foundation
Empower the next generation to become
stewards of the islands.
meritofoundation.org

Cultured Abalone
Learn how to purchase and cook up
locally-farmed red abalone.
culturedabalone.com

Santa Cruz Island Foundation
Learn about the cast of characters
who have called the islands home.
scifoundation.org/home.aspx

Commercial Fishermen of Santa Barbara
Buy freshly-caught seafood from
local fishermen, right off the boat.
cfsb.info

CONTRIBUTORS

The following experts, storytellers, poets, and students generously contributed their knowledge and wisdom to bring the Channel Islands to life:

Atwater, Tanya (20)
Bacon, Captain David (283)
Boser, Christina (204)
Boyce, Jennifer (188)
Bush, Doug (300)
Clark, Liz (6)
Coonan, Tim (196)
Cordero-Lamb, Julie (126)
deGruy, Mike (44)
deWet-Oleson, Kathy (228)
Dratch, Peter (208)
DuVall, Amelia Jade (42)
Earle, Sylvia (78)
Fagan, Brian (274)
Feinstein, Jake (260)
Francis, Jayden (88)
Francis, Laura (296)
Hastings, Sean (164)
Hauser, Hillary (84)
Hofman, Courtney (184)
Johnson, John R. (98)
Jordan, Chris (344)
Keane, Julia (350)
Long, Sydney (310)
Lopez, Casmali (116)
Love, Milton (270)
Lozano-Knowlton, Rocío (168)
Maassen, Morgan (62)

Miranda, Deborah A. (120)
Morris, Don (31)
Morten, Jessica (164)
Nichols, Wallace J. (56)
Pipkin, Scot (148)
Permé, Eric (368)
Reed, Dan (240)
Relis, Paul (358)
Riparetti Brown, Tommy (74)
Safina, Carl (304)
Sanjayan, M. (174)
Schuyler, Peter (36)
Schwemmer, Robert (156)
Sherman, Wilson (200)
Shrout, Sam (288)
Simon, Scott E. (258)
Steele, Bruce (236)
Taylor, Liz (326)
Ufberg, Max (328)
Vague, Captain Tiffany (283)
Valoyce Sanchez, Georgiana (108)
Vega, Jessica (246)
Wagner, Emma (340)
Wheeling, Kate (328)
Williams, Ian (14)
Wilson, Edward O. (212)

Photos

While these pages can't literally take you to the islands, the following photographers and organizations have generously contributed their images to help spark your imagination:

Boreham, Greg (180, 194-195, 210-211)
Chen, James (334-335)
Davis, Katie (342-343)
Dewey, Bill (144-145, 152-153)
Faulkner, Bill (30)
Hsieh, Wayne (12-13)
Jordan, Chris (344-347)
Klug, Douglas (220, 222-223, 226-227, 232-233, 256-257, 261, 294-295, 308-309, 311, 316)
Maassen, Morgan (62-71, 82-83, 89)
Muhs, Daniel R. (33)
Liz Clark Collection (6-7)

NASA (50)
National Park Service (30, 32)
Pedal Born Pictures (4, 56, 59, 94, 266, 273)
Pitcher, Lincoln (endpaper)
Santa Cruz Island Foundation (293)
Schwemmer, Robert (42-43, 45, 106-107, 114-115, 118, 130-131, 133, 138, 160-161, 215, 352-353, 364-365, 369, 384-385)
Searls, David "Doc" (331)
Simon, Scott E. (248-249)
U.S. Geological Survey (172-173)
Waiya, Mati (102-103)
The Wishtoyo Chumash Foundation (102-103)

Thank You

Island Visions would not have been possible without support and feedback from:

Lynn & John Seigel-Boettner
Sally Kurnick
Kevin Buddhu
Kim Geritz
Patty Malone
Janis Spracher
Anand Varma
Mark Unger

Glen & Dana Fritzler
Ernie Brooks
Julia Baugh
Beth Abrahamson
Cesar Viramontes
David Teton-Landis
Russ Bradley
Tony Smith

SELECTED BIBLIOGRAPHY

GENERAL

- "Channel Islands National Marine Sanctuary." National Oceanic and Atmospheric Administration, U.S. Department of Commerce, https://channelislands.noaa.gov/.

- "Channel Islands National Park (U.S. National Park Service)." National Park Service, U.S. Department of the Interior, www.nps.gov/chis/index.htm.

- Daily, Marla. "Islapedia." Islapedia, Santa Cruz Island Foundation, www.islapedia.com/.

- "From Sea to Shore Lecture Series." National Park Service, U.S. Department of the Interior, 2010, https://www.nps.gov/chis/learn/photosmultimedia/from-shore-to-sea-lecture-videos.htm.

- Monterey Bay Aquarium, https://www.montereybayaquarium.org/.

- "West of the West." West of the West, http://www.teachchannelislands.org/.

CHAPTER 1

- Langin, Katie. "Evolution Works in Fast, Localized, Mysterious Ways." *Slate Magazine*, 6 Feb. 2015. https://slate.com/technology/2015/02/santa-cruz-island-scrub-jay-evolution-surprising-biodiversity-in-neighboring-populations.html

- Livingston, D.S. *Island Legacies: A History of the Islands within Channel Islands National Park*. Department of the Interior, 2016, https://www.nps.gov/chis/learn/historyculture/upload/CHIS-Historic-Resource-Study-FINAL.pdf.

- Meiri, Shai, Natalie Cooper, Andy Purvis. "The Island Rule: Made to Be Broken?" *Proceedings of the Royal Society B: Biological Sciences*, vol. 275, no. 1631 (Nov 2007): 141–148, doi:10.1098/rspb.2007.1056.

- Schoenherr, A., C. R. Feldmath, & M. Emerson. *Natural History of the Islands of California*. Berkeley: University of California Press, 1999.

- Tyson, Peter. "Gigantism & Dwarfism on Islands." Public Broadcasting Service, November 1, 2000. http://www.pbs.org/wgbh/nova/article/gigantism-and-dwarfism-islands/.

CHAPTER 2

- "How Does the Ocean Affect Climate and Weather on Land?" *Ocean Explorer*, National Oceanic and Atmospheric Administration, https://oceanexplorer.noaa.gov/facts/climate.html.

- "Ocean Zones." *Ocean Explorer*, National Oceanic and Atmospheric Administration, https://oceanexplorer.noaa.gov/edu/curriculum/section5.pdf.

- "Volumes of the World's Oceans from ETOPO1." National Oceanic and Atmospheric Administration, https://www.ngdc.noaa.gov/mgg/global/etopo1_ocean_volumes.html.

CHAPTER 3

- Akin, Marjorie H., James C. Bard, Kevin Akin. *Numismatic Archaeology of North America: a Field Guide*. Routledge, Taylor & Francis Group, 2016.

- "Blue Dicks." *Nature Collective*, https://thenaturecollective.org/plant-guide/details/blue-dicks/.

- Erlandson, Jon M., et al. "The Kelp Highway Hypothesis: Marine Ecology, the Coastal Migration Theory, and the Peopling of the Americas." *The Journal of Island and Coastal Archaeology*, vol. 2, no. 2, 2007: 161–174. doi:10.1080/15564890701628612.

- Gamble, Lynn H. *The Chumash World at European Contact: Power, Trade, and Feasting among Complex Hunter-Gatherers*. University of California Press, 2011.

- Gamble, Lynn H. "Structural Transformation and Innovation in Emergent Political Economies of Southern California." *Hunter Gatherer Archaeology as Historical Process*, The University of Arizona Press, 2011: 227–247.

- Gill, Kristina M., and Jon M. Erlandson. "The Island Chumash and Exchange in the Santa Barbara Channel Region." *American Antiquity*, vol. 79, no. 3, 2014: 570–572.

- Hudson, Dee Travis. "Chumash Canoes of Mission Santa Barbara: the Revolt of 1824." *The Journal of California Anthropology*, vol. 3, no. 2, 1976: 5–15.

- Kennett, Douglas J, et al. "Historic Chumash Settlement on Eastern Santa Cruz Island, Southern California." *Journal of California and Great Basin Anthropology*, vol. 22, no. 2, 1 July 2000: 212–222.

- Kovacs, Kangkang. "A Journey of 21 Miles and Thousands of Years." *Santa Barbara Independent*, 13 Sept. 2010, https://www.independent.com/2010/09/13/journey-21-miles-and-thousands-years/.

- Lawler, Andrew. "Secrets of a Small Island." *Hakai Magazine*, 9 Nov. 2015, https://www.hakaimagazine.com/features/secrets-small-island/.

- McGrail, Sean. *Boats of the World: from the Stone Age to Medieval Times*. Oxford University Press, 2004.

- Tainter, Joseph A., et al. *The Way the Wind Blows: Climate Change, History, and Human Action*. Columbia University Press, 2000.

Chapter 4

- Junak, Steve. *A Flora of Santa Cruz Island*. Santa Barbara Botanic Garden in Collaboration with the California Native Plant Society, 1995.

- Junak, Steve, and Linda Ann Vorobik. *A Flora of San Nicolas Island, California*. Santa Barbara Botanic Garden, 2008.

- Knapp, Denise A. "Ecosystem Restoration on Santa Catalina Island: A Synthesis of Resources and Threats." *Catalina Island Conservancy, Oak Ecosystem Restoration on Santa Catalina Island, California: Proceedings of an on-Island Workshop*, February 2-4, 2007, 2010: 35–216.

- Lombardo, Carmen A., and Kate R. Faulkner. "Eradication of feral pigs (Sus scrofa) from Santa Rosa Island, Channel Islands National Park, California." *Proceedings of the fifth California islands symposium* (DH Browne, H. Chaney, and K. Mitchell, editors). Santa Barbara Museum of Natural History, Santa Barbara, California. 2000.

- Moody, Aaron. "Analysis of Plant Species Diversity with Respect to Island Characteristics on the Channel Islands, California." *Journal of Biogeography*, vol. 27, no. 3, 2000: 711–723. doi:10.1046/j.1365-2699.2000.00435.x.

- Philbrick, Ralph N. *The Plants of Santa Barbara Island, California*. Santa Barbara Botanic Garden, 1972.

- Power, Paula J., et al. "Native plant recovery in study plots after fennel (Foeniculum vulgare) control on Santa Cruz Island." *Monographs of the Western North American Naturalist* (2014): 465-476.

- "Public Law 96-199." U.S. Government Publishing Office, https://uscode.house.gov/statutes/pl/96/199.pdf

- Redmon, Michael. "Justinian Caire - Owner of Santa Cruz Island." *The Santa Barbara Independent*, 15 Aug. 2013, https://www.independent.com/2013/08/15/justinian-caire/.

- Rick, Torben C., et al. "Ecological Change on California's Channel Islands from the Pleistocene to the Anthropocene." *BioScience*, vol. 64, no. 8: 680–692. doi:https://doi.org/10.1093/biosci/biu094.

- "Treaty between Spain and Portugal Concluded at Tordesillas; June 7, 1494." *Avalon Project - Documents in Law, History and Diplomacy*, https://avalon.law.yale.edu/15th_century/mod001.asp.

- "United States Chunie v. Ringrose." *OpenJurist*. https://openjurist.org/788/f2d/638/united-states-chunie-v-ringrose.

Chapter 5

- "About Island Fox." Friends of the Island Fox, http://www1.islandfox.org/p/about-island-fox.html.

- "DDT - A Brief History and Status." Environmental Protection Agency, https://www.epa.gov/ingredients-used-pesticide-products/ddt-brief-history-and-status.

- "Facts Statistics: Pet Statistics." Insurance Information Institute, https://www.iii.org/fact-statistic/facts-statistics-pet-statistics.

- "Island Fox Update 2018." Friends of the Island Fox, http://www1.islandfox.org/2018/07/2018-channel-island-fox-update.html.

- "Meat Consumption." The Organisation for Economic Co-operation and Development, https://data.oecd.org/agroutput/meat-consumption.htm.

- "Pet Industry Market Size & Ownership Statistics." American Pet Products Association, https://www.americanpetproducts.org/press_industrytrends.asp.

- "Recovery Plan for Four Subspecies of Island Fox (Urocyon littoralis)." U.S. Fish and Wildlife Service, 2015.

- "Sunscreen Chemicals and Coral Reefs." *Ocean Service*, National Oceanic and Atmospheric Administration, https://oceanservice.noaa.gov/news/sunscreen-corals.html.

Chapter 6

- Foster, Michael S., and David R. Schiel. *The Ecology of Giant Kelp Forests in California: a Community Profile*. U.S. Fish and Wildlife Service, 1985.

- "Kelp Losing Their Grip on the Seafloor." *Earth Observatory*, NASA, https://earthobservatory.nasa.gov/images/85105/kelp-losing-their-grip-on-the-seafloor.

- Klein, JoAnna. "Watch a Great White Shark Hunt Through a Kelp Forest for Its Next Meal." *The New York Times*, 5 Apr. 2019, https://www.nytimes.com/2019/04/05/science/shark-kelp-video.html.

- Leet, William S. *California's Living Marine Resources: a Status Report*. California Dept. of Fish and Game, 2001.

- Love, Robin Milton. "KELP The World's Great Forest Under the Sea." *MARE: Marine Activities, Resources & Education*, The Regents of the University of California, 1994, https://mare.lawrencehallofscience.org/sites/mare.lawrencehallofscience.org/files/images/MAREKelp_Forest_Bkgnd.pdf.

- "Ocean Acidification." Woods Hole Oceanographic Institution, https://www.whoi.edu/know-your-ocean/ocean-topics/ocean-chemistry/ocean-acidification/.

Chapter 7

- a_sams18. "Kelp: The Sea Weed That Could Save Mankind." *NationSwell*, 26 Feb. 2014, https://nationswell.com/sea-weed-save-mankind/.

- "About Giant Sea Bass." *Spotting Giant Sea Bass*, UC Santa Barbara Marine Science Institute, https://spottinggiantseabass.msi.ucsb.edu/aboutBass.jsp.

- Dillman, Terry. "Commercial Fishing's Contribution to Santa Barbara Economy." *Fishermen's News*, 1 Dec. 2015, https://www.fishermensnews.com/story/2015/12/01/features/commercial-fishings-contribution-to-santa-barbara-economy/364.

- "California Market Squid." *Monterey Bay Aquarium Seafood Watch Reports*, 9 Jan. 2019, https://www.seafoodwatch.org/-/m/sfw/pdf/reports/s/mba_seafoodwatch_camarketsquidreport.pdf.

- Cho, Renee. "Making Fish Farming More Sustainable." *State of the Planet*, Columbia University Earth Institute, 25 Apr. 2019, https://blogs.ei.columbia.edu/2016/04/13/making-fish-farming-more-sustainable/.

- "Fishing & Farming Methods." *SeafoodWatch*, Monterey Bay Aquarium, https://www.seafoodwatch.org/ocean-issues/fishing-and-farming-methods.

- Greenberg, Paul. "How Mussel Farming Could Help to Clean Fouled Waters." *Yale Environment 360*, 9 Mar. 2013, https://e360.yale.edu/features/how_mussel_farming_could_help_to_clean_fouled_waters.

- Haas, Hannah J., et al. "Black Abalone (Haliotis Cracherodii) Population Structure Shifts through Deep Time: Management Implications for Southern Californias Northern Channel Islands." *Ecology and Evolution*, vol. 9, no. 8, 2 Apr. 2019: 4720–4732. doi:10.1002/ece3.5075.

- Leeworthy, Vernon R., Desiree Jerome, Kelsey Schueler. 2014. *Economic Impact of the Commercial Fisheries on Local County Economies from Catch in all California National Marine Sanctuaries 2010, 2011 and 2012*. Marine Sanctuaries Conservation Series ONMS-14-05. U.S. Department of Commerce, National Oceanic and Atmospheric Administration, Office of National Marine Sanctuaries, https://sanctuaries.noaa.gov/science/conservation/ca_fullreport.html.

- "Market Squid." *California Sea Grant*, https://caseagrant.ucsd.edu/seafood-profiles/market-squid.

- "Our Catch." *Commercial Fishermen of Santa Barbara*, http://www.cfsb.info/our-catch.

- "Our Model." GreenWave, https://www.greenwave.org/our-model.

- *The State of World Fisheries and Aquaculture 2014*. Food and Agriculture Organization of the United Nations, http://www.fao.org/resources/infographics/infographics-details/en/c/231544/.

- *The State of World's Fisheries and Aquaculture 2016*. Food and Agriculture Organization of the United Nations, http://www.fao.org/publications/sofia/2016/en/.

- *The State of Fisheries and Aquaculture in the World 2018*. Food and Agriculture Organization of the United Nations, http://www.fao.org/state-of-fisheries-aquaculture.

- Vojkovich, Marija. "The California Fishery for Market Squid (Loligo Opalescens)." *California Cooperative for Oceanic Fisheries Investigation*, vol. 39, 1998, http://calcofi.org/publications/calcofireports/v39/Vol_39_Vojkovich.pdf.

- Wilcox, Meg. "Farmed Scallops Are Coming to a Plate Near You." *Civil Eats*, 18 Sept. 2018, https://civileats.com/2018/09/11/farmed-scallops-are-coming-to-a-plate-near-you/.

Chapter 8

- Booth, Stephanie. "That's the Last Straw." *NationSwell*, 1 Apr. 2019, https://nationswell.com/thats-the-last-straw/.

- Borenstein, Seth. *Science Says: Amount of Straws, Plastic Pollution Is Huge*. Phys.org, 21 Apr. 2018, https://phys.org/news/2018-04-science-amount-straws-plastic-pollution.html.

- "Brief Oil and Gas History of Santa Barbara County." County of Santa Barbara Planning and Development, Energy Division, https://web.archive.org/web/20180807032905/http://www.sbcountyplanning.org/energy/information/history.asp.

- Houseworth, James, and William Stringfellow. "A Case Study of California Offshore Petroleum Production, Well Stimulation, and Associated Environmental Impacts." *An Independent Scientific Assessment of Well Stimulation in California*, vol. 3, 9 July 2015: 28–111. https://ccst.us/wp-content/uploads/160708-sb4-vol-III-2.pdf.

- Madrigal, Alexis C. "Disposable America." *The Atlantic*, Atlantic Media Company, 21 June 2018, https://www.theatlantic.com/technology/archive/2018/06/disposable-america/563204/.

- O'Connor, Marie Catherine. "Study: Your Fleece Jacket Is Awful for the Environment." *Outside Online*, 26 July 2019, https://www.outsideonline.com/2091876/patagonias-new-study-finds-fleece-jackets-are-serious-pollutant.

- Ortel, Brooke. "A Different Path: Living in Southern Chile with Bureo Co-Founder Ben Kneppers." *The Cleanest Line*, Patagonia, 8 Feb. 2016, https://www.patagonia.com/blog/2016/02/a-different-path-living-in-southern-chile-with-bureo-co-founder-ben-kneppers/.

- "Petroleum & Other Liquids." *Independent Statistics and Analysis*, U.S. Energy Information Administration, https://www.eia.gov/dnav/pet/hist/LeafHandler.ashx?n=pet&s=f000000___3&f=m.

- Ritchie, Hannah, and Max Roser. "Plastic Pollution." *Our World in Data*, 1 Sept. 2018, https://ourworldindata.org/plastic-pollution.

- Solheim, Erik. "The Missing Science: Could Our Addiction to Plastic Be Poisoning Us?" The United Nations Environment Programme, https://www.unenvironment.org/news-and-stories/story/missing-science-could-our-addiction-plastic-be-poisoning-us.

INDEX

An aerial view of Prisoners Harbor on *Limuw* (Santa Cruz Island).
Photo by Robert Schwemmer

Behind the Vision

This book started with Santa Barbara Middle School's annual 9th grade Channel Islands Expedition. Immersed in the living classrom that is the islands, students on these trips had the opportunity to learn from educators of all kinds: rangers to sea lions, fishermen to giant coreopsis. One of those educators was Mike deGruy, a world-renowned ocean filmmaker and storyteller. Mike inspired two SBMS graduates to work with their former teacher to gather knowledge from these diverse experts into a tome to share with the world.

Jacob Seigel Brielle / Editor

Jacob didn't have a TV growing up. He was obsessed with books. Stories on the page took him to new worlds and helped him better understand his own. After college, he co-founded Pedal Born Pictures—a creative agency dedicated to shedding light on stories hiding in plain sight—with his brother Isaac. It was fitting that he finally ended up creating his own book about the fantastical—and very real—world right out his window. Jacob edited the content in these pages and wrote the musings that stitch them together.

Isaac Seigel-Boettner / Illustrator

Isaac could often be found doodling in the margins of his notebook during class. That didn't mean he wasn't listening. While at SBMS, he took a "junk art" elective, learning how to not burn himself with hot glue while building the worlds that existed within his mind. Now he works as the creative director at Pedal Born Pictures, translating stories and ideas into whatever medium best helps bring them to life. Isaac created all of the illustrations in this book, and fine-tuned the layout to make this multi-narrative collection sing.

Brian McWilliams / Mentor

Brian is the Headmaster of SBMS. He was Jacob and Isaac's teacher back before they could grow beards. Brian's ultimate goal is to help students discover their passions and purpose by exploring the world around them. Like Mike, he firmly believes that this is best done by diving headfirst into the oceans of wonder and possibility and immersing oneself in topics that matter. Brian helped captain this book from day one, rallying support to make *Island Visions* a reality.